Crime and Punishment in African American History

JAMES CAMPBELL

palgrave
macmillan

First published 2013 by
PALGRAVE MACMILLAN

Palgrave Macmillan in the UK is an imprint of Macmillan Publishers Limited, registered in England, company number 785998, of Houndmills, Basingstoke, Hampshire RG21 6XS.

Palgrave Macmillan in the US is a division of St Martin's Press LLC, 175 Fifth Avenue, New York, NY 10010.

Palgrave Macmillan is the global academic imprint of the above companies and has companies and representatives throughout the world.

Palgrave® and Macmillan® are registered trademarks in the United States, the United Kingdom, Europe and other countries.

ISBN 978–0–230–27380–1 hardback
ISBN 978–0–230–27381–8 paperback

This book is printed on paper suitable for recycling and made from fully managed and sustained forest sources. Logging, pulping and manufacturing processes are expected to conform to the environmental regulations of the country of origin.

A catalogue record for this book is available from the British Library.

A catalog record for this book is available from the Library of Congress.

10   9   8   7   6   5   4   3   2   1
22 21 20 19 18 17 16 15 14 13

Printed in China

For Zoë, with love.

Contents

List of Illustrations

Acknowledgments

This book evolved out of a course that I have taught for the past several years. I would like to thank students at the University of Portsmouth and the University of Leicester whose comments and enthusiasm for the subject have influenced the pages that follow in many different ways. The book has also benefited enormously from feedback on draft chapters by David Brown, Kate Dossett, George Lewis, and Vivien Miller. I am grateful to them all, as well as to Palgrave Macmillan's anonymous reviewers and, in particular, the series editor, Stephen Tuck, who offered valuable advice on the manuscript at a late stage. My thanks also to Jenna Steventon for steering the project through the editorial process at Palgrave Macmillan so smoothly, the Arts and Humanities Research Council, the British Academy, and the British Association for American Studies for funding that supported my research, and the University of Leicester for a period of study leave during which I was able to write much of the manuscript. Finally, I thank my family for their love and support and, above all, Zoë Hilton, who has made the years that I've spent writing the book wonderful.

The authors and publishers wish to thank the following for permission to use copyright material:

Corbis Images UK Ltd. For the images on pp. 124, 132, 173 and 179, © Bettmann/Corbis, for the image on p. 198, © Vernan Bryant/Dallas Morning News/Corbis, and for the image on p. 217 © Ed Silvera/Demotix/Demotix/Demotix/Corbis

Library of Congress for all other images reproduced in the book.

Every effort has been made to trace the copyright holders but, if any have been inadvertently overlooked, the authors and publishers will be pleased to make the necessary arrangements at the first opportunity.

Introduction

In February 2012, the killing of Trayvon Martin in Sanford, Florida, catapulted issues of race, crime, and punishment to the forefront of the American political and news agenda. Returning home from a 7-Eleven store, the African American teenager was followed and shot dead outside a gated community by George Zimmerman, a white, volunteer neighborhood watch captain of Latino descent who claimed he acted in self-defense. The Sanford police agreed. Following a cursory investigation, no arrests were made and the killing was quickly ruled a justifiable homicide. Within weeks, however, protests against the police handling of the case—led by Martin's family and joined by hundreds of thousands of supporters—swept across the nation. The Sanford police chief was suspended, the investigation reopened, and Zimmerman eventually arrested and charged with second-degree murder. At the time of writing, George Zimmerman is yet to stand trial, but the name of Trayvon Martin is already enshrined in the long history of African American crime and punishment. Indeed, the national and international prominence of the case is partly a consequence of the many ways that it resonates with that history. It evokes past practices of white vigilantes assuming pseudo-police powers over African Americans, law enforcement officers neglecting white-on-black violence, and equal justice resting on mass protest movements rather than the rule of law. Through these connections, the case raises questions about the past and current state of civil rights, race relations, policing, and the criminal law in the United States.

This book takes up these questions by exploring the intersection of African American history and criminal justice history over the course of nearly four centuries. It investigates how African Americans have engaged with, influenced, and experienced crime and punishment from the seventeenth century to the present. It asks how black experiences of law enforcement have changed over time, why these changes have occurred, and what significance they have had within

1

and beyond black communities. It looks at forms of policing, court procedures, and punishments, tracing their evolution in different regions and jurisdictions. It also explores the circumstances in which the legal system has deferred to, or sometimes been supplanted by, extrajudicial authorities such as slaveholders, the Ku Klux Klan, and lynch mobs. While these subjects mostly defy sweeping generalizations, the analysis presented here reveals notable continuities over time in the outcomes and implications of African Americans' encounters with the criminal justice system. These encounters have often been discriminatory and violent, but their form and consequences have varied across the United States according to local circumstances and have changed considerably over time as the relationship between race and law enforcement has been remade in different eras according to evolving political and economic interests, powerful protest movements, and developing ideas about law, justice, and punishment.

In approaching this subject matter, *Crime and Punishment in African American History* introduces and interrogates six major themes that resonate across the past four centuries:

The black freedom struggle. The African American history of criminal justice is an integral part of the history of the black freedom struggle. Although popular memory of the civil rights movement is dominated by demands for the right to vote and integrated schools, black political activism has always been rooted in campaigns for equal justice and for protection from racial violence and unjust punishment. Nonetheless, civil rights gains have not always translated into improvements in the treatment of African Americans in terms of criminal justice. On the contrary, African American political and social advances have often been met with an intensification of racial repression justified in the name of crime control. In the aftermath of both the American Civil War and the modern civil rights movement, for example, criminal justice mechanisms were used to strip large numbers of African Americans of recently acquired citizenship rights. More pervasively, black political activists from slave rebels to student sit-in demonstrators have regularly been subject to criminal justice sanctions.

Labor. The forms and function of law enforcement against African Americans have consistently been tied to issues of labor control. From slavery, through the peonage and chain gangs of the Jim Crow era, and the mass incarceration that accompanied deindustrialization in the late-twentieth century, the arrest, prosecution, and punishment of black workers has served the interests of landholders, industrialists, and government through providing a subordinate and cheap labor force.

Violence. In the black past, violence has permeated law enforcement and there has rarely been a clear-cut divide between extralegal punishment and the justice system. On the contrary, law and violence have often been closely intertwined. Slave courts readily dispensed with even the pretense of due process in periods of slave uprisings, and in the 1850s slaveholders seized runaways under the barely regulated legal procedures of the Fugitive Slave Act. In the segregation era, black defendants were sentenced to death in courtrooms surrounded by baying mobs, and prisoners worked in convict leasing camps alongside tenants trapped in debt peonage. African Americans are today rarely subject to extralegal policing by white vigilantes, but new forms of militarized law enforcement, parole, and civil injunctions have created a parallel system of crime control in many black communities that operates outside standard judicial procedures.

Resistance. African Americans have continually resisted white-dominated law enforcement and extralegal punishment. Through armed self-defense, political mobilization, and legal challenges, black resistance has challenged and destabilized white supremacy, driving an ongoing process of criminal justice reform that sometimes has mitigated the system's harshest features, though rarely threatened their foundations and often resulted only in the evolution of new forms of repression. The earliest slave laws developed to contain insurrections and escapes; a multifaceted movement against lynching forced allegations of black criminality to be heard in southern courtrooms; discriminatory trials were liable to challenges in federal courts and international protests; militant black organizations in the 1960s protected civil rights workers from Klan violence, and ongoing grassroots campaigns contest the contemporary war on drugs and prison-industrial complex.

Gender and class. African American crime and punishment has always been related to the construction of boundaries, divisions, and ideas about gender and class. The outcome of rape prosecutions against black defendants has reflected the social status of white female victims as well as the racial identity of their alleged attackers; laws criminalizing mixed-race marriages and sexual relationships were used from the Civil War to the 1960s to police racial boundaries, and the denigration of black womanhood has in many periods led police to neglect vice in urban black neighborhoods. Racially discriminatory law enforcement has also routinely been used to defuse class tensions among whites, though not infrequently poor whites have also been caught up in penal mechanisms targeted primarily at the black population.

Place. The African American history of crime and punishment has been heavily conditioned by local context. From the slave era to the present, the South has been exceptional in the pervasiveness and severity of racial violence, discriminatory criminal justice, and coercive penal practices. This broad southern distinctiveness, however, masks significant variations among and within different states, and it has not developed in isolation, but rather in dialogue with the rest of the nation and with the federal government and judiciary. The African American experience of criminal law in the northern and western states likewise stems from distinctive local conditions, but also reflects deep entanglements and influences across county, state, and regional borders.

This book is heavily influenced by a new and diverse body of scholarship that has developed on issues of crime and punishment in African American history over the past 30 years. Making use of previously neglected sources, such as local court records and African American newspapers, historians have provided original insights into the "everyday" black experience of law enforcement and extralegal violence. Through detailed, local case studies of subjects including slave law, lynching, convict leasing, police brutality, discriminatory prosecutions, and the death penalty, this work has focused on how law enforcement works in practice and found a history filled with diversity, tensions, divisions, and conflicts underlying and complicating the well-worn narrative of violent white supremacy and racist criminal justice in the American past. It has, moreover, provided an important counterpoint to legal histories that draw mainly on appeals court and legislative records to examine the federal and constitutional dimensions of violence and law enforcement in black history, but which sometimes neglect both the influence of nonlegal factors on the administration of criminal justice and the impact of legal outcomes outside of the courtroom.

Building on the new understandings of African American crime and punishment opened up by grassroots studies, this book joins many individual stories into a longer narrative in order to present a wide-lens interpretative history. This approach aims to highlight connections, continuities, and change across time and place. It also allows for consideration of how African American crime and punishment relates to broader themes in American history and makes the case more forcefully than a local study possibly can for incorporating issues of race, crime, and punishment as a central component of wider historical debates. It presents, for example, the long history of African American crime and punishment as a powerful counterpoint to the promises of America's founding documents and the nation's rhetorical and constitutional commitment to freedom, justice, the rule of law, and equal protection. It reveals an engrained alternative tradition—a genealogy of injustice—in which violence has played as prominent a role as legal process, white supremacy has been as influential as egalitarian principles, and black resistance has played a primary role in the evolution of the criminal justice system. But it warns against essentializing this tradition by demonstrating that it stemmed from different causes and took different forms in different places and at different times.

Few previous studies have attempted to analyze together the social and legal histories of African American criminal justice and extra-legal law enforcement over the long sweep of the American past. There are, however, a number of historical, legal, and social-science analyses of long-term shifts in issues of race, law, and criminal justice that provide a broad interpretative framework for this book. The most prevalent view—and the view with which most Americans today would likely concur—argues that criminal law has become more equal, less violent, and fairer in its treatment of African Americans over time. Assessing developments in African American criminal justice from slavery to the present, legal historian Randall Kennedy found "dramatic discontinuities" between the eras of slavery, segregation, and the present and identified the modern civil rights movement of the 1950s and 1960s as a major turning point after which the history of African Americans and law enforcement changed profoundly. Kennedy also criticized late-twentieth century scholarship and political activism that identified with the struggles of black defendants and convicts and called for constraints on the powers of law enforcement. In Kennedy's view, this work was detrimental to the interests of black America and undermined attempts to deal with more pressing legal concerns, such as the underenforcement of law in black communities ravaged by illegal drugs and high rates of intraracial violence. Adopting a more polemical and less nuanced stance, the conservative black scholar Thomas Sowell maintained that the "battle for civil rights was fought and won" in the past and dismissed continued African American agitation as representing the socially destabilizing "politicization of the law." From this perspective—which law professor Paul Butler calls "the celebratory tradition"—change in issues of race and criminal justice appears either as a product of, or inseparable from, broader changes in civil rights law that have affected all aspects of American race relations and the black experience.[1]

Alternative interpretations focus more on continuity than change, draw a clearer distinction between the history of African American crime and punishment and the course of the wider civil rights struggle, and are less sanguine about the evolving black experience of law enforcement. The theme of continuity has recently been evoked by law professor Michelle Alexander who describes the vast scale on which African Americans are imprisoned in the twenty-first century as constituting a "new Jim Crow," much as historians studying earlier eras have described convict leasing as "worse than slavery," and the system of peonage that flourished in the South from Reconstruction to the mid-twentieth century, as "slavery by another name." Diverse explanations have been put forward for the persistence of racial discrimination in law enforcement. Derrick Bell argued that progress toward racial justice has occurred only when the interests of black and white Americans converge, and throughout American history this has invariably been only a temporary condition. As characterized by former federal judge and historian Leon Higginbotham, African American legal history has been a "journey" from "total racial oppression" to only "muted shades of freedom" in which legal reforms have struggled to erase the precept of black inferiority that was cultivated through slavery and segregation and continues to influence judicial processes. William Stuntz, by contrast, focuses on new factors that allowed discrimination to flourish in the second half of the twentieth century, such as declining local community influence over criminal justice outcomes and a massive expansion in prosecutors' discretionary power that came at the expense of legal due process. In Doris Provine's assessment, discrimination in American criminal law has "morphed … rather than disappeared," as jurists and politicians in recent decades have embraced an ideology of color-blind jurisprudence that fails to address the persistence of structural and unconscious racism.[2]

The way in which the history of African American crime and punishment is written and understood is consequently of profound importance to interpretations of criminal justice in the present. In a recent study, criminologists James Unnever and Shaun Gabbidon argue that "centuries of subordination," and "criminal justice injustices" have forged a unique African American worldview marked by a profound "cynicism" about modern law enforcement that contributes to high rates of offending. Anthropologist John Hartigan similarly argues that Americans' views on race, crime, and punishment in the present are "in part, based on the relevance they attribute to the past." Among those who consider race a key variable in twenty-first-century criminal justice, history is "ever present, with certain actions and attitudes being continually repeated," while for proponents of the view that the civil rights movement largely eroded the pertinence of race to the enforcement of criminal law, the past is confined to history and crime and punishment in the present considered "an entirely contemporary matter." The way in which the past is understood also has relevance to efforts to reform criminal justice processes and outcomes in the present, by revealing the circumstances in which change has occurred in the past and the factors that have limited or distorted intended outcomes. The history of African American crime and punishment can readily appear to be a strange, foreign country if reduced to a one-dimensional narrative of extreme and explicit violence, discrimination, and lawlessness, or with a focus limited to legal decision making. This study argues that it should instead be interpreted as a multifaceted and constantly evolving story of conflict and struggle entwined with wide-ranging social, legal, economic, and political forces.[3]

Crime and Punishment in African American History is a relatively short book that seeks to draw out major themes across a broad time period. Writing it has consequently entailed making difficult decisions about content and emphasis. Inevitably, specialists in the field will have little trouble pointing to important issues that are neglected or could have been discussed in greater depth. I have been guided by a number of considerations in reaching the choices I have made. First, I have sought to highlight the diversity of African American criminal justice history over time and space. Second, I have sought to reflect recent developments in the historiography. Third, although the book attempts to tell the story of the "everyday life" of African American crime and punishment, this can often be most effectively done through events that, in themselves, are extraordinary. The book does attempt to paint broad pictures of trends and patterns in law enforcement, but it often does so through illustrative case studies that, apart from their analytical value, also provide the most engaging entry point to the subject matter.

The book is divided into three sections. Part One examines the era of slavery and the reconstruction of the relationship between race, crime, and punishment that occurred in the late-nineteenth century. These chapters demonstrate the overwhelming extent to which law and violence combined first to uphold the slaveholders' rule and then to secure white supremacy in the decades after emancipation. At the same time, they also reveal conflicts over the early history of African American crime and punishment, as ideas about race evolved and white elites struggled to secure and adapt the legal and extralegal pillars of their power amidst dramatically shifting social and political contexts. Chapter 1 focuses on slave resistance and crime and the everyday forms of control and punishment that slaveholders used to prevent and regulate these activities. Slaveholders' power was all but unconstrained by law and it was backed up by the work of overseers, patrols, police officers, and magistrates. It also drew on broad support from nonslaveholding white Americans, though by the mid-nineteenth century this support was deeply fractured, particularly outside of the southern states. Chapter 2 moves inside the courtroom to explore the trials of slaves and free African Americans charged with the most serious criminal offenses, including murder and rebellion. It traces the varied and evolving judicial processes that enslaved defendants encountered, the diverse factors that influenced trial outcomes, and the blurred division between legal and extralegal justice. Chapter 3 takes the story into the decades after the American Civil War when African Americans, the federal government, and reactionary white southerners fought to shape and administer a new system of criminal justice according to wildly divergent hopes and ideas about the future of black freedom.

Part Two focuses on African American crime and punishment in the era of segregation from the 1890s to the 1940s, highlighting the interaction of legal and extralegal practices and forms of black resistance. Chapter 4 examines systems of convict leasing, chain gangs, and peonage as connected forms of labor control and criminal punishment operating within and outside legal boundaries. Chapter 5 traces the equally connected histories of lynching and criminal trials in the South and questions both the significance and limitations of campaigns by civil rights groups and workers' organizations against mob rule and discriminatory prosecutions and executions. Chapter 6 moves beyond the southern states and uncovers the relationships that existed between law and violence in crime, policing, and punishment in the rapidly expanding black neighborhoods of major cities in the American Northeast and Midwest.

Finally, Part Three engages with themes of change and persistence in African American crime and punishment from the civil rights era to the present. In this period, the most explicit and public acts of racial discrimination and violence were largely purged from American law enforcement. As has happened repeatedly since the era of slavery, however, new developments in policing and punishment since the 1960s have ensured that the discriminatory and repressive impact of criminal justice on African American life survives and thrives in Obama's America as it did in Lincoln's. An epilogue considers recent efforts to address injustices of the past through prosecuting the white killers of black civil rights activists, memorializing the victims of lynching, and campaigning for reparations for the survivors of racial atrocities. It argues for the importance of remembering these events as elements of ongoing historical processes.

Part One

Slavery to Freedom

1

The Slaveholders' Rule

*[A] judicious freedom in the administration of our police laws
for the lower order must always have respect for the confidence
which the law reposes in the discretion of the master.*
— *State v. Boozer*, South Carolina Court of Appeals, 1850

On Highland Plantation in West Feliciana Parish, Louisiana, Bennett
H. Barrow was the law. Owner of more than 200 slaves in the mid-
nineteenth century, Barrow punished his human property with abandon.
Some days Barrow whipped all of his cotton pickers for shirking work,
other times he had "a general whipping frolic" for no particular reason.
He thrashed slaves for stealing, including two house servants who broke
into his storehouse and were whipped "worse than I ever whipped any
one before." Eight or ten slaves who stole some hogs were ducked before
they were beaten. When the slave Demps hit his wife Hetty and locked
her up, Barrow intervened, "turning her loose and fastening him." He
whipped Dave and Jack for their "rascality" and planned to chain them
at nights and on Sundays "till I think they are broke in." Later he built a
jail, where he imprisoned Darcas for, "pretending to be sick, repeatedly,"
and some slaves who were bad mannered when he gave them a dinner
in his ballroom. Jack was dressed up in a sheet and had feathers stuck in
his ears while three slave couples were forced to "ride" him around the
quarters as punishment for quarrelling. When Barrow's slaves ran away,
as they often did, he hunted them down. He shot Jerry in the thigh when
he heard he was planning an escape, only for Jerry to abscond anyway a
week later. Recaptured, Jerry was jailed, but another slave set him free
to steal a pig. Locked up again and put in the stocks, by morning Jerry
had disappeared once more, the jail door and stocks again broken down

by another slave. Barrow used "Negro dogs" to hunt runaways, too. On one occasion they "tore ... naked" one of Mrs. Wade's slaves who had "been drawing a knife & pistol on persons about town," and then gave him "another overhauling" when he got home.[1]

The roots of African American crime and punishment rest amidst the struggles that played out between slaves and their owners on plantations like Highland, on farms, in towns, and cities across America from the seventeenth to the nineteenth century. Crime was scarcely the issue; power, property, racial supremacy, mastery, and forced labor were all at stake. "The power of the master must be absolute," wrote North Carolina chief justice Thomas Ruffin in 1829, "to render the submission of the slave perfect."[2] There was hardly any aspect of a slave's conduct that slaveholders might not consider worthy of punishment and the law placed few constraints on the brutal and dehumanizing penalties they could inflict. But the submission of the enslaved was never perfect. Slaves resisted their bondage persistently and in doing so they forced the war of slave control beyond the plantation and into public spaces where the slaveholders' power was still fearsome, but also more contingent and contested. The right to inflict violence on slaves was extended to all whites, patrols were established to keep watch over the southern countryside, and police forces were established that gave cities a militaristic air. Laws also clamped down on the status of free African Americans and federal legislation provided for the capture of runaways anywhere in the nation and demanded their return to bondage even from states that had abolished slavery. These policies ensured that slavery functioned well enough to remain profitable and—at the local level—relatively stable in the nineteenth-century South, but they also had unexpected and contradictory implications and elicited fierce opposition, especially outside of the slave states.

Slave societies in the United States

In 1790, slightly less than 700,000 African Americans lived as slaves in the young United States. When conflict over slavery led the nation to Civil War, 71 years later, the enslaved population had increased to almost four million. In the intervening years, the importation of slaves from Africa had been prohibited and slavery had slowly been purged from the northern states in a process that prompted the growth of free black communities, mostly in large cities. By contrast, in the southern states slavery had flourished, though it had also changed in profound ways (see Illustration 1.1).

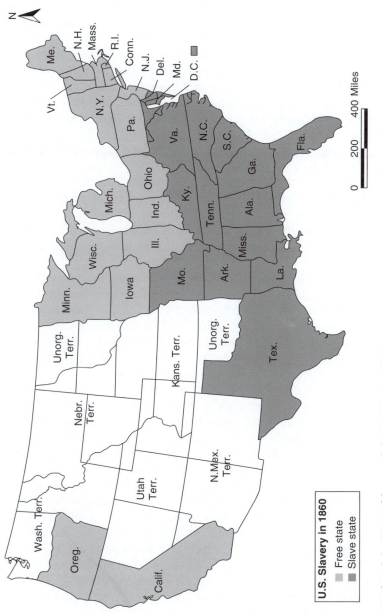

Illustration 1.1 Map of free and slave states in 1860

In the revolutionary era, slavery's powerbase lay on the Eastern Seaboard, in the tobacco farms of Virginia and the rice fields of low country South Carolina. By the mid-nineteenth century, slaveholding men from these regions remained committed to the peculiar institution and were still among the leading pro-slavery voices on the national stage, but the driving force of slavery's expansion lay further west in the Black Belt that stretched from backcountry South Carolina and Georgia across Alabama, Mississippi, and beyond. There, thousands of white men, many ambitious, others adventurous, some desperate, were lured by the potent combination of cheap land and the opportunity to get rich through the cultivation of cotton and sugar using enslaved black labor. By 1860 almost two million slaves, or more than 50 per cent of the total slave population, toiled on the cotton plantations of the Deep South to meet the massive demands of textile factories in Great Britain and the northern United States.[3]

Back east, in the Upper South states of Virginia and Maryland, the economic, social, and cultural development of slavery proceeded along very different trajectories. Colonial population growth made land scarce and expensive, limiting opportunities for economic and social advancement, particularly among poorer whites, but also for the sons of men of even moderate means. Coupled with rising prices for slaves, increased land values consolidated the wealth of the established Chesapeake elite to the extent that by the revolutionary era planters such as George Washington had more slaves than they could usefully employ on their own land. This led to a diversification of economic interests that had profound implications for African Americans. Most slaves in the Upper South continued to work on farms, but large numbers were hired out to toil for men and women other than their owners. Many acquired a skilled trade, and some were set to work in the factories and mills of emerging cities such as Baltimore and Richmond that symbolized the growth of the market economy and the slow onset of industrialization in the region. Over one million more slaves were removed from the eastern seaboard between the American Revolution and the Civil War, with the vast majority sold westward, away from their families and communities, through the cruel processes of the domestic slave trade. As such, across the states of Kentucky, Maryland, and Virginia, the percentage of slaves in the total population declined throughout the antebellum era. The free black population, by contrast, grew. There had been few free blacks in colonial America, but from the revolution to the early-nineteenth century substantial numbers of slaves secured freedom through manumission and self-purchase, particularly in the Upper South where white support for black freedom drew on the revolutionary ideas of the age and slaveholders' evolving economic interests. In Maryland and Virginia there were less than 10,000 free blacks in the 1780s, but by 1810 there were 65,000. Thereafter, new legal restrictions constrained black slaves' access to freedom, as slaveholders began to fear the impact of free African Americans on the slave population, but still by 1860 free people accounted for 13 percent of all African Americans in the Upper South. In the Deep South, by contrast, the continued expansion and profitability of slavery meant that free people were never more than 1.5 percent of the region's non-white population and mostly were people of mixed-race descent concentrated in cities like New Orleans and Charleston where they carved out a clearly defined status between enslaved and white society.[4]

The pre-Civil War South, then, was a dynamic and varied place and slavery was a diverse and changing institution. Whether slaves lived on vast sugar plantations in Louisiana or were hired out on short contracts in Baltimore informed all aspects of their lives, including culture, family, and community structures. It also shaped opportunities for resistance and criminality and forms of white dominance and control. Yet the everyday experiences of slavery were also determined by factors that transcended regional and temporal differences, not least the personal proclivities, characters, and circumstances of individual slaves and their owners, ideologies and interests of gender and class, the forms of labor and management associated with different staple crops, the often unintended consequences of market transactions, and the ratio of blacks to whites in local populations.[5]

Slave resistance

In the early hours of August 22, 1831, Nat Turner, a slave in Virginia, murdered his seven-year-old owner, Putnam Moore, Moore's mother, Sarah, and her husband, Joseph Travis. From the Travis house, Turner and a small band of rebels moved on to neighboring farms, killing the white residents they encountered, seizing weapons, and gathering new recruits. Between 50 and 60 slaves and a handful of free African Americans roamed across Southampton County killing at least 57 white people before the insurrection was crushed by white militias on August 24. Turner alone escaped, hiding-out for more than two months before he was captured and hanged.[6]

The Turner rebellion was the deadliest in the history of North American slavery. Slaves in New York set fire to a building on Broadway in 1712 and killed nine white people in the ensuing chaos. In 1739, several scores of slaves marched south toward Florida from Stono, South Carolina, killing 21 whites before they were hunted down by the militia. Two hundred slaves revolted in the Louisiana plantation belt in 1811 and in 1839 slaves mutinied aboard the *Creole*, a ship transporting them from Virginia to New Orleans, and secured freedom in the Bahamas. But these were rare occurrences. Slaves in North America recognized that demographic, geographic, and political conditions militated strongly against rebel success, in contrast to the circumstances that facilitated more frequent and larger-scale insurrections in other parts of the Americas, including Brazil and the Caribbean. In a slave society such as Jamaica, where a rebellion in 1831 hastened slavery's abolition throughout the British Empire just three years later, slaves comprised more than 85 percent of the population, the rugged mountain terrain offered cover from which to engage in guerrilla warfare, and white reinforcements could not be speedily called on. Outside the Anglo-American world, the persistence of the trans-Atlantic slave trade until the mid-nineteenth century further encouraged rebellions in Brazil and Cuba, perpetuating slave populations with disproportionate numbers of men and people born free in Africa, more fragile bonds of family and community, and stronger African cultural influences than typically existed in the United States after Congress outlawed the importation of slaves in 1808.[7]

The scarcity of large-scale slave rebellions in the United States belied the insecurity of the nation's slaveholders. Rumors of revolt were commonplace and several major conspiracies were betrayed or uncovered before they began, including in Louisiana in 1738, New York in 1741, Richmond, Virginia, in 1800, and Charleston in 1822. Between 1785 and 1831, a total of 96 slaves were convicted of insurrection in Virginia alone and more than one hundred other slaves in the state were found guilty of murdering whites.[8] In the fall of 1856, slaveholder paranoia fuelled fears of impending slave rebellion across the South. Originating in Texas in September, alleged plots were uncovered far to the east in Virginia and Georgia and around the iron works of Tennessee and Kentucky. Although the solidly pro-slavery Democrat James Buchanan was elected president in 1856, the threat of revolt was magnified by the context of growing political opposition in the northern states to slavery's expansion, embodied in strong support for the Republican Party that was contesting its first national elections that year.[9]

In response to the growing strength of the antislavery movement in the North and calls for slavery's immediate abolition after 1830, southern slaveholders constructed a powerful pro-slavery ideology. In this telling, slaves in the South were contented and docile and acquiesced in their condition, while acts of slave crime and resistance were interpreted as products of poor management or, more commonly, nefarious abolitionist or free black influences. In reality, however, it was the actions of slaves themselves that most shook slaveholders' faith in the security of their institution. Notwithstanding the relative scarcity of organized, politically conscious rebellions, resistance was endemic to the slave condition and slaveholders recognized all too clearly that individually innocuous expressions of slave autonomy were the building blocks of profound threats to white supremacy. Historian William Dusinberre uses the term "dissidence" to describe the everyday, mostly nonviolent acts through which slaves commonly contested white domination. Insubordination, work slowdowns, damaging and breaking tools, arson, and the theft of all manner of property including crops, money, personal belongings, and livestock were an ordinary part of slave life. So was the illicit purchase of alcohol, gambling, secret gatherings, short-term absenteeism, learning to read and write, and running away. Slaves also perpetrated acts of violence against whites that were of more limited design and intent than uprisings. They assaulted, stabbed, poisoned, and murdered white owners, overseers, patrollers, and strangers, sometimes in a sudden, passionate rage, on other occasions after careful and deliberate planning.[10]

Writing in the 1970s, Eugene Genovese denied that any of this constituted a real threat to the slaveholders' rule. While recognizing the realities of slave agency and white brutality, Genovese understood slavery in the United States as a paternalistic institution in the sense that slaveholders and their human property were bound together by reciprocal duties and obligations and that slaves accepted central tenets of the white world view. In consequence, slave resistance was manageable and tended to reaffirm rather than challenge dominant structures of power. Theft, for example, "weakened [slaves'] self-respect," running away was a safety valve "drawing off those who might have led insurrections," and violence against brutal slaveholders was sufficiently rare that it highlighted that most slaves would remain subservient, "so long as their expectations did not suffer a severe jolt." To this end, slaveholders commonly encouraged or, at least, tolerated, the strong and fulfilling families and communities that slaves created on plantations and across local neighborhoods. By the nineteenth century, many also provided religious instruction and plots of land that slaves used to grow crops and rear livestock. These practices brought slaves spiritual comfort, material benefits, and even opportunities for resistance, but they also bound them more closely to their owners' properties and helped sustain a labor force that was healthy, productive, and profitable.[11]

Recent scholarship demonstrates powerfully that, although paternalism was "important for the master's self-image, [it] meant little to the typical slave."[12] If slaves accommodated to their condition, it was because of violent domination rather than an acceptance of slaveholders' moral legitimacy. Slaves who worked to improve their lives within the confines of slavery on Louisiana sugar plantations, for example, have been described as "realists" who recognized that escape, "was almost impossible, and the power of the local militia and whites could not be surmounted[.]"[13] Yet slaves also developed an autonomous "moral economy" of their own. Acts that whites punished as crimes, slaves viewed as legitimate acts of resistance. When Parker, a slave in Virginia, killed his owner with an axe, he declared, "[t]hey may hang me, but I shall go to heaven."[14] Frederick Douglass interpreted his decision to fight back against Edward Covey, a man his master had tasked with "breaking" him, not as an illegal assault on a white person but, "a turning-point in my 'life as a slave' ... [that] ... revived a sense of my own manhood ... and inspired me with a renewed determination to be a *free* man." When slaves stole their owners' property they likewise mostly viewed the act as an assertion of economic independence and the taking of what was rightfully theirs, though slave communities were sufficiently complex as to encompass a multitude of attitudes on such complex moral issues.[15]

Among the most pervasive acts of resistance, running away illustrates how pragmatic considerations shaped views on crime and resistance within slave communities. In the antebellum era, thousands of slaves escaped to the free states of the North, though many more who tried were recaptured or killed. Slaves mostly absconded for temporary periods, however, usually running by cover of night and hiding out close to home. It was often dangerous to move further afield. Slaves could exploit knowledge of the geography of their own neighborhoods to stay one step ahead of their pursuers and they could turn to friends and relatives for food, sustenance, and shelter, but they could not assume unconditional support. Aiding runaways involved sacrifice on the part of those who remained in bondage. Slaves gave from their own meager rations and risked stealing from whites even though they faced vicious punishment if caught harboring a fugitive. But there were also rewards to be gained from betraying a runaway and though strong bonds of racial solidarity reached across the

United States, facilitating many slaves' flight to liberty, fugitives took particular risks when they sought refuge among slaves in places where they were strangers.[16]

The slaveholders' rule

From the emergence of the plantation system in the mid-eighteenth century until the Civil War, policing and punishment in the experience of most African American slaves was primarily the prerogative of slaveholders, overseers, drivers, and patrollers who exercised barely regulated power on farms, plantations, and across the southern countryside. For all that law codified race and slavery, in the United States legal institutions and the state played a secondary role in regulating the institution's everyday workings. As South Carolina slaveholder and politician James Henry Hammond explained in 1845, "on our estates we dispense with the whole machinery of public police and public courts of justice. Thus we try, decide, and execute the sentences, in thousands of cases, which in other countries would go into the courts."[17] Frederick Douglass concurred, describing Colonel Lloyd's plantation in Maryland as, "a little nation of its own, having its own language, its own rules, regulations and customs. The laws and institutions of the state, apparently touch it nowhere."[18] Douglass overstated the point; slaveholders depended on nonslaveholding whites, the legal system, and the federal government to maintain their dominance. Nonetheless, he captured that slave control was about white supremacy and the compulsion of black labor, as well as the regulation of crime, and, as such, slaves could not be allowed recourse to state authorities to challenge everyday matters of plantation discipline. "If the state of slavery is to exist at all," wrote pro-slavery ideologue Chancellor William Harper of South Carolina, "the master must have, and ought to have, such power of punishment as will compel [slaves] to perform the duties of their station."[19]

Neither African slavery nor white supremacy had emerged fully formed in the colonies of North America. On the contrary, understandings of race were highly malleable in the seventeenth century and although there is evidence that Africans were owned as lifetime slaves in the Chesapeake Bay region as early as the 1620s, what legal historian Christopher Tomlins calls, the "institutional contours ... [and] ... means ... to ensure slavery's indefinite perpetuation," developed later, in piecemeal fashion, and in response to changing economic, political, and demographic conditions rather than a predetermined racial ideology. Certainly, there was no axiomatic association of blackness with slave status in the institution's formative decades. White indentured servants, American Indians, and Africans were all subject to varying forms of "unfreedom," and many among the first generation of Africans brought to North America in the seventeenth century were able to forge relatively autonomous lives as a result of the instability of early colonial society and their own cultural background as "Atlantic creoles," cosmopolitan men and women familiar with European judicial systems, religions, and languages as a result of encounters along trade routes that touched the African coast.[20]

Notwithstanding the opportunities for black independence in early-colonial America, the legal rights and social status of Africans and their descendents were gradually eroded and connections between race and slavery strengthened beginning in the mid-seventeenth century. Over the course of the next several decades, colonial legislatures legalized hereditary, lifetime slavery, identified the condition explicitly with imported Africans, and cut off routes to freedom for black men and women such as conversion to Christianity. Expansive legal codes imposed strict regulations on the lives of people of African descent. They prohibited marriage between Africans and Europeans, limited interracial trade, outlawed large gatherings of slaves, provided mechanisms for returning runaways to their owners, and introduced severe punishments for slaves who assaulted whites or were involved in insurrections. This codification of racially based slavery accompanied the consolidation of landholdings and political power in the hands of autocratic elites who were anxious to secure a stable, pliant, and substantial labor force and secure their dominance against threatening interracial alliances of African slaves, Native Americans, and indentured Europeans.[21]

Most significantly for the history of African American criminal justice, colonial law did little to regulate slaveholders who violently abused their own slaves even to the point of death. In 1669, the Virginia House of Burgesses provided that slaveholders could not be prosecuted for murder for killing a slave through punishment. The situation was similar in South Carolina, where a fine of £700 was the limit of the law's sanction for any free person convicted of slave homicide. In other colonies, the law regulating slave murder was not explicitly articulated, but in practice few slaveholders stood trial for killing their own human property anywhere in seventeenth- and eighteenth-century North America. The Virginia legislation was premised on slaves' status as property: "It cannot be presumed," reasoned Virginia's lawmakers, "that prepensed malice (which alone makes murther ffelony) should induce any man to destroy his owne estate." Such thinking persisted in the mid-nineteenth century when James Henry Hammond claimed that laws prohibiting slaveowners from killing or maiming their human property were "so seldom violated that they are forgotten."[22]

In the colonial era, only South Carolina and Georgia criminalized nonfatal violence against slaves, mandating fines of up to £100 for such brutality as dismemberment, castration, burning, and the cutting out of eyes and tongues. From the late 1780s, however, new laws were introduced to limit the violence that white southerners could inflict on their own human property. In 1788, Virginia for the first time made whites who killed slaves in the course of inflicting corporal punishment liable to prosecution for murder. By the early 1820s, most other southern states had followed suit, either through legislation, constitutional provisions, or judicial rulings. South Carolina made slave murder a capital offense in 1821, and introduced a $500 fine and six months imprisonment for killings that occurred in a moment of unpremeditated passion. In 1841, the same punishment was extended to cases of cruelty to slaves, while in Florida the code of 1828 criminalized the infliction on slaves of "cruel and unusual punishment" by any party, including slaveholders. Louisiana, Alabama, and Texas all provided for abused slaves to be sold at auction, while Maryland passed a law in 1860 freeing slaves whose owners were convicted of slave abuse three times. Nonetheless, in most states slaveholders remained exempt from prosecution if they killed a slave who had committed an act of resistance or insurrection and in practice few slaveholders ever faced legal proceedings for killing slaves in any circumstances, although there were occasional exceptions that usually stemmed from a community's collective sense that a slaveholder had violated even the broad limits of permissible slave treatment. In an 1858 case heard in Sandersville, Georgia, a slaveholder was convicted on testimony from his own daughters of murdering his 13-year-old slave through the infliction of inhuman punishment. Similarly, when the slaveholder Michael Boylan whipped to death his slave Stepney, he was arrested by a local sergeant who found him sitting in a drunken stupor alongside Stepney's still warm, dead body, a coffin, "and a hole dug to receive it." Reporting the case, the *Savannah Republican* commented, "we are shocked to record such a crime in our midst and trust the law will be rigidly enforced against the offender."[23]

That southern courts occasionally prosecuted slaveholder cruelty by the nineteenth century was rarely evidence of concern to protect the enslaved. Rather, when law intruded on the master–slave relationship, it did so in the interests of the wider white society. Too much brutality could inspire slave resistance. As Justice Brockenbrough of Virginia explained in the 1820s, there was a "danger that oppression and tyranny, against which there is no redress, may drive [slaves] to despair."[24] Moreover, the conviction of murderous slaveholders also served the South's cause in the propaganda war with antislavery campaigners who arrayed instances of violent slave abuse in support of their cause. In 1853, a self-styled "New York merchant" highlighted cases of slaveholder brutality as evidence of slavery's "infernalizing" impact on southern white society. Responding to the conviction in South Carolina of Thomas Motley for the murder of a slave torn apart by bloodhounds after being shot, whipped, and tortured in a vice, the merchant surmised that the roots of the crime lay in Motley's childhood exposure to violence against slaves that "encrusted [his heart] in cruelty."[25] Southern whites countered such analysis with reports stressing that slaveholder brutality was uncommon, condemning the practice when cases came to public attention, and calling for stringent legal consequences for the guilty.

This concern was disingenuous. The infliction by white women and men of physical abuse on African American bodies remained throughout the era of slavery not only common and legal, but often impetuous, sometimes sadistic, and not infrequently murderous. The documentary record is replete with evidence that the lash was liberally applied, usually to the bared bodies of slaves for insolence, slow or unsatisfactory work, running away, fighting, drinking, gambling, and almost any other form of conduct to which a white person took exception (see illustration 1.2). Mary Ann Helam was struck fifty lashes for refusing to marry the man her owner, Latham Brown, had selected to be her husband. Robert F. W. Allston of South Carolina punished his slaves when they failed to demonstrate what he defined as "honesty, truth, diligence, and cheerfulness in their work." Wallace Turnage, once a slave in Alabama, recalled seeing "the skin fly" from the naked backs of two women who were whipped by their overseer for picking insufficient cotton."[26] Beyond the lash, other corporal atrocities were inflicted on slaves as forms of punishment according to slaveholders' whims and imagination. Slave bodies were mutilated, eyes punched out, limbs and ears severed, noses slit, and Achilles tendons slashed. Iron collars, chains, and bells were fitted to slaves to cause pain and humiliation and to prevent escape and some slaveholders devised even more inventive tortures. Colonel M'Quiller,

Illustration 1.2 Wilson Chinn, a branded slave from Louisiana—Also exhibiting instruments of torture used to punish slaves, c.1863. Courtesy of Library of Congress, Prints and Photographs Online, Miscellaneous Items. <http://www.loc.gov/pictures/item/96524703/>

of Cashaw County, South Carolina, had his slaves rolled down a hill while locked inside a hogshead lined with nails, while the fugitive slave Charles Ball told of a master in Georgia who pumped cold water over the head and shoulders of recalcitrant slaves until they were rendered insensible. For enslaved women, and for some enslaved men as well, rape at the hands of white masters, overseers, and others was a further form of violent abuse used to assert white mastery that the law did nothing to inhibit.[27]

Slaveholders' legally sanctioned powers of violence over the enslaved stemmed from slaves' dual status as persons and property. Slaves were chattel—they could be bought, sold, and inherited—and their treatment, as far as possible, was their owners' business. But the primacy of plantation justice was also rooted in cultural, economic, and geographic conditions in the southern states. It reflected that the South was an overwhelmingly rural place, in parts a frontier society, where state power and the machinery of law enforcement had limited reach. In the post-Revolutionary Northeast, economic, social, and cultural developments encouraged the growth of state power to maintain order among increasingly concentrated, diverse, and anonymous populations, especially in big cities. By contrast, in the less populated, more geographically dispersed and culturally homogenous jurisdictions of the South, state authority was distrusted as an unnecessary and potentially dangerous imposition on the capacity of local whites to regulate society according to shared community values and beliefs, including patriarchy, white supremacy, and a code of honor. Honorable men were expected to seek personal redress, often through ritualized violence and shaming practices, such as dueling and brawls, not only in response to violence, but also slights, insults, and other attacks on the person, character, and status of themselves, their families, and household dependents. In a society where status and power were functions, in part, of exercising mastery over slaves, recourse to the protection of outside authorities was considered a dishonorable admission of personal vulnerability. The judicial system was not rejected entirely (in fact, slaveholders often went to court to resolve civil disputes involving slaves), but criminal law was usually "subordinated to the needs of the community, and ... applied with the utmost severity or indifference, depending on the consensus of the public."[28]

Evolving ideas about race, slavery, and criminality further discouraged legal intervention in the relationship between slaveholders and their human property. In the colonial period, white planters viewed the enslaved—at the time predominantly African born—as culturally alien and "intestine enemies." Law had little place in policing the warlike conditions of the master-slave relationship; white domination (and survival) instead demanded that all whites exercise constant vigilance and unremitting brutality in their dealings with slaves. By the nineteenth century, however, the stern patriarchy of colonial mastery had given way to an ideology of domestic paternalism that slaveholders developed to defend slavery from abolitionist attacks and to justify the institution to themselves. In the paternalistic imagination, slaves were no longer threatening enemies, but racially inferior and dependent members of extended white families. In this ideological context, slave crime was mostly perceived as a product of racial incapacity rather than malign intent and slave control was akin to disciplining an unruly child—a matter for "the domestic forum" rather than the courts.[29]

Slaveholders who identified themselves as paternalists acknowledged that whipping was a necessary tool of their domestic rule, but they maintained that it was a last resort applied dispassionately, consistently, and in accordance with principles of justice and humanity. James Henry Hammond, for example, questioned whether the corporal punishment of slaves was any less humane than the English practice of transporting thieves to Australia. Plowden Weston, owner of more than 300 slaves and four plantations in South Carolina, instructed his overseers that "no person should ever be allowed to break a law without being punished, nor any person punished who has not broken a well-known law." A minister in Tennessee wrote that on some plantations tribunals operated, "where complaints are referred, grievances redressed, and disputes settled," and Jefferson Davis, future president of the Confederacy, had his slaves tried and sentenced by a jury of their peers. Other slaveholders sought to maintain a façade of benign mastery by delegating whipping to an overseer or driver, or paying a fee to have slaves flogged at a local jail. One planter believed that slaves dreaded the "solitariness" of imprisonment, "and to be deprived from the little weekly dances and chitchat," but violence was the true purpose of slave imprisonment. It was rumored that the Charleston workhouse annually raised more than $10,000 in fees from slave floggings, while the former slave William Anderson, who claimed to have been jailed 60 times, vividly described the New Orleans calaboose as "a hell on earth," where each day, from sunrise until late afternoon, as many as one hundred victims were tied to a ladder and whipped. Such jails did not allow all slaveholders to keep faith in their paternalistic fantasies. South Carolina planter Charles Manigault kept secret from his fellow slaveholders that he sent his Charleston house slaves to be flogged at the city workhouse for fear that it would compromise his benevolent reputation.[30]

Even if Manigault's reputation had suffered among his slaveholding peers, he could rest secure that the law was never likely to intrude on the manner in which he judged and punished his slaves. When the punishment of slaves was debated in the courts, it was invariably at the instigation of slaveholders themselves and it was more likely to be in the form of a civil cause for damages than a criminal prosecution. Cases of fraud and breach of warranty, for example, arose between slave purchasers and sellers when recently traded slaves ran away, disobeyed orders, or acted in other ways their new owners had not anticipated when agreeing the sale. In the courtroom, white litigants advanced competing understandings of race and criminality depending on their self-interests. Sellers usually had a stake in depicting the slave at issue as trustworthy, virtuous, and hard working, but corrupted through poor management on the part of the purchaser. Conversely, purchasers argued that slave insubordination was a product of inherent characteristics that had been fraudulently obfuscated on the auction block.[31]

Slaveholders also pursued legal redress when slave hirers maimed or killed slaves in their employment. As many as 15 percent of southern slaves were hired out—sometimes for a few days, often for a year—under contracts that sought to regulate hirers' powers, but frequently gave rise to disputes between hirers and owners, particularly in cases of ill treatment. The issues at stake were most famously dissected in the North Carolina case of *State v. Mann* (1829) that arose when John Mann shot his hired slave Lydia in the back when she ran from a whipping. An indebted former mariner who could not have paid substantial damages in a civil case and had no slaves of his own, Mann was convicted on a criminal charge of assault by a jury comprising slaveholders whose verdict protected the property interests of wealthy men like themselves. On appeal, however, Mann's conviction was overturned. Chief Justice Thomas Ruffin reasoned that the law could not recognize the difference between slaveholders and slave hirers that was implicit in the trial jury's guilty verdict without compromising the stability of the slave regime. It was, instead, necessary that hirers enjoy, "the full dominion of the owner over the slave" even though they lacked the financial investment in the slave's person that was believed to check excessive slaveholder brutality. While Ruffin collapsed the distinction between hirer and owner in defining questions of slave control, however, not all southern justices concurred with his judgment. In *James v. Carper* (1857), concerning the whipping of a hired slave suspected of theft (incorrectly, as it turned out), the Tennessee Supreme Court reasoned that the safety of slaves and, hence, the interests of slaveholders, demanded that slave hirers not be allowed to inflict or order chastisement without "reasonable" cause and that, in any case, the punishment could not be more than "moderate." While *Mann* overturned a criminal conviction, *Carper* upheld a civil claim for damages, safeguarding slaveholders' property rights and affirming the primacy of whiteness in structuring the social order without affording slaves themselves the protection of the criminal law.[32]

The law's failure to protect slaves from white violence extended also to free African Americans, who suffered from underenforcement of the law most egregiously as a result of restrictions on black testimony against whites in criminal trials that were enforced across the South. A notable case occurred in 1851, when William Johnson, a slaveowning free black barber in the city of Natchez, Mississippi, was shot dead by Baylor Winn, a man with whom he had been involved in a long running property dispute and had recently sued for trespass. Although Winn was indicted as a free man of color, a jury decided that he was actually white. In a decision that revealed the legal conflicts and uncertainties that often surrounded racial identities in the slave South, the jury was swayed by evidence showing that Winn had once voted and testified in a court of law, civil rights that only white men could perform. The only two eyewitnesses to Johnson's murder were African Americans, and with Winn ruled white they could not speak against him and the prosecution case collapsed.[33] William Johnson was an unusually prosperous free black man and well connected in white society. He used law regularly in the conduct of his business. Yet, like all African Americans, he was an easy target for white criminals. Unless there were white witnesses willing to speak up in court, whites walked free when charged with crimes against blacks and it was irrelevant whether the victim were enslaved or free.

Patrols and policing

Touring the southern states in the 1850s, the landscape architect Frederick Law Olmsted noted that law enforcement in the slave states depended "upon the constant, habitual and instinctive surveillance and authority of all the white people over the blacks." Although slaveholders reified their personal bonds with slaves as the basis of a paternalistic and stable social order, in practice the business of slave control could never be confined to individual relationships or kept within plantation boundaries. Slaves knew worlds beyond their own-ers' property. Their day-to-day affairs routinely took them to neigh-boring farms and plantations, local stores and trading posts, and into villages, towns, and cities. Many travelled on their owners' business or, at least, with their owners' permission, running errands, working as hired hands for local employers, and buying and selling goods in markets, including their own produce. Slaves also developed family and kinship ties that were the basis of resilient communities and they formed networks of strategic alliances, not only with fellow bondsmen and women but also free African Americans and nonslaveholding whites, that stretched across and beyond their immediate neighbor-hoods. In places beyond the purview of their owners, from isolated backcountry roads to grog shops, waterways and crowded city streets, slaves were subject to the surveillance and control of patrols, militias, justices of the peace, night watchmen, and police officers who collec-tively constituted a more formalized, but equally violent and discre-tionary, counterpart to the mechanisms of plantation punishment.[34]

Slave patrols were established early in the colonial era, usually under the authority of county governments or militias. They trailed roads and pathways, interrogating slaves and whipping those who could not furnish a pass or adequately explain their business. They also searched slave quarters hunting for runaways, stolen goods, and anything that might appear out of the ordinary, and they broke up slave gatherings including religious services.[35] Decades after aboli-tion, many former slaves still had vivid memories of abuse suffered at patrollers' hands. Former Georgia slave Neal Upson, recalled that "petterollers … 'most nigh kilt some slaves … when dey didn't have no pass" and Millie Barber remained emotionally scarred years later from watching her father stripped and flogged by patrollers after he risked secretly visiting his wife and children on a neighboring planta-tion.[36] Yet patrollers also faced resistance from the enslaved. At a secret slave dance in Texas, ropes were tied across approaching roads to trip patrollers' horses and buy time to escape. Slaves also learned patrols' schedules and routes (in nineteenth-century Georgia, patrols were required to visit plantations just once every two weeks), and they hid, ran, and fought to evade punishment. When patrollers tried to confiscate a bottle of whiskey from an enslaved woman in Arkansas, it was reported that, "she snatched a palling off the fence and nearly beat them poor white trash to death," and in Cape Fear,

North Carolina, patrol work was scaled back after slaves began to burn patrollers' barns and kill their cattle.[37]

Nor were slaveholders uniformly supportive of the patrols on which their mastery depended. In colonial times, slaveholders had routinely served as patrollers themselves, but in the antebellum era they increasingly paid fines or employed substitutes to avoid patrol duty. Patrol work therefore became a more explicitly lower class occupation and disputes over patrollers' conduct became a lightning rod for class tensions within southern white society. Some patrols were criticized for overzealous interference in the affairs of slaveholders, while others were disparaged as lax and inefficient. Prominent planters, including Georgia's Chief Justice Joseph Henry Lumpkin, barred patrolmen from their plantations, and Henry Davis's master went so far as to teach his slaves how to put patrollers' bloodhounds off their scent by covering their feet in mud. Grand jury reports, however, also recorded regular complaints that patrols failed to prevent slaves running away, committing theft, and threatening white women in their neighborhoods.[38]

In the urban South, paramilitary style city guards and night watches began to replace slaves patrols soon after American independence. Charleston, the largest city in the late-eighteenth-century South, but still with a population of just a few thousand, formed the region's first police force in the 1780s, and by 1801 a small city night watch in Richmond was supplemented by a state appointed public guard of 100 men formed following an attempted slave rebellion that originated on the outskirts of the city. The guardsmen were quartered in the state armory, served three-year terms, and worked under similar regulations as governed US troops. The New Orleans gendarmerie, formed in 1805, operated along similar lines, with the first recruits carrying swords, living in barracks, and half of the men patrolling the city on horseback, although reforms in the 1830s created a more recognizably civilian police, unarmed and without uniforms in response to criticisms from white residents that the force was dominated by immigrants and resembled a standing army that threatened republican liberties. The reforms also reflected the declining proportion of slaves in the New Orleans population, and in other southern cities where European immigration was more limited the militia-style forces remained.[39]

The early adoption of policing in the urban South—long before similar developments in far larger northern cities—was testament to the extensive and varied opportunities for slave autonomy that were inherent to city life. A demand for flexible and short-term labor made slave hiring especially common in cities and allowed many skilled bondsmen to choose their own employers, keep a portion of their wages, and rent rooms independent of white supervision. More pervasively, the urban built environment fundamentally compromised white supervision of black conduct. Alleyways, grog shops, and private dwellings provided ready opportunities for slaves to gather surreptitiously, runaways could hope to blend into the anonymity and diversity of urban crowds, and the railroads, canals, and harbors that made cities hubs of commercial trade networks facilitated escapes. Cities were also home to substantial communities of free African Americans and impoverished white people, many of whom were European immigrants or sailors with little experience of the South's racial mores. Relationships across the color line could be fraught with tension and violence. The free poor competed with slaves for work, and claims to racial supremacy were integral to the status and identity of the white working class. At the same time, however, urban interracial subcultures flourished based around shared working, residential, and social spaces and experiences. Even though race invariably trumped class as the primary determinant of poor whites' political loyalties, city authorities nonetheless were particularly fearful of the implications of friendships and associations that crossed the racial divide.

The primary work of the first police forces in the urban South was to enforce strict municipal black codes that stipulated precise regulations of slave conduct. Slaves out on the public streets were expected to carry a pass from their master and public gatherings of even a handful of slaves were prohibited. Violations of slave pass ordinances accounted for much of the business brought before city mayors who held daily court sessions where they dispensed speedy and summary judgments, usually within hours of an arrest, to prevent delay in returning slaves to work. In Charleston, Mayor Robert Hayne reported that 768 slaves appeared before him in 1837, almost all charged with, "being out at night without tickets or ... found in the dram shops or other unlawful places." About one-third were sent to the workhouse for corporal punishment, 309 received small fines—rarely more than $1—and only a handful were remanded for trial on more serious charges. Similarly in Savannah, more than 80 percent of 3000 slaves jailed between 1809 and 1815 were accused of violating the city's 10 p.m. curfew, disorderly conduct, suspicious activity, and running away.[40] Hundreds more were arrested and whipped by police officers without even the limited formality of a Mayor's Court appearance, but aside from occasional crackdowns—usually prompted by insurrection scares or the appointment of a new mayor or police chief—the bonds of urban slavery overall remained relatively lax. By the 1850s, southern police forces were roughly double the size of their northern counterparts relative to population, but still they had insufficient manpower to keep watch over slaves and free African Americans in all of the clandestine spaces that cities offered for illicit activities.

What is more, for all that slaveholders demanded strict control of urban slaves, as individuals they regularly opposed excessive police interference that threatened their own authority or compromised their slaves' productivity. In Richmond, Thomas Massie complained about the arrest of his slave Billy for being without a pass, and condemned the city watchmen as "a set of worthless lazy fellows, who would take up occasionally inoffensive servants, merely to show they did something." An editorial in the New Orleans *Daily Picayune* concurred, complaining that slaves were "frequently arrested when there are not the slightest grounds for supposing them to be fugitives from service, and positive losses and annoyances to their owners are the result." Slaveholders also impeded the work of the police by demanding warrants before allowing their property to be searched, many more paid fines rather than have their slaves suffer a potentially incapacitating whipping, and still others routinely ignored the prohibition on allowing slaves to hire their own time, a practice that could be highly profitable, but which gave slaves unprecedented independence.[41]

Neither patrols nor city police forces drew much distinction between slaves and free African Americans. The presumption in southern law was that black skin equated to slave status and free blacks were required to register at local courthouses and carry papers attesting to their liberty. Like slave pass laws, this regulation often went unenforced. It is estimated, for example, that as few as 20 percent of free blacks in Virginia complied with the registration requirements, but the fear of arrest was ever-present and there is evidence from Richmond that in times of high labor demand free blacks without papers were rounded up and hired out to pay off their jail fees. For some, the consequences of arrest could be even more severe. In the antebellum era, free African Americans were prohibited from entering most southern states and were subject to reenslavement if they did not leave their home states within 12 months of manumission. A similar fate could befall free black sailors whose ships docked in southern ports. Under Negro Seaman's Acts, first passed in South Carolina in 1822, these men were imprisoned until their vessels departed. If a ship's captain refused to pay the costs of imprisonment or to remove a black sailor from the state, the sailor could be sold into slavery. Under pressure from Britain and the northern states, the provision for enslavement was replaced within a year by a requirement that black sailors leave the state, but this policy was reversed in 1835 and similar legislation regarding black seamen was enacted in other Deep South states in the 1830s and 1840s.[42]

Legal restrictions on free African Americans' liberties functioned as a surrogate for slavery in a society where blackness and freedom were considered incompatible and dangerous. African Americans were not the only free people who threatened slave control in the Old South, however; nonslaveholding whites also conspired with slaves, aiding runaways, engaging in interracial sexual relationships, and trading stolen and illicit goods. Illegal trading enabled slaves to obtain liquor, new clothes, and other goods prohibited by their owners, while it provided rural poor whites with food stolen by slaves who had easy access to plantation supplies. In towns and cities, white shopkeepers also welcomed the cash and high prices that slaves were typically forced to pay as a preferable alternative to the credit and discounts they usually had to offer white customers. Historian Jeff Forrett has argued that poor whites traded with slaves for rational business reasons rather than out of hostility to slavery as an institution, but for slaveholders the issue posed a serious threat to black subordination.[43] In 1855, a state committee in Georgia found no less than "2200 foreign grog-shop keepers" who supplied slaves with liquor, but the law struggled to clamp down on the practice. As Frederick Law Olmsted recognized, these were cases where "[t]he law which prevents the reception of the evidence of a negro in courts ... strikes back, with a most annoying force, upon the dominant power itself."[44]

In order to compensate for the prohibition on black witnesses and combat interracial crime, southern legislatures and courts in the 1850s began to restrict white legal privileges, despite the dangerous implications this posed to the ideology of white supremacy in a society based on racial difference. In South Carolina, petitions were submitted calling for the disfranchisement and public whipping of white offenders and the latter penalty was eventually introduced in 1857 for those convicted of a second offense. States also increased fines and prison terms for trading with slaves and relaxed the standard of proof required for a guilty verdict in an attempt to counter low conviction rates that stemmed from the inadmissibility of black testimony against white defendants. When Grady, a white man in

Georgia, was convicted of inducing three slaves to steal from their owner and escape to Boston, the key prosecution witness was a Mr. Moreland, the slave's owner. Moreland was white, but the testimony he relayed to the court was based largely on what he had been told of the crime by one of the slaves involved and Grady appealed that Moreland's evidence was at odds with Georgia's laws of 1838 and 1850 under which slave testimony was inadmissible against whites. In rejecting the appeal, however, Justice Lumpkin ruled that the verdict was consistent with the law's intent "to make the white man responsible directly, for crimes committed or attempted, through the agency of negroes." Slaveholders also turned to extralegal sanctions to punish whites involved in illicit trading with slaves, including expulsion from church congregations, mob violence, and the formation of organizations such as the "Savannah River Anti-Slave Traffick Association" that was formed in the 1840s to regulate the hundreds of African Americans whom slaveholders claimed spent nights at illegal gatherings, drinking, dancing, and stealing. Yet none of this stopped the trade, and prosecutions of whites in fact increased in the mid-nineteenth century, reflecting growing white poverty and heightened slaveholder anxieties about slave control in an era of abolitionism.[45]

Fugitives and freedom

Speaking in the 1930s, Bernice Bowden recalled how black fishermen in Virginia, including her enslaved father, "could look up the Potomac River and see the ships comin' in."[46] Because the South did not exist in isolation, slave resistance, crime, and punishment was connected to developments beyond the region's borders. In the 1790s and early 1800s, news of the black rebellion against French rule in Haiti had spurred rebels in the Chesapeake and by the 1830s, with slavery abolished in the northern states and abolitionist influences increasingly prominent in the South, thousands of slaves, especially in the Upper South, fled in search of freedom to Illinois, Ohio, and Pennsylvania, and further north into New York, New England, and Canada. Jacob Green, enslaved in Kentucky, ran away repeatedly in the 1840s. Once he reached as far as Utica, New York, before he was recaptured. On route back south, a crowd of black people in Cleveland tried and failed to free him before his ship left the port, but he dived overboard with the aid of the vessel's captain and a group of black and white abolitionists helped him escape to Zanesville, Ohio. After four months, he was arrested and claimed as a slave once more. He spent a year in bondage in Kentucky, before fleeing to Lexington while out driving his master's carriage. There he stowed away on board a ship bound for Cincinnati. Forced to hide in a cellar after he was spotted by his master's nephew, Green was discovered by a black servant who contacted an agent on the underground railroad. At night fall, Green was smuggled out to a safe house and from there to Buffalo and, finally, Toronto.[47]

The legal status of slaves outside the South was complex and changing. Even as northern states slowly abolished slavery through the early decades of the nineteenth century, they were bound by the Fugitive Slave Act of 1793, which empowered slaveholders to seize runaways anywhere in the nation. Most northern states also tolerated slaves brought within their borders for temporary periods under what were known as sojourner laws. Beginning in the 1820s, however, antikidnapping and personal liberty statutes were passed in the North that facilitated African Americans' claims to freedom. Slaves had routinely been leased out in "free" Ohio in the 1830s, for example, but under the state's 1841 Law of Freedom, they were automatically freed on stepping foot in the State. In the *Prigg* (1842) case, however, the US Supreme Court struck down similar legislation in Pennsylvania and in 1850 Congress enacted a new Fugitive Slave Law as part of a sectional compromise that turned on whether slavery should be permitted in new states carved from territories in the West that the United States had captured from Mexico during the war of 1846–8. The law gave slaveholders new powers to pursue runaways into free states, required federal marshals, private citizens, and judicial officers to assist in the chase, and swept away the legal rights of alleged fugitives who could not testify in their own defense and were denied a jury trial, leaving even African Americans born free in the North liable to what amounted to legalized kidnapping.[48]

Hundreds and possibly thousands of slaves escaped to "free" northern territory during the 1850s, many fleeing along the East coast from Maryland and Virginia and still more crossing from Kentucky and Missouri into the Upper Midwest. In total, records survive of 191 African Americans claimed as slaves under the Fugitive Slave Act between 1850 and 1860, of whom 157 were remanded into bondage and only 34 set free by commissioners empowered by federal judges to conduct the summary proceedings. These cases frequently engendered intense sectional conflict (see Illustration 1.3). Vigilance committees were established by abolitionists from Massachusetts to Ohio, which worked to protect free blacks and fugitives alike from

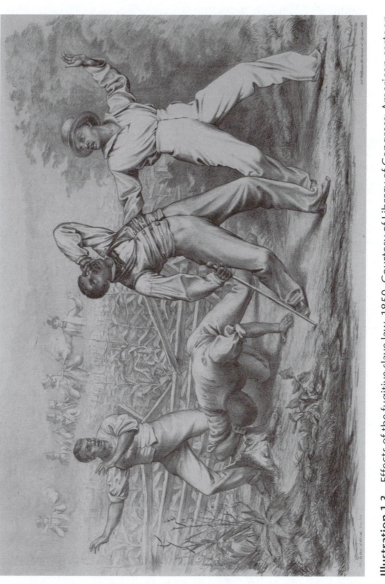

Illustration 1.3 Effects of the fugitive slave law, 1850. Courtesy of Library of Congress: American cartoon print filing series. <http://www.loc.gov/pictures/item/2008661523/>

slave-catchers. In Boston, a vigilance committee led by the Reverend Theodore Parker orchestrated popular protests in October 1850 that so intimidated slave-catchers sent to seize Ellen and William Crafts that they abandoned their efforts and the Crafts were able to escape to Britain. The following February, a runaway named Shadrach was rescued by armed abolitionists from a Boston courtroom and was able to travel to safety in Canada. Yet when Thomas Sims was arrested as a fugitive two months later, one hundred Boston policemen were stationed outside the courthouse to prevent a repeat of the scenes and Sims was eventually taken to the South under armed guard in the middle of the night. Elsewhere, in September 1851, Edward Gorsuch, a slaveholder from Maryland, tracked two of his slaves to the farmhouse of William Parker, a black man, near Christiana, Pennsylvania. With six male relatives and three federal marshals in tow, he demanded the return of his property, but rioting ensued as local blacks and whites defended the fugitives. Gorsuch was killed and Parker and the fugitives escaped to Canada. Thirty-six blacks and two whites involved in the rioting were indicted in Philadelphia for treason, but the case collapsed for lack of evidence. Three years later, back in Boston, the arrest of Anthony Burns as a fugitive two months after his escape from Richmond, Virginia, led to rioting that left one marshal dead. When Burns was returned to Virginia on June 2, an estimated 50,000 people took to the streets of Boston in protest and more than 2000 soldiers were stationed along the route to maintain order.[49]

Far from securing slaveholders' claim on their human property, fugitive slave cases exacerbated sectional tensions over slavery's future. Even so, in law the support that federal authorities provided for the slaveholders' cause was reaffirmed in the 1850s by the US Supreme Court in the case of *Dred Scott v. Sandford* (1857). Born and raised a slave in Missouri, Dred Scott had sued for his freedom in the late 1840s on the grounds that for long periods he had lived with his owner, John Emerson, in the free territories of the Midwest. The case wound through the legal system for a decade until it reached the Supreme Court where Chief Justice Roger Taney ruled that no African American—slave or free—had any rights that the law was bound to respect.[50]

The violent and arbitrary mechanisms of everyday slave control stretched from farms and plantations to the US Congress. They were wide ranging and they enabled slavery to function satisfactorily, at least from the perspective of most southern whites. But issues of

African American policing and punishment also presented challenges to the slaveholders' rule, due to the fact that slavery could never be reduced in practice to the simple binary divisions between master and slave and black and white that were enshrined in statutes and idealized in pro-slavery rhetoric. The slave South was embedded within an Atlantic World context in which antislavery thought burgeoned from the late-eighteenth century, and although US slavery still flourished in the mid-nineteenth century, it did so in a nation that was becoming ever more starkly divided legally, socially, economically, and politically by the issue of abolition. Slave resistance consequently had powerful political implications, because it forced conflict over slavery's future onto terrain that slaveholders could not unambiguously control. It generated divergent definitions and understandings of slave crime, opened up violent punishments inflicted on plantations to national scrutiny and debate, made slave policing dependent on nonslaveholding whites, and required the federal government to intercede on the South's behalf in the legal affairs of nonslave states. Slaves might suffer at the hands of a man like Bennett Barrow in the 1840s much as they had done a century earlier, but even as slaveholders continued to dominate the small worlds of their own plantations, slave resistance ensured that they had to struggle mightily to contain growing tensions and weaknesses in their rule.

2

Slavery and the Criminal Law

When it was determined to hang the poor fellow ... his judges could not know, nor do I suppose, they much cared, whether he were innocent or guilty.
—Richard Hildreth, *The White Slave; or, Memoirs of a Fugitive,* 1852

In 1800, following an audacious but doomed slave conspiracy near the city of Richmond, Virginia, Thomas Jefferson, then Vice-President of the United States, debated the rebels' fate with his good friend, Virginia governor James Monroe. At the head of the conspiracy was Gabriel, a skilled blacksmith owned by local planter Thomas Prosser. Like many slaves in the region, Gabriel was hired out to work in Richmond where he lived with some autonomy and was exposed to the political debates about freedom and equality that dominated national politics at the time. Inspired by religious faith, the revolutionary rhetoric of the age, the ongoing slave rebellion in St. Domingue, that would lead to the founding of Haiti as the world's first black republic four years later, and intense divisions of class and party politics among white Virginians, Gabriel led as many as 1000 African Americans, enslaved and free, in plotting to seize control of Richmond, secure their own freedom, and spark further revolt across the region.

Scheduled for August 30, torrential rain caused Gabriel's rebellion to be postponed and when two of his enslaved conspirators subsequently revealed the plot to a local white man, the militia was swiftly mobilized to defend the capital and capture the rebels. Ten slaves implicated in the insurrection had been hanged by the time that

38

Monroe sought Jefferson's advice on how many more he should allow to die. Jefferson considered this an important but difficult question. He believed that in Washington there was "a strong sentiment that there has been hanging enough" and was concerned for the impact further executions might have on Virginia's reputation: "[t]he other states & the world at large will forever condemn us if we indulge a principle of revenge, or go one step beyond absolute necessity," Jefferson warned. Yet, the practical implications of sparing rebel slaves were equally unpalatable. "I doubt whether these people can ever be permitted to go at large among us with safety," Jefferson cautioned, concurring with Monroe's earlier assessment that a pardoned rebel could never become "a useful servant." Jefferson suggested that the Virginia legislature might pass a law to sell out of state those condemned slaves not yet put to death. Within months, Virginia adopted the policy, but it came too late for those involved in Gabriel's plot. Although Monroe recommended that all executions be stayed until the legislature could next meet, he was overruled by his councilmen who demanded more and immediate killing.[1]

The broad scope that the law allowed slaveholders, patrols, and the white population at large to inflict violence on African Americans meant that even slaves suspected of committing the most serious crimes were routinely judged and punished without recourse to legal institutions, but thousands of enslaved men and women nonetheless faced criminal trials and punishment at the hands of the state. There were no hard and fast rules as to when slaves would be brought before the courts rather than subjected to informal discipline, but most slave trials concerned crimes that were committed in public spaces rather than private farms or plantations and when the accused was beyond the direct control of a white master or overseer. In most cases, the alleged crime was also sufficiently serious as to warrant the infliction of severe corporal punishment, including the severing of limbs or the death penalty and somewhat less often there was disagreement among whites as to the guilt of the accused or the appropriate sanction. Above all, state criminal justice apparatus was deployed in cases of insurrection that posed a fundamental threat to white society that could not be left to individual owners to address independently.

Enslaved defendants confronted a justice system that was less an alternative to plantation justice than an extension of the slaveholders' power cloaked in legal garb. Although some states moved to extend significant procedural rights to slaves in the antebellum era, slave trials were invariably shot through with unregulated judicial discretion, community influence, and white supremacist assumptions about race and criminality.

Slave penal codes, meanwhile, mandated the death penalty for offenses that struck at slaveholders' security and supremacy, including, in most jurisdictions, insurrection, arson, striking, raping, or poisoning a white person, or even attempting the act. From the first recorded slave execution in 1641 until slavery's abolition in 1865, at least 1720 black slaves suffered the death penalty, though this figure almost certainly undercounts the true total. Many thousands more were sentenced to be whipped, sold and exiled, branded, and in other ways tortured.[2]

This sanguinary and despotic system of slave "justice" also shaped the trials of free African Americans—in the North as well as the South—yet at the same time it also mapped out boundaries and limits to slaveholders' authority. As pro-slavery legal scholar, Thomas Cobb, of Georgia, argued, the criminal trial of slaves recognized that there were circumstances when "[t]he right of the master to control his slave [was] subordinate to the right of the State to hold the slave amenable to its laws". Cobb's explanation spoke to a tension at the heart of African American crime and punishment in a slave society: while slaveholders might seek to protect personal interests—including their property investment in enslaved criminals—Cobb reasoned that only the state could consistently act for the greater good of white society.

The slave criminal trial

Amidst the relatively fluid racial order of the mid-seventeenth century, there was no systematic attempt to distinguish the experiences of black and white defendants in criminal law. Beginning in the 1690s, however, as slave populations grew and racial categories hardened, new codes were enacted in all of the English colonies outside of New England providing for slaves to be tried in separate courts from whites that operated outside the common law. The earliest distinct slave courts were in South Carolina, where trials were conducted after 1690 by two magistrates and five freeholders (and after 1740 by one magistrate and two freeholders in noncapital cases) and Virginia, where a panel of at least four justices of the peace—known as a court of oyer and terminer—sat in judgment on slaves from 1692. Other colonies followed suit. In slave courts from Georgia to New York, and by the nineteenth century as far west as Louisiana, panels of magistrates and freeholders together conducted examinations, passed judgments, and imposed sentences. There was no trial by jury and legal precedents and common law due process rights of the accused were disregarded. Until the antebellum period, there were also few rules of evidence in slave trials and no mechanism to appeal against convictions. Such legal technicalities were unnecessary. The courts were designed not to uphold justice but to protect against slave resistance. As North Carolina chief justice John Taylor explained in 1821, "our ancestors" established slave courts out of "a sense of common danger, and the duty of self-preservation".[3] Especially in times of slave rebellion, slaveholding colonists considered a quick and certain method of trial and punishment for slaves to be imperative. While white defendants could spend months in jail waiting for the next scheduled court session to convene, slaves were examined within five to ten days of indictment in Virginia and within six days in South Carolina. Whether judged innocent or guilty, enslaved defendants were speedily executed or returned to work. Within a week of the outbreak of a rebellion involving several hundred slaves in Louisiana in 1811, for example, a judge and five slaveholders sat as an examining tribunal in St. Charles Parish and condemned to death 21 slaves in hearings that lasted just two days. According to reports, the convicts' bodies were mutilated and their heads displayed on poles at points around New Orleans and along the lower Mississippi River for months afterwards.[4]

In the conservative and aristocratic legal and political environments of South Carolina and Virginia, as well as in Louisiana, which was influenced by the distinctive legal cultures of France and Spain, the examination of enslaved defendants outside of common law survived until the Civil War. Over time, new procedural regulations were introduced, including defense attorneys, peremptory challenges, and requirements for unanimous verdicts in capital cases. Louisiana and South Carolina also permitted appeals from the decisions of slave courts, though the separate trial system for slaves meant that higher courts did not need to extend to enslaved defendants all of the due process protections reserved for whites. In an 1851 case concerning coerced slave confessions, for example, the Louisiana Supreme Court declared itself "not prepared to say the same strictness should be observed" as in cases involving free defendants.[5] There was no appellate process in Virginia, but from 1800 the state governor did review all capital convictions and was empowered to convert death sentences to sale and transportation out of the United States. Few of these provisions interfered with the courts' primary repressive purposes, but they reflected slaveholders' concern to maintain a façade of justice as well as growing criticisms from politicians and legal professionals within the three states of the continued denial of due process to enslaved defendants. In 1822, for example, the Governor of South Carolina, Thomas Bennett, described court proceedings against 128 slaves arrested in Charleston for conspiring in an insurrection plot supposed to have been led by a free black man named Denmark Vesey as "a violation of Law" and contrary to the "rules which universally obtain among civilized nations, in the judicial investigation of crime." In 1829, US Supreme Court justice William Johnson similarly described the proceedings of South Carolina slave courts as "summary" and "arbitrary"[6] and in the late-1840s, Judge John Belton O'Neall joined the attack, calling the system "the worst … which could be devised" and criticizing the influence on court decisions of local "passions and prejudices." South Carolina governor James H. Adams took up the theme in the 1850s, describing the courts' decisions as "rarely in conformity with justice or humanity" and eventually he moved to outlaw them.[7]

In the majority of slave states, separate slave trial systems were abandoned beginning in the Revolutionary era. In Pennsylvania, the system ended at the same time as the abolition of slavery itself in 1780, Delaware introduced trial by jury for slaves in 1789, and in 1793 North Carolina placed slave trials under the jurisdiction of the regular county courts. A concern with swift justice remained, however, and if the county court was not scheduled to convene within 15 days, the case could be heard summarily by three justices of the peace and a 12-man jury. Under both modes of trial, only slaveholders could serve as jurors, a rule designed, as explained by North Carolina Chief Justice John Taylor in 1826, "to protect the property of the owner, by infusing into the trial, that temperate and impartial feeling, which would probably exist in persons owning the same sort of property." This dual system lasted until 1816 when slave trials were transferred to the state's superior courts. Trial by jury was extended to slaves in Georgia in 1811, although in contrast to white defendants who were tried in superior courts, slave trials in Georgia took place until 1850 in inferior courts where there was no requirement for justices to have legal training. Further west, the Missouri Constitution of 1820 included provision for slaves to be tried in regular courts with a jury and similar systems prevailed in Alabama and Mississippi, although in the latter state a variation of the oyer and terminer system operated from 1822 to 1833 in which magistrates sat with a 12-man jury. Courts comprising slaveholders and justices were retained for noncapital cases.[8]

Southern whites hailed the extension of trial by jury to enslaved defendants as evidence of a commitment to justice that was consistent with paternalistic rhetoric. In ruling on an appeal against the conviction of a slave in 1856, North Carolina Chief Justice, Frederick Nash, wrote, "[t]he slave stands at the bar, clothed with the same privileges that the white man enjoys, and the trial is conducted by the same rules."[9] Justice Nisbet of the Georgia Supreme Court similarly claimed that the decision to grant slaves and free African Americans the same trial rights as whites in capital cases, "reflects distinguished honor upon the State and exhibits in clear and strong lights, the humanity of our laws towards them."[10] In Florida, Chief Justice Charles DuPont described the equal treatment of slave and master in the courtroom as "the crowning glory" of the southern slave system.[11] This rhetoric bolstered pro-slavery arguments in the face of increasingly vehement abolitionist attacks on the South, which themselves often drew attention to the workings of slave law. In one of the most comprehensive abolitionist critiques of the southern legal system, George Stroud condemned the "cruel enactments" of slave penal codes, which William Goodell similarly described as "despotic" and "barbarous."[12] Yet the audience for expressions of faith in the justice of slave law not only comprised northern abolitionists, but perhaps more importantly southern slaveholders themselves who sought reassurance that their financial stake in human property was protected in the courtroom and that law enforcement was consistent with justice and their pretensions of paternalistic interest in the slaves' well-being. Indeed, even in the colonial era, New York had permitted the trial of one enslaved defendant to be moved before a jury when his master offered to pay a fee and, in the wake of the suspected slave insurrection of 1741, authorities elected voluntarily to examine the accused before a jury to lend greater credibility to the proceedings.[13]

The incorporation of slave trials into regular court sessions had significant legal implications. The evolutionary nature of the common law meant that legal arguments upheld in the trial of white defendants set precedents that would apply equally when slaves stood in the dock. Likewise, judges could not disregard due process in slave cases without considering the potential ramifications of their decision-making for future white defendants. This provided some assurance that testimony in slave trials would be weighed fairly and in accordance with established procedures and it also meant that rulings and verdicts against slaves could be appealed to higher courts where appellate judges commonly insisted that rules of legal formalism were strictly adhered to even if this meant reversing a slave's conviction on a technicality. Trained and experienced in law, many of the appellate judges who ruled on the form and substance of slave trials were genuinely concerned to uphold due process for enslaved defendants and, unlike most politicians in the South, they were usually elected to long terms on the bench and so could afford to write opinions that might not chime with popular pro-slavery sentiments.[14]

Between 1830 and 1860, a total of 185 slave convictions were appealed across nine southern states of which 111 resulted in reversals.[15] Strikingly few of these cases involved protestations that a convicted slave was innocent. The North Carolina Superior Court, for example, granted new trials in 18 of 32 cases involving slave defendants between 1848 and 1865 and in 12 of these cases the basis for the new trial was a technical error on the original indictment.[16] In one case, a slave convicted of burning a corn crib had his conviction overturned because the statute on which the prosecution was based concerned only the burning of barns.[17] In a similar case in Alabama, the conviction of Clarissa, a slave condemned to death for attempting to poison a white person, was quashed because the indictment in the case did not specify that the jimson weed Clarissa had allegedly used in committing the crime was poisonous. In 1841, the murder conviction of Isham, a slave, was overturned in Mississippi on the grounds that the prosecution case had included a coerced confession.[18] In some cases, errors on the indictment even spared slaves convicted of raping white woman, including Martin in North Carolina in 1832. Southern supreme courts also repeatedly threw out coerced confessions by slave defendants. In 1858, Alabama went so far as to rule slave confessions inadmissible on broader grounds than applied to free defendants due to slaves' supposed lesser familiarity with the workings of law and greater susceptibility to threats of violence or promises of reward.[19]

Crimes, convictions, and punishments

A lack of evidence makes it difficult to assess how far appeals court decisions shaped the routine administration of slave prosecutions in lower trial courts. In all states, slave conviction rates varied significantly with the type of crime charged. Slaves were most likely to be acquitted when prosecuted for offenses that were difficult to prove, indicating at least a nominal concern with truth on the part of justices and juries. Slaves accused of violent crimes, for example, were more often convicted than those tried for crimes against property, reflecting that prosecutors could usually call eyewitnesses to testify to assaults and murders, but were more reliant on circumstantial evidence in cases of theft and burglary. In Georgia, only 10 percent of slaves charged with property crimes were convicted or pleaded guilty between 1850 and 1865, compared with 42 percent tried for crimes against the person. Infanticide was equally difficult to prove. In a society with high rates of infant mortality, courts struggled to distinguish between deaths from natural causes and those caused by deliberate suffocation or neglect. As a result, conviction rates were usually lower for slave women charged with murder than for enslaved men who more often perpetrated public acts of violence or killed in ways that left physical evidence on the victim's body. Prosecutions for arson and poisoning were difficult to sustain for similar reasons. In a sample of cases from Georgia between 1755 and 1865, there was a conviction rate of only 46 percent for arson (11 out of 24) compared with 81 percent for murder (87 out of 107).[20]

Enslaved defendants probably evaded conviction more often in common law jurisdictions than in South Carolina's freeholders' courts or Virginia's courts of oyer and terminer, but the available data is far from conclusive. In a sample of 17 counties in Tennessee between 1825 and 1861, 113 out of 160 capital cases involving slaves reached a verdict, of which 55 ended in acquittals. At 66 percent, this conviction rate was broadly similar to that for white defendants in the state. The situation was comparable in Georgia where changes to the slave trial system drove a decrease in capital slave trial conviction rates from 94 percent to 71 percent between the colonial period and the Civil War. In Savannah, only 15 percent of prosecuted slaves were convicted and in upstate Greene County trial conviction rates for blacks and whites were almost identical, though it is significant that across the state charges against whites were far more often dismissed at earlier stages of the prosecution process. In states with separate slave courts, there were fewer opportunities for charges to be dropped before trial than in common law jurisdictions and magistrates consequently heard prosecutions based on the flimsiest of evidence, but still conviction rates were high. In South Carolina between 1818 and 1860, nearly 70 percent of 1071 slave defendants prosecuted in Anderson and Spartanburg districts were found guilty and there were convictions in 57 percent of a sample of 751 slave examinations from seven counties in Virginia between 1786 and 1865.[21]

Irrespective of the statistical evidence, common law prosecutions of slaves were no guarantee against procedural irregularities or convictions based on dubious proof. In a case from Elbert County, Georgia, in 1839, David Bond took out a warrant for burglary against Edmond, a slave, after discussing with a fortune teller what might have happened to money that had gone missing from his home. Edmond was subsequently convicted on the basis of the circumstantial evidence that he seemed to have "plenty of money." Likewise, Allen, a slave, was convicted of rape in North Carolina solely on the testimony of his white alleged victim who was said to have proved in court, "all the requisites that constitutes in law the offence." Before cases even came to court, evidence and confessions were commonly extracted from slaves under torture, and the exclusion of this testimony at trial was probably exceptional rather than the norm. In 1857, three slaves were executed near Natchez, Mississippi, for the murder of Duncan Skinner, a plantation overseer, on the basis of testimony extracted from slaves tied up and whipped by local planters after a coroner's jury had initially ruled the death accidental. Six years later, the slave Jane confessed to burning down the house of her master, A. J. Smith, while he whipped her. She later pleaded guilty to arson in a South Carolina court and was hanged.[22]

In slave courts, trial proceedings were even less regulated. As South Carolina attorney general, Robert Y. Hayne, explained in 1822, the very purpose of the courts was to "hear and determine the matter brought before them in the most expeditious and summary manner." Justice Elihu Bay concurred, noting that the absence of due process reflected the threat of slave insurrection and warning that superior courts "ought not to be eagle eyed … in finding out and supporting every formal error or neglect." Slave courts kept few written records of their business, but those that survive indicate that convictions were often highly questionable. The most high-profile examples of the repressive function of slave courts occurred in times of slave insurrections. In 1822, 35 black men were hanged in Charleston, South Carolina, and a further 40 banished from the United States by courts hastily convened to investigate the reported conspiracy headed by Denmark Vesey. The proceedings were mostly conducted behind closed doors and the prosecution case was largely built around evidence obtained from a small number of black witnesses who were themselves implicated in the insurrectionary plot. Historian Michael Johnson argues in a controversial analysis that the evidence of these witnesses, obtained under torture and the threat of execution, was so tainted that it is likely there was no conspiracy at all and the alleged participants were instead framed by white Charlestonians led by the city's mayor, James Hamilton, in order to justify a politically expedient crackdown on the city's African Methodist Episcopal Church and free African American community. This interpretation overstates the case. It overlooks, for example, evidence corroborating elements of the slaves' testimony that suggests the stories of an insurrectionary plot were far more than an elaborate fabrication elicited by fear. Nonetheless, it was undoubtedly the case that the Charleston authorities were little concerned with establishing the truth of the allegations in their courtrooms.[23]

Nat Turner's 1831 rebellion in Southampton County, Virginia, also led to a brutal crackdown by the courts. As in Charleston nine years earlier, several slaves were convicted and sentenced to death based on the circumstantial testimony of just one or two witnesses, who in most cases were slaves themselves and very possibly anxious to tell their white interrogators whatever they wanted to hear. Frank was condemned solely on testimony from Becky, a slave, who swore only that a week prior to the rebellion she had been in the slave quarters at Solomon Parker's plantation, where several of the rebels were later recruited, and heard the accused commit to "help kill the white people." Becky's evidence was also decisive in the examination of Isaac and Jim. On this occasion, a second enslaved witness—Bob—corroborated that both prisoners frequently went to the Parker plantation, but still there was no evidence that directly implicated them in the rebellion.[24]

Had Frank, Isaac, and Jim been tried by a jury, their fate probably would have been little different. All across the South, due process and even law itself was easily disregarded in times of heightened slave unrest and white insurrectionary fears. On June 2, 1802, an insurrectionary plot was uncovered in Bertie County, North Carolina. The plot was tied to a wider conspiracy stretching across eastern Virginia that inspired terror among local whites coming just two years after Gabriel's aborted attack on Richmond. By June 16, at least nine slaves had been hanged and by the end of the month 15 were dead, but in the state legislature there was unease about the legal process. Incriminating testimony had been obtained and documented by a "committee of inquiry" that was hastily assembled to prevent a lynching. The committee offered pardons to slaves who gave up the names of the leading conspirators, but the dubious validity of this evidence was acknowledged later in the year when the legislature adopted an evidentiary rule from the state's old slave courts, ruling that in future insurrection prosecutions slave testimony would only be admitted when corroborated by "pregnant circumstances" that gave the court good reason to trust the witness.[25]

Trial by jury was of little more benefit to slaves in North Carolina 30 years later. When news of Nat Turner's rebellion reached the state, white men in the neighborhood where Harriet Jacobs lived as a slave took up arms and marauded through black communities, "acting out their brutal will." Slaves were flogged, their possessions seized or vandalized, and some threatened with execution until saved by slaveholders described by Jacobs as, "the better class of the community," but who were minded principally to prevent the destruction of their valuable human property.[26] While the rights of slave defendants in southern law steadily expanded, the growing abolitionist threat only increased recourse to such extralegal forms of slave control. A vigilance committee hanged 12 slaves and five whites in Mississippi in 1835, and in the fall of 1856, when fears of slave insurrection swept across the South, vigilantes captured, whipped, and executed slaves from Texas to Tennessee. Against the backdrop of the Civil War, at least 30 slaves were executed in the fall of 1861 by a vigilance committee that conducted investigations into a reported conspiracy in Second Creek, near the city of Natchez, Mississippi.[27]

Even in more peaceful times, it was precisely in those jurisdictions where slave defendants had most legal protections that they were least likely to appear in court on criminal charges. In Leon County, Florida, just 17 slaves and free African Americans constituted less than 2 percent of the defendants in more than 1000 criminal trials held in two periods for which records remain from 1826 to 1833 and 1841 to 1869. Nine of these 17 cases involved murder, indicating that lesser offenses were handled in lower courts or outside the legal system altogether. Similarly in Warren County, Mississippi, which included the city of Vicksburg, only 47 enslaved defendants appeared in court between 1841 and 1859. By contrast, in states where slaves were tried in separate courts from whites and had minimal procedural safeguards, they stood trial more regularly and for a wider range of offenses. In Richmond, Virginia, with a similar slave population as Vicksburg, 444 slaves faced criminal trials in the 30 years before the Civil War and in the same period 321 slave trials were held in the district of Spartanburg, South Carolina.[28] In contrast to the murder cases that comprised most slave trials in Florida and Mississippi, Spartanburg and Anderson districts saw 43 percent (453) of black defendants between 1818 and 1860 charged with property crimes and only 12 percent (106) with violent crimes against the person. Apart from a substantial number of unspecified offenses, the most significant categories among the remaining cases were gambling, Sabbath violation, rioting, and harboring runaways. A similar diversity of cases characterized slave trials in Virginia, where it is estimated that more than 3000 slaves were prosecuted between 1706 and 1785 and as many as 9000 over the following 80 years.[29]

Evolving procedural safeguards for enslaved defendants did not impact significantly on rates of slave executions, even though the number of crimes for which slaves could be put to death declined in most states in the decades after independence. Georgia removed all forms of theft from its death penalty statutes in 1816 and narrowed the circumstances under which slaves could be executed for arson and burglary, while in North Carolina attempted rape was the only offense that carried the death penalty for enslaved but not white convicts by the time of the Civil War. These changes were consistent with developments in penal thought that reshaped criminal punishments across Western societies from the late-eighteenth century and were evident elsewhere in the South in the construction of state penitentiaries and the abolition of most corporal punishments for white convicts. Slave executions nonetheless increased in frequency during this period. At least 1259 slaves were put to death between 1790 and 1865, with 96 percent executed for murder, insurrection, or rape. Relative to population, this represented an eight-fold increase in rates of slave executions between the 1790s and the 1860s.[30] In Alabama and Virginia alone between 1840 and 1860, 285 African Americans were hanged compared with only 22 whites, even though both states had majority white populations. Across the South, meanwhile, practices such as burning at the stake, public execution, and branding persisted for African American convicts long after they were abolished for white criminals. The last recorded slaves to be burnt alive in South Carolina were William, a runaway from Georgia executed near Greenville in 1825 for murdering a white man, and Jerry, who was convicted of rape with intent to murder. In 1841, the heads of three free blacks and one slave executed in St. Louis were displayed in local stores as a grisly warning, while public hanging for slaves continued in 1850s Louisiana after white executions were removed behind prison walls.[31]

Property, class, and gender in the courtroom

In *Kirkwood v. Miller* (1858) the Tennessee Supreme Court condemned the lynching of slaves in the state two years earlier. Upholding the claim of a master who sued for the value of a slave murdered by a mob amidst rumors of a slave uprising, the Court ruled that "vague, unde-fined apprehensions about a 'rising or insurrection of the slaves,' ... cannot be allowed to save parties from liability for the destruction of their neighbor's property."[32] Similar considerations were at stake in all slave trials and were a primary reason why the courts had any con-cern with justice at all. The execution of a slave represented a consid-erable financial cost to the slave's owner and often also to the state treasury, which was usually required to pay some level of compensa-tion, if rarely a slave's full value. Mississippi paid one-half the assessed value for executed slaves, Missouri offered no compensation at all, and Alabama and North Carolina limited compensation in cases where slaveholders were adjudged to have contributed to the crime through ill-treatment of the convict or some other "failure" of mastery.[33]

Slaveholders were also liable for various costs involved in prosecut-ing their slaves and for damages resulting from the crime committed. In several states, including Missouri, Louisiana, and North Carolina, the owners of convicted slaves were required to pay all court costs, prison fees, and, in cases of theft, to provide restitution for stolen property to the victim.[34] By the nineteenth century, slaveholders were also responsible in most states for furnishing slaves with defense coun-sel, a policy based on the paternalistic notion that masters had a duty of care toward their human property. A desire to protect property investments rather than a concern with justice prompted some slave-holders to retain leading attorneys to represent enslaved defendants. In one Florida case, for example, Abraham Dupont appointed future federal judge McQueen McIntosh to defend his slave, Luke, charged with "malicious destruction of property" for shooting a neighbor's mules that had wandered onto the Dupont plantation.[35]

Even in cases that ended in acquittal, a criminal prosecution was potentially an expensive business for the owner of an accused slave. Slaveholders might be required to post security to guarantee a slave's good conduct and future appearance in court, while slaves held in jail awaiting trial were unavailable for work and at risk from illness and neglect. In 1856, the slave William spent six months awaiting trial for murder in Savannah in a jail that the local grand jury condemned as "entirely incompatible with health."[36] Once legal proceedings had concluded, even slaves who received noncapital sentences might still be incapacitated for several days or weeks by the effects of the severe corporal punishments that courts could impose. Some slaves in state custody never returned to their owners at all. A slave sent to the

New Orleans calaboose to be whipped slit his own throat rather than endure a flogging, while a slave convicted of a capital offense took his own life in a Kentucky jail while on remand awaiting sentence. The state Supreme Court rejected a claim for damages, ruling that the state was only liable for the value of slaves who had been "executed or condemned."[37]

In another case, also from Kentucky, a slave accused of a "heinous" crime escaped from a county jail along with a recaptured runaway who had been incarcerated by his owner for safekeeping, and when Sarah escaped from jail in Merriwhether County, Georgia, her execution for murder had to be delayed for two months until she was recaptured. Such incidents were perhaps in the mind of Tennessee slaveholder Elijah Moore in 1854. As the *Athens Post* reported, Moore's slave Tom was often "insolent" to his master's family, but Moore chose not to have him arrested, as he "was desirous of having his labor in the crop at this particular time". Beyond the short-term loss of jailed slaves' labor, the permanent scars of the lash and the branding iron that marked the bodies of enslaved convicts had longer-term implications for slaveholders: as symbols of the bearers' criminality and resistance to white authority, they could affect a slave's price on the auction block. As Andrew Boone, a former slave in North Carolina explained, "[a] nigger scarred up or whaled an' welted up wus considered a bad nigger an' did not bring much. If his body wus not scarred, he brought a good price."[38]

There was a tension implicit in these cases between the security of the white population at large and the property interests of individual slaveholders. While the criminal law functioned against the interests of African Americans, by the nineteenth century it did not unambiguously serve the interests of the ruling race. Indeed, it could not, because white society was not always of one mind. This was dramatically apparent in Richmond, Virginia, in 1852. In that year, Jordan Hatcher, a 17-year-old slave was hired out, like hundreds of other young, enslaved men in the city, to work in a tobacco factory. One February morning, William Jackson, a white overseer, attempted to whip Hatcher for the poor quality of his work. Hatcher retaliated and in the ensuing struggle he struck Jackson across the head with an iron poker, fracturing his skull and causing injuries that proved fatal the following day. After Hatcher was convicted of murder and sentenced to death, a petition containing the signatures of 60 prominent Richmond citizens called upon Virginia Governor Joseph Johnson to spare Hatcher from the gallows mainly on humanitarian grounds and due to the fact that the fatal blow that killed Jackson "was struck under circumstances tending greatly to aggravate the boy [Hatcher], without premeditation and with no design to kill." This consideration was uppermost in Johnson's mind when he commuted Hatcher's death sentence to sale and transportation. Explaining his decision to the General Assembly, Johnson argued that as "Hatcher was in a state of great excitement and suffering when he struck the blow," the crime was not murder, "but *manslaughter*, without intent to kill," and it would have been treated as such had the defendant been a white man. Finally, "though the *letter of the law* prescribed the *penalty of death*," Johnson believed that it would be, "contrary to the spirit of the laws and of our age, and contrary to *mercy and humanity*," to execute Hatcher.[39]

In reality, the fate of Jordan Hatcher, like that of many other slave defendants, was entangled with the identity of his victim. Had Hatcher killed his owner, he would most likely have been hanged, but William Jackson's lower-class status militated against execution when weighed against the costs to the slaveholding class. Sale and transportation had by this time served as a routine and prudent alternative to the death penalty in Virginia for more than 50 years. Although 628 slaves were executed in the state between 1785 and 1865, hundreds more were spared and sold, shifting the burden of compensation from the state treasury to slave traders.[40] As commonplace as sale and transportation had become, however, it was controversial and the Hatcher case split Richmond's white community. There was outrage among tobacco factory owners—who more often hired slaves than owned them—and the white working class, which included men who identified with William Jackson. While slaveholders endorsed sale and transportation as a means of reconciling control of slave crime with their property interests in slave defendants, white workers, who competed with hired slaves like Hatcher for jobs, considered their precarious social status challenged by a commutation that implied "that a *negro is as good as a white man*." The Richmond press further railed that sale and transportation undermined the work of the courts, compromised slave discipline, and burdened other states with Virginia's criminal slaves. Sale out of the state was, according to one newspaper editor, no punishment at all, though slaves themselves, torn away from their homes and families, would surely have disagreed. "It would be better," argued the *Dispatch*, "to pass a law making the loss fall upon the master who is so unfortunate as to own a felon." Controversy over sale and transportation persisted in Virginia until the sentence was replaced in 1858 with labor on the public works for life, but this proved an equally problematic punishment. During the Civil War, when slave convicts were hired out to companies including the Covington and Ohio Railroad, many escaped to enemy lines and fearful whites submitted petitions and threatened mob violence to prevent the employment of enslaved prisoners in their communities.[41]

With similarly divisive consequences, considerations of gender also shaped white community responses to slave trials. At least 151 enslaved women were put to death between 1641 and 1865, with a small increase in the number of women among all executed slaves from 7.4 percent before 1790 to 9.3 percent over the following 75 years until slavery's final abolition. The relative infrequency with which enslaved women stood trial meant that whites rarely perceived female slave crime as a serious threat, but enslaved women were, in fact, disproportionately involved in the most serious offenses. A study of capital slave trials found that female defendants were charged with more serious crimes than men, most commonly murder, arson, and poisoning, and their victims were frequently their masters and mistresses. In contrast to enslaved men who mostly toiled as field hands, substantial numbers of women were house servants and their crimes reflected the particular forms of oppression and opportunities for resistance presented by the rhythms of their daily work and the proximity of white authority figures.[42]

Celia was 14 when she was first raped by her owner, Robert Newsome. In 1855, she was 19, the mother of two children by Newsome, and pregnant once more when, in the midst of another attempted rape, she struck Newsome a fatal blow and then burned his dead body in a furnace. Celia was afforded a rigorous defense from a three-man legal team and might have been spared the gallows under a Missouri statute that the defense contended gave all women, even slaves, the right to defend themselves from sexual assault. But the judge disagreed, refusing to instruct the jury in this aspect of law and Celia was found guilty in a verdict that affirmed the law's subservience to the slaveholding class and notions of white mastery and dominance. Even so, Celia's trial had implications outside the courtroom as well. Reacting to details of Newsome's abuse of Celia published in the press and stoked by the emotive arguments of the young woman's court-appointed defense counsel, many in the local white community opposed the verdict and some unknown persons went so far as to break Celia out of jail to ensure that the state Supreme Court could hear an appeal before the death sentence was carried out. Once the scheduled execution date had passed, Celia was returned to custody, but the Supreme Court refused to interfere in the judgment of the jury and Celia went to the gallows on December 21, 1855.[43]

In 1846, white community sympathies shaped by ideas about gender and respectability did conspire to spare Nelly, an enslaved teenager, from execution after she was indicted by a coroner's jury in Missouri for infanticide. The identity of the child's father was unknown, but local rumor suggested it was Henry Edwards, Nelly's owner, who had recently died. Even before the case came up for trial, hundreds of whites from across the state orchestrated a successful campaign that led the governor to pardon Nelly without a jury ever hearing the evidence against her. Public and private considerations worked together to influence the governor's decision. Nelly was said to have been "ignorant" and of "little mind" at the time of the killing, while it was believed that a trial would be "unpleasant" to community morality and cause suffering to ladies who would be called to testify. In particular, the white women of the Edwards family might be shamed if the trial made public that Henry Edwards had sexually abused his young slave. The petitioners also noted that Edwards' widow had "small means" to raise and educate her ten children, implying that she could scarcely afford the cost of losing Nelly to the hangman's noose. Finally, sparing Nelly, a young, female, slave who had suffered sexual abuse, was consistent with southern slaveholders' paternalistic self-image.[44]

Issues of gender and white respectability could also work together with victims' class identities to influence the trials of black men accused of raping white women. In contrast to the post-Civil War decades, when alleged black rapists were frequently lynched by mobs, in the antebellum period white southerners more often allowed enslaved men accused of raping white women to have their day in court and for all that the odds were stacked against the accused in such cases, neither conviction nor severe punishment was a foregone conclusion. On the contrary, white women from lower class backgrounds or whose social conduct was considered immoral or deviant could find that their allegations carried little weight in court when they accused black men of rape. After the slave Cato was sentenced to death for the rape of a white woman in Florida in 1860, for example, the state Supreme Court ordered a new trial, citing evidence that Susan Leonard, the alleged victim, was a "common prostitute." Similarly, in Virginia, almost half of slaves sentenced to death for rape between 1789 and 1833 were recommended to the governor as fit objects for mercy by the judge or jurors on account that the victim had consented to or encouraged the crime. In these cases, evidence about the victim's standing in the local community was often critical to determining the enslaved convict's fate. When a slave named Dick was sentenced to death in Leesburg, Virginia, for the rape of a white woman, his owner, Hamilton Rogers, petitioned the governor for clemency, but others in the community criticized the appeal. They described the victim, Pleasant Coles, as a woman of "unblemished character," and claimed that Rogers was seeking to use his wealth and status to protect his financial investment in the slave. Conscious of lower-class opposition to clemency, Governor John Floyd refused to intervene in the case and Dick was hanged.[45]

Free African Americans

Thomas Jeremiah was a free African American harbor pilot and fisherman in late-colonial Charleston. Born a slave, "Jerry" was one of the wealthiest black men in North America by the 1770s and probably a slaveholder, yet in 1775 he was arrested on charges of insurrection, tried without a jury, and condemned to death on the testimony of two slaves who alleged that he was plotting a slave uprising in conjunction with the British. Lord William Campbell, royal governor of South Carolina, was horrified by the proceedings, which he considered a travesty of justice, but he was powerless to reverse the death sentence. Independence was still a year away, but American and British forces had already clashed at Lexington and Concord and in South Carolina a provincial congress, headed by Henry Laurens, a prominent slaveholder committed to protecting American liberties from British tyranny, wielded great political influence. In a series of letters exchanged with Campbell, Laurens warned that if Jeremiah were not executed, he would be lynched by a mob in front of the governor's mansion.[46]

Freedom did not spare African Americans such as Thomas Jeremiah from the oppressive strictures of southern criminal justice. As with the trial and punishment of slaves, by the eighteenth century the political interests and racial ideology of the slaveholding class took precedence over questions of culpability and justice when free blacks stood in the dock. Charged with minor crimes—misdemeanors under the jurisdiction of local magistrates—free blacks were commonly whipped like slaves rather than fined or jailed like whites. When fines were issued, free blacks might be hired out for years at a time to pay off the debts. On trial for their lives, they faced the same loosely regulated courts as slaves or, at best, confronted all-white juries and a penal code that in many states grew more severe over time as reforms to manumission laws drove an increase in the free black population, growing sectional tensions exacerbated fears of the danger that black freedom posed to the peace of the slave states, and the emergence of pro-slavery arguments centered in part on slavery's civilizing influence on people of African descent led southern whites to draw firmer connections between race and criminality. David Christy, a supporter of African colonization schemes, argued, for example, that crime was rampant among free black settlers in Canada and pointed to disproportionately high rates of black imprisonment in the northern United States to contend that freedom had a detrimental effect on African Americans' moral character.[47] Virginia governor William Smith also railed against high rates of free black imprisonment, while in Edgefield, South Carolina, grand juries presented free African Americans as "a common nuisance," and "a corrupting set of vagabonds."[48]

Coupled with free African Americans' involvement in antislavery activities, such as the planned Gabriel Prosser and Denmark Vesey uprisings, David Walker's incendiary articles calling for slave insurrection in 1829, and Nat Turner's rebellion two years later, this rhetoric of inherent black criminality drove the passage of increasingly repressive criminal laws that particularly targeted the large free black communities of the Upper South. In Virginia, free African Americans lost the right to trial by jury in 1833, except in capital cases, while Maryland allowed free blacks to be sold out of the state as slaves for a second felony conviction from 1835 and in 1858 introduced sale into slavery for life as the standard punishment for all free blacks convicted of felonies. In addition, fixed-terms of enslavement, ranging from two to five years, were mandated for misdemeanors including petty theft. Under these new statutes, 89 free blacks were enslaved across Maryland within two years. Virginia similarly provided for free black penitentiary inmates to be leased out to labor on public works, including canals, roads, and bridges in 1858, and two years later introduced sale into slavery. Among the first men sentenced under the new law was Floyd Cousins, found guilty of burglary and sold to a "southern gentlemen" for $700 to labor on a cotton plantation.[49]

Racial disparities in criminal justice were less severe outside the South, but they were stark nonetheless and equally rooted in the history and ideology of slavery. In the years to 1750, 41 percent of all slave executions in British North America occurred in the northern colonies (72 of 175), a figure highly disproportionate to the 6 percent of slaves who lived in the region. As well as indicating a propensity for resistance and criminality among northern slaves, the high rate of slave executions in the North reflected the particular importance of the courts as mechanisms of slave control in colonies with relatively small, urban centered slave populations, and the prevalence of ideas about race that were engrained in understandings of crime and punishment in northern colonies as early as the seventeenth century. Puritan sermons in New England dating back as far as the Salem witchcraft trials of the 1690s identified a primal connection between blackness and crime, and northern crime narratives by the late-eighteenth century included sensationalized accounts of black-on-white rape that drew on and reinforced persistent racial discrepancies in law enforcement. In Connecticut, for example, five men were executed for rape between 1700 and 1830. All were black and in each case the alleged victim was a white woman.[50]

With abolition, separate courts and penal codes for blacks and whites were replaced in the northern states with unified criminal laws, yet racial distinctions persisted, notably segregation laws and the exclusion of black jurors, a customary practice that assumed legal sanction through new restrictions on black voting rights in the antebellum North that left African Americans ineligible for jury selection across most of the region. Race riots in the 1830s in which police joined with white mobs further contributed to an atmosphere of violence and intimidation against African Americans in northern law enforcement that contributed to high rates of black imprisonment. By 1830, African Americans in Pennsylvania comprised less than 3 percent of the state population, but 46 percent of the inmates at Philadelphia's Walnut Street penitentiary. A majority of black prisoners were arrested in Philadelphia itself, many having migrated to the city from rural areas and been forced into petty thievery and other minor offenses by poverty, segregation, and employment discrimination.[51]

In the mid-nineteenth century, abolitionists criticized violent discrimination against black Americans in the administration of criminal justice outside the southern slave states. The American Anti-Slavery society argued in 1838 that the exclusion of African Americans from trial juries and the processes of law enforcement was a primary reason why "the colored class furnish more than their fair proportion to the population of our prisons."[52] In 1849, the conviction and death sentence of Washington Goode for the murder of Thomas Harding in Massachusetts heralded the most vociferous accusations of the antebellum era that race exercised a pernicious influence on northern law enforcement. The state charged that Goode had acted out of jealousy after learning of Harding's relationship with Mary Ann Williams, a woman who had carried on an affair with Goode the previous summer. Defense counsel countered that the prosecution relied on contradictory and circumstantial evidence from "prostitutes and men of the lowest character," and argued that, even if Goode were guilty, he should not be sentenced to death as he had been threatened by Harding and was intoxicated at the time of the killing. In an indication of how engrained racist ideas about criminality had become even in the heartland of the abolitionist movement, Washington Goode's defense attorney sought to exploit white racism on behalf of his client, claiming that the "cruel social prejudice" of American society had left Goode "half savage ... ignorant and unenlightened." By contrast, when abolitionists sought to explain the case, they concentrated on the impact of racism on the administration of justice. When Massachusetts Governor George Briggs refused to commute the death sentence, the prominent antislavery campaigner Wendell Phillips charged that Briggs was using the specter of a black murderer on the gallows to bolster public support for capital punishment amidst growing calls for its abolition.[53] Frederick Douglass's newspaper, *The North Star*, similarly editorialized that Goode was the victim of "the debasing influence of Southern institutions" on northern law enforcement.[54]

The incipient public activism of northern blacks on issues of crime and punishment could have no counterpart in the South while slavery survived. Free black victims of crime in the South did regularly turn to the courts for redress when they fell victim to crimes committed by fellow African Americans, but slaves' responses to crime necessarily took more subtle and constrained forms. Slaves could try to influence white witnesses, who routinely offered testimony that was based on what they had heard from slaves and this evidence sometimes served to secure the acquittal of black defendants. Sam, a slave in South Carolina, for example, was found not guilty of the rape of a white woman in part because white witnesses reported to the court that Sam's wife—whose word would have held little sway on its own— claimed to have been with her husband throughout the night of the alleged offence. Slaves also established their own disciplinary mechanisms that functioned according to alternative notions of justice than prevailed under the slaveholders' law. As historian Dylan Penningroth notes, slaves "[s]ometimes ... set up special committees that publicly questioned suspects and used such divination objects as string-tied Bibles and graveyard dirt to detect thieves."[55] Slaves' disputes with each other were also heard in church courts, which mostly regulated moral offenses, such as adultery and drunkenness, but also concerned themselves with crimes against person and property. Betsey and William, an enslaved couple, were investigated for striking each other by the Philadelphia Baptist Church in Spartanburg District, South Carolina, for example, and in Richmond, Fanny Randall, a free black woman, was brought before the First African Baptist Church in the 1850s accused of stabbing.[56]

Ideas about race and practices of law enforcement that would define the black experience of criminal justice until late in the twentieth century were established in African Americans' earliest experiences of trial and punishment. Thousands of enslaved defendants appeared in American courts before white officials for whom justice was a secondary concern. Trials were quick, rules of due process warped and readily ignored, and legal processes sometimes circumvented altogether by white vigilantes or state-sanctioned militias. The main function of the criminal law of slavery was to uphold the interests of white, slaveholding elites, and the primary purpose of court hearings and clemency proceedings was very often to establish precisely what those interests were and how competing white concerns might be reconciled. A range of factors weighed on the decision-making process of justices, jurors, and governors: the security of white society against slave resistance; the value of slaves as property; the rights of owners to protection of their financial investments; patriarchal gender ideologies; growing class divisions among whites exacerbated by economic downturns, immigration, and the rising price of slaves, and intensifying abolitionist attacks on slavery from outside the South that were fueled by reports of rank injustices in slave trials. Mastery was central to these factors, but so was white supremacy and so, too, was the retention and control of the black labor force. For these reasons, the injustices of the slave trial system infused the prosecution and punishment of free African Americans across the United States in the antebellum era in ways that would persist long after slavery's abolition.

3

Reconstruction

No state shall make or enforce any law which shall abridge the privileges or immunities of citizens of the United States; nor shall any state deprive any person of life, liberty, or property, without due process of law; nor deny to any person within its jurisdiction the equal protection of the laws.
— Fourteenth Amendment to the US Constitution, 1868

On September 22, 1865, several months after the Confederacy had lost the Civil War, a state convention in Alabama resolved that "hereafter there shall be neither slavery nor involuntary servitude in this State."[1] Five days later, Burt, formerly a slave, but now a free man, was convicted in an Alabama court of murder in the first degree for killing a white man. Burt was sentenced to hang and his execution set for November, but he won a reprieve. With regret, the state Supreme Court overruled the conviction and discharged Burt from custody. Though the court did not doubt that Burt was guilty, the statute "providing for the punishment of *slaves* ... for murder" had been repealed with the abolition of slavery and neither the indictment nor the conviction could stand. "The discharge of the prisoner is one of the evils resulting from the war," one justice noted, though he added ruefully that it was, "not by any means the greatest that has been brought about by that calamity." The abolition of slavery enabled other black prisoners who had been tried and convicted as slaves to escape the hangman's noose. At its January term in 1866, the Alabama Supreme Court discharged George, convicted of assault and battery with intent to rob, and Nelson, convicted of murdering a slave.[2]

Emancipation transformed the American South. As the legal status of four million African American men, women, and children shifted from slavery to freedom, the implications reverberated far and wide. In the following months and years, constitutional amendments and congressional legislation placed African Americans on an equal footing with whites in the eyes of the law. The practical implications of black freedom, however, were uncertain, and shaped equally by local context as by national legal and political developments. In the realm of criminal justice, the era of Reconstruction and its immediate aftermath witnessed African Americans participating in the administration of southern law enforcement for the first time as police officers, jurors, witnesses against white defendants, sheriffs, and judges. Particularly in regions where Union soldiers or Freedmen's Bureau agents were stationed or where black political influence was strong, black defendants sometimes benefited from what historian Donald Nieman has called "remarkably even-handed" treatment in the courts.[3] Such conditions, however, were rare, short-lived, and did not guarantee justice in the courtroom for African Americans either as defendants or victims of crime. The archetypal black experience of Reconstruction-era southern criminal law was instead characterized by discrimination, violence, and the violation of legal rights, as white southerners strived to prevent the legal system from interfering with customary practices of white domination of black life and labor. Where whites could control the courts and shape "justice" to their own ends, they did so, and where they could not they bypassed judicial processes altogether and turned to violent terror to police black conduct. In both circumstances, the consequence was that southern law enforcement failed to protect African Americans' person and property while at the same time black men and women were arrested and prosecuted in extortionate numbers, often for trivial offences, and sometimes on entirely spurious charges.[4] Black communities resisted these developments, but by the late-nineteenth century hopes of evenhanded southern law enforcement had been violently subsumed beneath the insatiable demands of white employers for cheap and pliant black labor and the white supremacist imperatives of segregation.

Emancipation, black codes, and racial violence

Emancipation was a drawn-out process that occurred across the four years of the American Civil War. Abraham Lincoln issued the Emancipation Proclamation on January 1, 1863, signaling for the first time publicly the adoption of the abolition of slavery as a central war aim alongside the preservation of the Union. Yet already tens of thousands of slaves had seized freedom amidst the upheavals of war by running away from their owners' farms and plantations. Many headed straight for Union lines, taking advantage of disruption on the southern home front and the absence from local communities of the hundreds of thousands of white men who joined up to fight for the Confederacy. As early as May 1861, an attorney in Alabama warned that "*anarchy*" would prevail on the home front, "and the slaves become our masters," if the army continued to accept all of the men who had volunteered, and by 1864 the residents of Swift Creek, South Carolina, called for the discharge of one local man renowned for controlling slaves with a pack of dogs in order to prevent, "the depredations Committed on us by the black population such as breaking open dwelling houses ... robbing hen houses, killing Cattle Hogs &c and stealing everything the can lay their hands on" [*sic*]. In Georgia, planters complained that 20,000 slaves—worth $15 million—had escaped and they called for summary executions under military law as the only effective remedy. The old forms of punishment were no longer sufficient. Captured runaways might be whipped by their masters, but they would still remain, in the words of one planter, "a leaven of corruption in the mass & stand ready to make any other attempts that may promise success." Prosecution through the courts, meanwhile, would involve, "long litigation ... large expense & doubtful conviction," and, in any case, there were so many runaways that the local jails could not hold them.[5]

The fears of black crime and rebellion that had plagued southern white society in the antebellum era were promptly converted after the Civil War into memories of a more peaceful and innocent time. In the rose-tinted recollection of the Richmond *Daily Dispatch*, just months after the southern surrender, a single burglary or murder in the pre-war years had been "a matter of excitement for weeks," and there had been no need for a large police force. Sarah Clayton, a white woman who lived through the Civil War in Atlanta, believed that immorality was "inborn" among African Americans but that under the disciplinary influence and moral guidance of slavery it had rarely led "to more than lying and stealing."[6] In the wake of emancipation, however, planters complained that African Americans, "showed no disposition to work, and were wandering about the country ... plundering and stealing indiscriminately." Their fears coalesced in late-1865 around speculation that African American troops and freed people were planning insurrections to force the redistribution of plantation lands among the former slaves. The rumors proved unfounded, though they were exploited by governors in Alabama and Mississippi to justify establishing militia companies to police the freed people and protect white property. President Johnson approved the militias in a move that made no distinction between legal and extra legal, giving federal sanction to a campaign of terror against blacks.[7]

The intersection of law and extra-legal violence as mechanisms to control freed people would prove characteristic of the entire Reconstruction era, as courts and vigilantes strived together to coerce black labor, constrain burgeoning Republican political power, and sustain a social structure based on white supremacy. The determination of white southerners to use law as a surrogate for slavery was explicit in the enactment from 1865 to 1867 of wide-ranging black codes that sought to define and limit the rights, legal status, and freedom of African Americans. The codes afforded freed people several new rights that acknowledged the abolition of slavery. Former slaves were entitled to marry, they could sue and be sued, own and inherit property, enter into contracts, and testify in a wide range of civil and criminal court proceedings. They were also made subject in most instances to the same trial processes and punishments as whites. Yet there were notable caveats. African Americans could not marry white people; in several states they could not testify in cases that did not involve a black plaintiff, victim, or defendant, and they could not vote or serve as jurors. A central concern of the black codes, moreover, was to regularize white control of black labor. To this end, statutes forced African Americans to enter into restrictive contracts with white employers, criminalized the breach of those contracts, and limited labor mobility. Black men and women who did not work for whites faced arrest as vagrants and punishment via fines, imprisonment, and forced labor. "Vagrancy" was typically defined broadly so as to afford law officers extensive discretion in policing black conduct. In Georgia, the term encompassed persons without means to support themselves who were found "wandering or strolling about in idleness," "leading an idle, immoral or profligate life," gambling, trading in stolen property, or without fixed abode. Alabama additionally included "stubborn or refractory" servants and laborers who did not comply with the terms of their contracts, while Mississippi added persons "with no lawful employment or business."[8]

Once under contract, the rights of black workers were further curtailed. In Texas, employers could impose fines for impudence, fighting, and disobedience and they were entitled to twice the value of any property that workers stole or destroyed. Laborers who left before the end of their contract forfeited all wages earned and could be forcibly returned to work. Under the terms of enticement statutes it was also a criminal offense to encourage laborers to break their contracts, for example by offering alternative employment. Additional legislation further constrained freed people's capacity to make a living independent of white people and restricted opportunities to work away from rural farming occupations. In North Carolina, persons of color could not trade in livestock unless the transaction was witnessed by a white person. In Mississippi they could not rent or lease property outside of towns and in South Carolina a license was required for black men to practice a trade. Licenses were granted only to applicants judged of good moral character and on payment of a fee that ranged from $10 for mechanics and artisans to $100 for storekeepers. Apprenticeship laws also allowed for orphaned and impoverished black children to be bound out, usually until the age of 21, often to white employers who formerly had owned them as slaves, and in thousands of cases against their parents' will.[9]

The passage of the Black Codes in the mid-1860s played out against a backdrop of extreme racial violence that was inflicted on freed people by individual whites, mobs, and armed bands of nightriders that roamed the southern countryside terrorizing black communities much as patrollers had done during slavery. There is no complete record of the murders, beatings, rapes, and torture that occurred during the Reconstruction era, but in total thousands were killed between the end of the war and the late-1870s. A Congressional Report in December 1865 offers an insight to the early years of the terror. On David Parker's plantation in Gates County, North Carolina, former slaves were kept in chains, regularly whipped, and warned they would be shot if they attempted to leave. In Amite County, Mississippi, a militia company committed a series of "brutal outrages," including beatings and murders, and in Texas it was reported that freed people were "frequently beaten unmercifully, and shot down like wild beasts, without any provocation, followed with hounds, and maltreated in every possible way." Another federal agent in the state reported that planters "systematically tie up and whip the hands [Freedmen] employed by them for any, and all causes .... Numbers of them have reported that they are worse off now than when they were slaves." In South Carolina, hired assassins and groups of regulators murdered former slaves who refused to sign contracts and by 1866 there were reports from across the South that vigilante groups calling themselves

"Ku Klux" were organizing not only for purposes of labor control but in response to any evidence of black autonomy, political participation, education, and racial uplift. Originally formed as a social club by veterans in Pulaski, Tennessee, in 1866, within a year the Ku Klux Klan was described by a Nashville reporter as "a secret military force," thousands strong, "made up chiefly of discharged Confederate soldiers ... for the purposes of overthrowing liberty in this state."[10]

The racial violence that flared across the South in the months after the Civil War reflected the determination of white southerners to resist moves toward black economic and political autonomy, but it was facilitated by confusion and uncertainty in post-war southern law enforcement and the appointment and election of ex-Confederates as magistrates, sheriffs, and police officers. In areas close to federal encampments, the presence of soldiers—including tens of thousands of Africans Americans—provided freed people with some protection from the worst atrocities and successful prosecutions were brought against white defendants in provost courts. In the summer of 1865, for example, North Carolina governor William Holden demanded that three men held for trial in a military court for assaulting a freedman be returned to civilian custody where he was confident "that strict and impartial justice will be administered." The local commanding officer disagreed, however, defending the army's jurisdiction in the case as "a necessity in the transition state in which the States lately hostile to the government now are." In Richmond, likewise, US brevet major-general John W. Turner extended the jurisdiction of the local provost court to cover prosecutions of white defendants based solely on black testimony in December 1865, when the city's pro-Confederate mayor refused to hear such cases.

Military rule, however, was sparse across much of the South and did not always equate to justice for African Americans. In South Carolina, where provost courts comprising three-man panels of officers and civilians operated from mid-1865 to October 1866, extant records indicate that conviction rates were higher for black than white defendants, and the most severe sentences, including jail terms and hard labor, were typically reserved for freed people. Similarly in North Carolina, county police officers appointed to serve under US army authorities refused military orders and instead followed the commands of local white magistrates. "They have taken negroes, tied them up by the thumbs, and whipped them unmercifully," reported Colonel E. Whittlesey, an African American from Maine and assistant commissioner in the Freedmen's Bureau, and he added that "they did not think they were doing anything wrong at all." Dexter Clapp concurred. A black lieutenant-colonel from New York, Clapp testified before a Congressional committee that "[o]f the thousand cases of murder, robbery, and maltreatment of freedmen that have come before me ... in North Carolina, I have never yet known a single case in which the local authorities or police or citizens made any attempt or exhibited any inclination to redress any of these wrongs or to protect such persons."[11]

Republican Reconstruction

In May 1866, longstanding tensions between black Union soldiers and white city police in Memphis erupted in two days of violence that left 46 African Americans dead, saw five black women raped, and churches, schools, and dozens of private homes burned to the ground in black neighborhoods in the South of the city (see Illustration 3.1). Two months later, at least 38 people were killed and hundreds injured in New Orleans when police and civilians committed to white supremacy attacked African Americans parading in support of Republican attempts to reconvene a suspended constitutional convention and enfranchise black voters. Occurring in the wake of the Black Codes and amidst ongoing vigilante violence and the political dominance of ex-Confederates, the rioting in Memphis and New Orleans forced a shift in Reconstruction politics in Washington. African American victims of racist violence and discriminatory courts played a key role in bringing the situation in the South to a national audience. Many risked further reprisals in reporting crimes to white law officers and testifying before federal officials and congressional investigating committees. Dismayed by the widespread reports of abuses against the freed people and President Andrew Johnson's conciliatory stance toward whites who had fought against the Union in the Civil War, in 1866 Republicans in Congress began to set out plans for a radical overhaul of southern politics and society. Over the President's veto, they extended the life of the Freedmen's Bureau and passed a civil rights act and the Fourteenth Amendment to the Constitution to secure African Americans equal citizenship rights. After the Fourteenth Amendment was rejected in all of the former Confederate states apart from Tennessee, Congress passed in March 1867 the first of four military Reconstruction acts organizing the South into five districts, each under the command of a US Army general. Military reconstruction gave federal authorities oversight of black voter registration, the

THE RIOT IN NEW ORLEANS—THE FREEDMEN'S PROCESSION MARCHING TO THE INSTITUTE—THE STRUGGLE FOR THE FLAG.
[Sketched by Theodore R. Davis.]

THE RIOT IN NEW ORLEANS—SIEGE AND ASSAULT OF THE CONVENTION BY THE POLICE AND CITIZENS.—Sketched by Theodore R. Davis.
[See Page 555.]

Illustration 3.1 The riot in New Orleans–The freedmen's procession marching to the institute–the struggle for the flag–siege and assault of the convention by the police and citizens, 1866. Courtesy of Library of Congress, Prints and Photographs Online, Miscellaneous Items. <http://www.loc.gov/pictures/item/94510091/>

administration of elections, and the ratification of new state constitutions in the South. These measures facilitated black political participation and in the spring and summer of 1868 this proved instrumental in securing ratification of the Fourteenth Amendment, Republican Party victories in state elections across the former Confederate states, and the election of hundreds of African Americans to local, state, and national office.[12]

The Reconstruction legislation passed by Congress from 1866 to 1868 had profound implications for American criminal justice. Apart from defining as citizens all persons "born or naturalized" in the United States, the Fourteenth Amendment, for example, committed states to upholding "due process of law" and "equal protection of the laws" for all individuals, and it gave the federal government the power to enforce these provisions. In the short term, however, the Bureau of Refugees, Freedmen and Abandoned Lands, commonly known as the Freedmen's Bureau, had the most immediate impact on southern law enforcement. Established in March 1865 as an agency within the War Department, the Freedmen's Bureau was commanded by General Oliver Howard who oversaw the work of hundreds of agents stationed across the southern states. The Bureau's remit was broad. It included the provision of health care, welfare, and poor relief; negotiating labor contracts; resolving disputes between African Americans and white employers, and establishing educational provisions for freed people, as well as the protection of freed people's rights in matters of criminal law. The Bureau's larger mission was to win white Southerners over to a vision of freedom for the African American community based on a shared sense of racial equality, a task it spectacularly failed to achieve.[13]

In response to political developments in Washington and evolving circumstances on the ground in the South, the extent of the Bureau's authority and the scope of its powers in criminal matters fluctuated greatly from the time of its inception until the end of 1868 when its judicial role ceased. On March 30, 1865, Howard instructed Bureau assistant commissioners to assume responsibility for criminal cases in those parts of the South where the civil courts were not operational or refused to accept the testimony of black witnesses. Bureau agents monitored the conduct of civilian courts, investigated cases, made arrests, and established freedmen's courts that usually comprised one representative each of the freed people, white planters, and the federal government, though often assumed different formats and were sometimes administered by a Bureau agent alone. As southern states expanded black testimony rights in 1866 (in law if not always in practice), judicial power was returned to civilian authorities. However, even where African Americans could appear as witnesses in all cases, blacks were widely discriminated against in criminal prosecutions and by early 1867 the Bureau had resumed its earlier regulatory functions across much of the South.[14]

Wherever freedmen's courts were established, white southerners railed against what they perceived as an inherent bias toward the freed people (see Illustration 3.2). Mostly prompted by political considerations rather than evidence of malpractice, the accusation that carried most validity was that the Bureau's courts functioned with little regard to law and due process. Rare was the Bureau agent who was trained in the law and few had in-depth knowledge of the legal peculiarities of the state in which they served. African Americans did not always benefit from a lack of legal formalism in the freedmen's courts, however, and nor were they guaranteed fair and equal treatment in courts administered by the Bureau or military authorities. On the contrary, Bureau officers were often accused of adopting a paternalistic attitude toward the freed people, sharing prevalent southern white views of black inferiority, and supporting the interests of the planter elite. In York County, Virginia, local African Americans elected Daniel Norton, a black man, as their representative on the Freedmen's Court, but his appointment was rejected by Orlando Brown, the Bureau assistant commissioner in the state, on the grounds that an integrated court would not be tolerated by local whites and that a white representative would be "more accustomed to the form ... of a court of justice."[15]

Several factors limited the Freedmen's Bureau's capacity to provide an effective and just forum for African American defendants and victims of crime. The Bureau consistently lacked resources. Agents were in short supply and a single officer might hold responsibility for several counties, requiring freed people to travel great distances to record complaints and rendering impossible the close supervision of southern courts. Confronted by strong and often violent white resistance, Bureau officers in many areas depended on military support for their personal safety as well as to make arrests. In Georgia, Bureau officials appointed southern magistrates as subagents to extend the reach of their activities, but African Americans condemned this development as, "worse than if the Bureau had no Agents at all." A Bureau investigation later found that the magistrates had "shamefully abused" their power and "occasionally inflicted cruel and unusual punishments."[16]

THE FREEDMEN'S BUREAU.—Drawn by A. R. Waud.—[See Page 402.]

Illustrations 3.2 The Freedmen's Bureau, 1868. Courtesy of Library of Congress, Prints and Photographs Online, Miscellaneous Items. <http://www.loc.gov/pictures/item/9251496/>

In 1868, only two out of 341 reports of white on black violence in Georgia resulted in a conviction and by the time the Bureau's judicial functions ceased at the end of the year many African Americans had "decided that it was not worth their lives to testify against whites or even to complain to the Bureau about the violence they suffered at the hands of their ex-masters."[17] The Bureau's criminal justice work was further undermined by what historian James Oakes calls Bureau agents' "limited ideological framework." Anxious to stabilize the southern labor force to boost economic recovery in the South, and believing that African Americans would only work under compulsion, some agents routinely sided against black plaintiffs who made claims of violent, fraudulent, or otherwise unjust treatment at the hands of white employers. At a national level, there was also a concern, even among many radical Republicans, that the Bureau represented an unconstitutional federal intrusion into the affairs of the states.[18]

The most significant impediment to the Bureau's work, however, was southern white resistance, which varied across the South. The diverse experiences of agents in different regions are illustrated in the contrasting correspondence and monthly reports from Bureau offices in Demopolis, Alabama, and Augusta County, Virginia. The office in Demopolis oversaw freed people's affairs across five counties in western Alabama that were marked by extreme violence and lawlessness throughout the mid to late-1860s. In his final report, submitted on December 31, 1868, Bureau subassistant commissioner R. A. Wilson despaired at the state of criminal justice in his district. Wilson informed his superiors that "during the six months that I have administered the affairs of this Sub District, there has been substantially no administration of justice within its limits." The local circuit judge had resigned the previous July and since that time no court had been held in any county in the region. Several counties had been without a sheriff or justices of the peace for long periods and in the town of Demopolis itself a mayor had been appointed by the state governor who was, reputedly, "of consumed mind; and under bonds on a charge of murder." In the areas near to the Bureau office, Wilson had made efforts, "to have the law respected," but he was utterly unequipped to have any impact on law and order in those parts of his district that lay further afield. In fact, Wilson's main contribution to limiting white racial violence was his repeated advice to African Americans to avoid conduct that might provoke white hostility, such as organizing political meetings, asserting their legal rights, and carrying muskets.[19]

Circumstances in Augusta County, Virginia, were altogether less violent than in western Alabama, and the civil courts functioned throughout the years that a Freedmen's Bureau office was stationed in the county. The Bureau agent in Augusta, Roswell Waldo, submitted a final report on his district on the last day of 1868 that struck a positive tone in contrast to R. A. Wilson's commentary on affairs in Demopolis written the same day. In the previous month, Waldo noted, there had not been a single case in the local courts, "in which there was any reason to believe that injustice was manifested toward any colored party." Waldo had not always been so upbeat, however, and neither was he certain that the absence of overt injustice meant that freed people were receiving equal treatment from the civilian authorities. On the contrary, such was the resentment felt by many magistrates toward both blacks and whites who were sympathetic to the Republican cause, that Waldo sought to resolve as many cases as possible himself and only reluctantly involved the courts in matters concerning the freed people.

The Freedmen's Bureau withdrew from southern law enforcement as Republican governments came to power across the region in the late-1860s. Reflecting the new political influence of African American voters that stemmed from extensive grassroots political organizing and the "radical" Reconstruction legislation enacted in Washington, African Americans became involved in the administration of justice for the first time, serving as police officers, sheriffs, and magistrates, and sitting as jurors in criminal trials. In these capacities, black officers strived to shape a more equal justice system, but their authority was fragile and its limits evident as violent Democratic campaigns rapidly checked Republican political power. During election campaigns in the era of Congressional Reconstruction, the Klan (see Illustration 3.3) and other white supremacist groups served as, "the rough vigilante arm" of the Democratic Party.[20] Andrew Flowers, an African American justice of the peace, was whipped shortly after taking up his office near Chattanooga, and a black trial judge who was attacked by Klansmen in Rock Hill, South Carolina, "was never known to hold another court".[21] In Lincoln County, Tennessee, the Republican vote collapsed from 780 in 1867 to just 4 in 1868 following a brutal Ku Klux campaign that drove out the electoral commissioner and forced the local Freedmen's Bureau and county court to suspend their business.[22] In St. Landry Parish, Louisiana, the Republican vote similarly fell from more than 2000 in elections for the state's constitutional convention in April 1868, to zero in the presidential ballot just

TWO MEMBERS OF THE KU-KLUX KLAN IN THEIR DISGUISES.

Illustration 3.3 Two members of the Ku-Klux Klan in their disguises, 1868. Courtesy of Library of Congress, Prints and Photographs Online, Miscellaneous Items. <http://www.loc.gov/pictures/item/97516403/>

six months later, as the murder rate in rural parts of the state more than trebled to almost 150 per 100,000 inhabitants. The vast majority of killers in these cases were bands of white men and most victims were African Americans.[23]

When freedmen and Republicans held a rally in Camilla, Georgia, in September, 1868, whites stationed around the courthouse square shot dead 12 and injured dozens. Three years later, rioting was sparked in Meridian, Mississippi, by the arson trial of three freedmen who had organized protests against Klan violence in the region. The Republican judge and one of the defendants were murdered in the courtroom and over the next two days hundreds of Klansmen killed at least 30 freed people, set fire to black homes and churches in the region, and forced the town's Republican mayor to flee. With Democrats returned to local government, a grand jury refused to indict anyone for the violence.[24] In such circumstances, even a white Unionist in Blount County, Alabama, did not report that he was whipped at gunpoint by six Klansmen, reasoning that "a man might as well go and dig his grave" as take out a warrant in such a case and that any officer who tried to arrest a Klansmen "wouldn't live long."[25] Among thousands of others murdered during Reconstruction were leading black political figures. Ida Hutchinson recalled the assassination of Tom Ivory, a prominent Republican, in Alabama in 1875. A group of Klansmen fired on Ivory as he stepped off a train and then "cut his tongue out before he died." The murder sent a message and Hutchinson's family, along with 50 other colored people, left Alabama soon afterwards.[26]

In Washington, the decimation of the southern Republican vote prompted new measures to protect the freed people's rights. Between May 1870 and June 1872, Congress passed four enforcement acts, the third of which, popularly known as the Ku Klux Klan Act, empowered federal courts to punish individuals who conspired or acted to deprive citizens of equal rights and protection of the laws. It also allowed the president to suspend the writ of habeas corpus in counties experiencing organized violence on a scale deemed to constitute a rebellion against the United States and to use the military against anti-civil rights groups and individuals. Persons indicted under the act were subject to prosecution in US district or circuit courts and liable to up to six years imprisonment or a fine of no more than $5000. These were new and far-reaching powers that even some Republicans feared were unconstitutional, but only in the short term did they raise hopes that peace might be restored in the South. The most wide-reaching enforcement efforts occurred in 1871 in nine upcountry South Carolina counties where the Klan was implicated in a spate of arsons, murders, and hundreds of whippings of African Americans committed after Republican victories in elections the previous year. After a local grand jury refused to issue any indictments, President Ulysses S. Grant imposed martial law on the area and hundreds of local whites were rounded up by the army. Charges were procured against 831 men, but most were dropped and only 98 of the accused eventually either pleaded guilty or were convicted. A majority of the convicts were sentenced to prison terms served in New York, but by 1876 all had received a presidential pardon.[27]

Amidst ongoing white terrorism, waning concern with race issues among Republican voters in the North, a nationwide economic depression, and a hostile federal judiciary, the Democratic Party regained political control of every southern state legislature and governorship between 1870 and 1877 and across most of the region the justice system became enshrined once more as an unambiguous pillar of white supremacy. There remained, however, significant local variations in the course of criminal justice politics during this period. In Washington County, Texas, a substantial German-immigrant population helped Republicans control local government until 1884 with significant implications for law enforcement. White Republicans served as district court judges with jurisdiction in felony trials, justices of the peace who conducted preliminary hearings and summarily handled minor offenses, and county sheriffs responsible for the everyday business of arrests, juror selection, and prosecutions. African Americans were often appointed as deputy sheriffs, served on juries, and had their testimony taken seriously by the courts, resulting in only limited disparities between black and white defendants in conviction rates and sentencing. This was in stark contrast to a county like Chatham in Georgia, which encompassed the city of Savannah. No African Americans served on the Chatham County grand jury during the entire Reconstruction period, the city police was dominated by ex-confederates, and black conviction rates from 1866 to 1879 were one-third higher than for whites.[28]

Developments in local justice were different again in Warren County, Mississippi. From 1868 to 1875, with the state under Republican rule, African Americans had unprecedented access to law and influence over the justice system. They accounted for half of all magistrates in Warren County and 35 percent of grand jurors, though this was below their 70 percent share of the local population and the poor and property-less were especially underrepresented. African American participation in the administration of justice led to an increase in black complainants appearing before the Warren County courts, although the criminal trial court docket still remained dominated by cases brought by whites and there was little discernible shift in conviction rates: black defendants remained more likely than whites to be found guilty, as they had been under Democratic rule.[29]

The election of Vicksburg's first black sheriff, Peter Crosby, in 1873, initiated a concerted white backlash against African American political influence. Spurred by reports of corruption among black officeholders and the refusal of grand jurors to indict the accused— evidence, for Democrats, of a broader black tolerance of criminality— whites in Warren County formed People's Clubs that coordinated armed resistance. Overcoming traditional hostilities, rural and city-based whites, Irish immigrants and natives rallied to the cause of white supremacy, while the black community split into factions, dividing on matters of policy and along urban-rural lines, as well as between former slaves and those who had been free before the war. After whites had swept municipal elections in the summer of 1874, Crosby was confronted in December by a crowd of 600 white men, resigned his office and fled Vicksburg. Days later, he organized a small force of supporters—around 120 men—to march on the city, but they were massively outnumbered by informal white militias and mobs that killed at least 60 African Americans and disarmed surviving local blacks. After US troops moved in, Crosby was returned to office, but he was permanently ousted within a year after failing to strike a conciliatory deal with moderate whites. The return of Democrats to power in Warren County had an immediate impact on the administration of criminal justice. African Americans appeared less regularly on grand juries and there was a decline in prosecutions instigated by black complainants. By 1880, African Americans were only 15 percent of the Vicksburg police force, having accounted for 50 percent ten years earlier.[30]

Similar developments accompanied the return of Democratic rule across the South. Between 1870 and 1880, black police officers were entirely purged from cities including Mobile and Montgomery, Alabama, and Portsmouth, Virginia, and their numbers were slashed in Charleston, South Carolina, from more than 40 percent to less than 20 percent and in New Orleans from 28 percent to 7 percent. In Texas, a state police force established by the Republicans and in which African Americans had comprised one-third of the officers was abolished entirely when the Democrats won power in 1873. Rates of black imprisonment, meanwhile, soared. Mississippi's prison population jumped from 234 in 1871 to 997 in 1879; in Alabama the number of state convicts more than trebled to 779 in just three years from 1874 to 1877; and across the South, African Americans soon comprised nearly 90 percent of all convicts. Poverty, violence, and instability fueled black crime, but rates of incarceration were equally a product of discriminatory law enforcement and the profits to be made from contracting convict labor to private corporations. As a *New York Times* correspondent found during an investigation in North Carolina in 1880, black defendants routinely received severe sentences for minor crimes while whites were held liable just for the costs of their case or served only short jail terms for offenses as serious as burglary and even murder. Green Gilchrist was sentenced to five years in the penitentiary for stealing 75 cents that he claimed to have found "lying on the floor of a room"; a man named Crutchfield received a two-year term for the theft of a spade, and two further black defendants got seven years each for stealing, respectively, a tin of sardines and an old plow worth $7. All of the accused appeared in court without legal representation and confronted all-white juries.[31]

Across the South, African Americans were also targeted by new legislation that broadened the scope of grand larceny prosecutions to encompass thefts previously classed as misdemeanors, such as stealing farm animals, an offense that in Alabama carried a minimum two-year sentence. Such penalties both reflected and reinforced widely held white views on the links between black freedom and criminality. The *Atlanta Constitution* believed that "the enfranchisement of the black has worked the enfranchisement of his vices and the liberation of his proclivities to crime." John T. Brown, a white employee at the Georgia Penitentiary, agreed: "The only difference existing between the colored convicts and the colored people at large consists in the fact that the former have been caught in the commission of a crime, tried and convicted, while the latter have not. The entire race is destitute of character."[32]

The death penalty was also turned against African Americans as Republican influence on the justice system waned. There were no recorded state-sanctioned executions in Mississippi during the years of Reconstruction when routine extra-legal killing made the penalty redundant, but in the decade after the Democrats regained power 27 black men were put to death in the state, though only two white men met a similar fate. Likewise in South Carolina, just nine blacks and two whites were executed between 1865 and 1874, but in the following decade 56 blacks and five whites went to the gallows. In March 1877, shortly after Democratic candidate Wade Hampton was sworn in as state governor, following disputed elections the previous year, four black men were hanged for arson and murder before a crowd of 5,000 people in Aiken County in what historian Jeff Strickland has called a "symbolic demonstration ... of white supremacy on a scale not seen in South Carolina since slavery." Hampton's election had been largely predicated on the violent repression of black voters by white militias; in Edgefield and Aiken counties alone, more than 3000 white men had served in 58 companies. But with Democrats returned to power at all levels of local and state government, Hampton could depend on the law to enforce a more refined form of white supremacy. Indeed, with the passage of legislation disfranchising convicted felons across the South, the discriminatory administration of criminal justice contributed directly to the suppression of black political power.[33]

African American resistance and legal culture

Criminal law was an oppressive force in black life after the Civil War, but African Americans' engagements with the legal system amounted to far more than discrimination, violence, and injustice. An editor in Lynchburg, Virginia, commented in 1866 that African Americans "flock[ed]" to the city's courtrooms "in throngs ... . They crowd the bar in ranks several deep and fill the seats against the wall.—Many are drawn there as witnesses and many others, the majority, out of curiosity."[34] Whites were dismissive of freed people's attendance at court, but for African Americans it expressed a commitment to the rule of law and a refusal to accept white dominance and abuse of judicial institutions. This commitment was rooted in experiences of law during slavery. Although plantation justice had been the primary mechanism of slave crime control in the antebellum period, slaves were familiar with court proceedings as a focal point of everyday life where ordinary people sought resolution to disputes and conflicts according to highly localized and discretionary notions of justice rather than abstract ideas about "rights" as defined in distant legislative chambers. Independent of the sweeping constitutional changes emanating from Washington, therefore, freed people routinely invoked law as a tool to regulate local matters such as family relations, labor contracts, and property claims. As historian Dylan Penningroth argues, they used law pragmatically, taking "their concerns from the yard and the church into the courtroom, and sometimes back again, pursuing their interests wherever they saw an advantage."[35] Some black commentators even believed that the African American community was too reliant on the legal system and feared that the specter of black litigants arguing over minor personal disputes in the public courts played into white stereotypes of black disorder. Samuel Smith, of Savannah, Georgia, wrote to the *Colored Tribune*, an African American newspaper in the city, to complain of the frequency with which black women reported their husbands to legal authorities as a means of resolving family quarrels. Smith described these women as "dirty" and "worthless" and contrasted their actions with the way that white women resolved disputes: "White families quarrel and disagree as much as the colored do but you never hear of white women however low they may be running to the magistrate to have their husbands jailed."[36]

Notwithstanding the criticisms of black men, black women's recourse to the courts was an important means through which they laid claim to the rights of citizenship at a time when other expressions of political autonomy, such as voting, remained closed off. Black women's engagement with law in relation to their domestic affairs, however, had complex outcomes, because the courts not only served as a venue to assert rights and seek protection, but also as a mechanism through which whites could police personal relationships within the black community. The right to marry, for example, was an important marker of freedom and source of strength for African American couples, but it also exposed them to punishment for offenses such as bigamy, fornication, and adultery that white lawmakers criminalized as immoral but which were often committed unwittingly and commonly tolerated in black communities where the oppression and instability of slave life had long compromised commitments to permanent monogamy and rendered unnecessary the formal dissolution of marriages. In several states, formerly enslaved couples who cohabited were automatically declared married at the end of the Civil War, often contrary to their wishes and sometimes without their knowledge. As late as the 1890s, African Americans were convicted of bigamy after marrying a partner whom, unknown to them, the law considered to be their second husband or wife. In Katherine Franke's analysis, the vigorous prosecution of such cases in southern courts was both a reflection of racist white views of African American morality and an attempt to shore up the moral order in a period of rapid social change.[37]

Black communities used what little political power and influence they had to protest injustice in the courtroom. In Dinwiddie County, Virginia, a mass meeting of black Republicans in 1875 called on local judge Henry Jones "to grant us the right of an impartial jury, regardless of race, color, or of previous condition of servitude." In 1884, the Tennessee State Colored Convention issued a petition condemning "the continued, persistent and unlawful manner in which they are tried, condemned, hanged, and enslaved, by individuals who have been taught from cradle to the jury box, that the negro is naturally inferior to them, by men of reason and prejudiced views of them and their race." White southerners rejected such arguments and tried to convince themselves and African Americans that the justice system treated everyone equally. White newspapers highlighted cases in which African American defendants were acquitted and claimed this was evidence of the law's even handedness, but African Americans were rarely convinced and continued to focus on the inequities of the justice system. As one black resident in Nashville explained in 1885, "[w]e cannot see why we should be watched more vigilantly by the police, apprehended for smaller offenses, and condemned with less hesitation than are the whites; why we are excluded almost invariably from serving on juries."[38]

When security and justice could not be secured through the courts, many African Americans participated in grassroots movements of armed self-defense, while others signed up to serve in state militias. In South Carolina, 1000 black men served in 14 militia units under Republican Governor Robert Scott, although historian Carole Emberton concludes that Scott formed the units out of political expediency rather than a "high-minded commitment to civil rights." In South Carolina and Louisiana, black militiamen played a key role in preserving Republican rule, for example fighting against white paramilitaries to hold the state capitols after disputed gubernatorial elections in 1876. By contrast, in states such as Alabama and Georgia, where African Americans were excluded from the militia, Republican rule ended years earlier.[39] At a more local level, Republican-organized Union Leagues maintained night patrols, investigated violent outrages, provided guidance and support to black Republicans caught up in legal disputes and monitored the performance of law enforcement officers, investigating crimes and making citizen's arrests when authorities failed to act.[40]

Black communities also made less formal arrangements to protect against white terrorism. As one former slave from Arkansas recalled in the 1930s of African Americans in 1870s South Carolina, "[t]hey organized. They used to have an association known as the Union Laborers .... It was a secret order carried on just like any other fraternal order. They had distress calls. Every member has an old horn which he blew in times of trouble." John Hunter remembered similar preparations in the early-1870s when the Ku Klux were whipping Blacks in Enfield, North Carolina: "The young niggers got their guns and rigged up a plan to kill them and laid out in a place for them, but they got wind of it and stopped coming." Others acted alone or with the support only of their family. When white men warned H. B. Holloway, a former slave in Georgia, that they would visit his house that night to whip him, he armed himself with an ax and his two sons with a pistol and a Winchester rifle and together they fought off six masked attackers. With only vestiges of Republican rule in the South remaining in April 1876, the *Savannah Colored Tribune* persisted in advocating that African Americans fight fire with fire: "If it is necessary for the protection of the lives of colored people, or to save them from the constant outrages committed upon them ... to kill and destroy their persecutors and tormentors, let them be killed and destroyed, and that without hesitation or delay."[41]

Toward Jim Crow

In 1874, Democrats won control of Congress for the first time since the Civil War, bringing an end to the era of Republican dominance in Washington. Within three years, the last Union troops were withdrawn from the South in a deal that secured the White House for the Republican presidential candidate Rutherford Hayes following a disputed election in 1876. The retreat from the radical agenda was driven, too, by the US Supreme Court, which issued a series of rulings that undermined the constitutional basis of federal protections for black rights. In 1873, the Court heard an appeal brought by New Orleans butchers who claimed that their constitutional rights were violated by a monopoly on the slaughterhouse business established by the State of Louisiana. Dismissing the case, the court ruled that the Fourteenth Amendment protected only the rights of national citizenship and not those under the jurisdiction of the individual states. Two years later, in *United States v. Cruickshank*, the Court threw out the convictions of 98 white men charged in 1873 with conspiring to violate the Fourteenth Amendment rights of more than one hundred African Americans killed during the Colfax Massacre in Louisiana. Because the accused had killed as private citizens and not while acting in an official state capacity, the Court held that they should be tried according to the laws of Louisiana and were not subject to federal authority. Collectively, these decisions pushed civil rights lawmaking back to white-dominated southern state courts, reflecting the prevailing faith in states' rights among the justices and a concern that the legitimacy of the federal judiciary not be compromised by politically sensitive civil rights cases.[42]

Federal protection of black civil rights in the South did not end overnight in the mid-1870s. Justice Department attorneys and marshals brought more than 1,200 cases of electoral law violations between 1877 and 1893, when the legislation was repealed, and one study has found that prosecutors in northern Mississippi secured a conviction rate of 55 percent in cases brought under the Ku Klux Klan Act in the early-1880s that was five times that in the 1871 South Carolina trials. These convictions, however, went against the grain and were secured against considerable odds. The Justice Department was always underfunded and understaffed; US marshals were overworked and poorly paid; there was no federal detective force to conduct investigations, and, most important of all, there was persistent resistance to the Department's work from local whites through fraud, violence, and judicial inertia. Although Republican political power survived in parts of the South until the 1890s, when white Democrats moved to crush the remaining black electorate through lynchings, constitutional reforms, and race riots, the federal government offered no resistance.[43]

As the concern and capacity of federal institutions to protect African American rights collapsed, whites in the South also moved to entrench black subordination through extending racial segregation laws. Beginning in Tennessee in 1881, legislation formalizing separation of black and white citizens on public transportation and public accommodations was enacted in almost all southern states by the turn of the century, but it was the criminalization of interracial sex and marriage—anti-miscegenation laws—that most fully embodied the new legal order. As a powerful symbol of social equality, the rights of mixed-race couples were contested during the Reconstruction era, with the enforcement of laws prohibiting interracial unions varying according to the shifting dynamics of local politics and questions of constitutionality remaining unsettled. By the 1880s, however, the law was clear. In *Pace v. Alabama* (1883), the US Supreme Court ruled that a state law providing prison sentences of two to seven years for "any white person and any negro" who married or committed adultery or fornication did not violate the Fourteenth Amendment's equal protection clause, because it applied to both black and white partners in the relationship. Over the next half century, 343 persons would be charged in Alabama with violation of anti-miscegenation statutes and 177 convicted and sentenced to an average of three to four years in prison, irrespective of their race or gender and with the full backing of the federal courts. Within months of the decision in *Pace*, the Court further cemented the legal basis of white supremacy in ruling unconstitutional the Civil Rights Act of 1875, which had prohibited discrimination in public accommodations. In the Court's view, the Act did not fall within the scope of the equal protection clause of the Fourteenth Amendment, which it instead applied only to discrimination by the state and not by individuals acting in a private capacity.[44]

African Americans contested the passage and enforcement of segregation laws, often taking the fight to the courts and the streets. Middle-class black women led the challenge to segregation on the railroads in the 1880s, clashing with police and initiating lawsuits as they demanded access to "ladies' cars" where they might find protection from the rough culture of second-class passengers who traveled in smoke-filled, mixed-race carriages. During the 1890s, southern states moved to disfranchise African Americans and the US Supreme Court gave explicit constitutional sanction to racial segregation in *Plessy v. Ferguson* (1896), but still resistance persisted, notably through boycotts of segregated public streetcars organized in several of the South's major cities in the early-twentieth century. The southern justice system had, nonetheless, been set on a course of systematic racial discrimination and violence that it would pursue until the 1960s. The early years of Reconstruction had offered fleeting hope that a body of criminal law developed amidst the culture of racial slavery could be transformed to represent and protect the interests of all southerners. The late years of the nineteenth century demonstrated that in practice law enforcement remained a pillar of southern white supremacy just as surely as it had been before the Civil War.

Part Two

Jim Crow Justice

4

The Southern Penal System

[O]ne, two time they 'rrest me, an' I told 'um I hadn't done nothin'; an' they said, "Arrest you in egvance—you gonna do sumpin'."

—W. D. Stewart ("Bama"), Parchman Farm, Mississippi State Penitentiary, 1947[1]

In the early-twentieth century, reports of a new form of slavery began to emanate from the Deep South. An autobiographical account published in 1904 of the life of a young black man held in debt peonage in Georgia revealed a system of almost unspeakable injustice and barbarity. Orphaned and hired out by his uncle to work for a prominent white landowner—"the Captain"—in Elbert County, Georgia, until the age of 21, as a young man the author was arrested and viciously thrashed when he sought alternative work. He subsequently agreed to a series of one-year labor contracts and eventually bound himself to the Captain's plantation for a ten-year term. Shortly afterwards, the Captain began to lease black convicts from the state and warned his free laborers that if they broke their contracts they "could be run down by bloodhounds, arrested without process of law, and ... returned to our employer, who ... might beat us brutally or administer any other kind of punishment that he thought proper." When the contracts expired, the workers found themselves bound once more by debts owed to the Captain for provisions they had procured over several years from his plantation store. Arrested, shackled, confined with state prisoners in a "filthy" stockade, and subject to meager rations and beatings, the "Georgia Negro Peon" worked for three years clearing his debt to the Captain, before one day he was

87

unexpectedly taken to South Carolina and released with only the clothes on his back.[2]

The blurred divide on the Captain's Georgia plantation between felons, contracted workers, and peons was indicative of the criminalization of black life in the post-Civil War South. Excluded from the administration of justice, prosecuted under arbitrary and coercive vagrancy and contract laws, and denied due process in the courts, African Americans were subject to a network of forced labor practices that operated in the name of criminal punishment to support white supremacy and serve the economic interests of the state, landholders, private corporations, and law enforcement officers. These continually evolving systems included convict leasing, state- and county-run chain gangs, prison farms, penitentiaries, and peonage and they operated both within and outside the law. In tracing the development of convict labor in the South from Reconstruction to the mid-twentieth century, this chapter explores the intersection of social and economic forces with racial ideology, but it also uncovers persistent challenges to forms of criminal punishment from prisoners, civil rights groups, labor unions, progressives, and penal reformers. Furthermore, it highlights that although the conditions of post-civil war black convict life often bore similarities to slavery, the late-nineteenth century southern penal system was a unique product of the post-emancipation world concerned with creating a "New South" as much as perpetuating the Old. Finally, the chapter argues that although southern punishment developed in ways distinct from mainstream national trends, the region was always integrated into a broader penal culture. The thousands of African Americans who suffered and died at the hands of scarcely regulated private corporations and state officials from the Civil War to the Second World War were victims of American penology and economic modernization as well as southern violence and racism.

The origins of convict leasing

Criminal punishments in colonial America targeted convicts' bodies through public floggings, ears nailed to pillories, bare flesh seared with branding irons, and frequent recourse to the gallows. These practices survived the American Revolution, but in the aftermath of independence reformers argued that the old penal regime was contrary to the humanitarian spirit of the age, undermined respect for the law, discouraged convictions, and turned petty criminals into hardened villains. Jails, which functioned mostly as short-term lockups for a diverse, interracial, and mixed gender inmate population of convicted felons, defendants, debtors, and paupers, were decried as unsanitary sites of disease, moral decay, and corruption. Most of all, the death penalty was attacked as a violation of the social contract between the citizen and the state that failed to distinguish between offenses and offenders of different magnitudes, and provided an ineffective deterrent against crime. On the contrary, public hangings were often scenes of riotous violence.[3]

Penitentiary imprisonment promised punishment of a very different order. The prolonged denial of freedom was a sanction peculiarly suited to a nation newly built on ideas of freedom and independence. As conceived by penal reformers, the purpose of prison was rehabilitation and deterrence through forced confinement, solitude, religion, and celibacy, but in practice imprisonment in early national and antebellum America was founded on forced labor. When Pennsylvania's pioneering Eastern State Penitentiary opened in Philadelphia in 1829, convicts worked alone in their cells as part of a regime of perpetual solitary confinement aimed at reformation of the soul, but it was the Auburn penitentiary in New York that provided the model for most prison labor in the nineteenth century. After nights spent in solitary confinement, Auburn prisoners congregated for work in manufacturing shops that were situated within the penitentiary walls but managed by external contractors. Early penal reformers debated the relative merits of these different systems of convict labor and the utility of work as a means to the rehabilitation of the criminal mind. In practice, however, the Auburn system flourished because the potential profits from congregate labor offered a mechanism for states to recoup some of the expense of prison administration.[4]

In the antebellum southern states, the violent culture of slavery contributed to the perpetuation of corporal punishments for many white as well as black convicts and sustained ideological currents of honor and patriarchalism that jarred with such underlying principles of penitentiary imprisonment as the centralization of state power and the deprivation of white freedom. By the Civil War, however, every slave state apart from the Carolinas and Florida had constructed a penitentiary, with most operating the Auburn model of congregate labor. Politicians, lawyers, businessmen, and newspaper editors were the main supporters of the penitentiaries in the South. These were men tied into the economic and cultural currents of the Atlantic

World, familiar with ideas of penal reform emanating from Western Europe and the northern United States, and they promoted penitentiary imprisonment as an orderly and civilizing innovation that offered protection for commercial interests. The majority of southern whites, however—including aristocratic planters opposed to state centralization, evangelical Christians wedded to Old Testament notions of vengeful punishment, and poorer whites in backcountry regions distant from international markets—were less concerned about the protection of property and conceived long terms of imprisonment for whites as a secretive and unrepublican form of elite tyranny and persistently attacked the burden of imprisonment on state finances, such that penitentiaries were always broadly unpopular and anomalous institutions in the region.[5]

After the Civil War, the shallow roots of penitentiary imprisonment in the South were made plain, as the region's politicians grappled with rapidly rising numbers of black convicts and state budgets that were close to bankrupt. Most southern states lacked the financial resources and political will to rebuild penitentiaries destroyed by the war, or to repair and expand those still standing. Reconstruction-era southern governments, both Democrat and Republican, therefore leased prisoners to private individuals and corporations under a variety of initially short-term schemes. Convict leasing would eventually prove highly profitable to southern governments, but in these early years the system served only to limit the drain of penal administration on the public purse. Under the terms of the first leases in Mississippi, the state paid tens of thousands of dollars to various contractors, including Confederate war hero and Ku Klux Klan grand wizard Nathan Bedford Forrest, for expenses including convicts' maintenance and transportation. When the Smith and McMillen Company signed Alabama's first lease in 1866 to work convicts on the Alabama and Chattanooga Railroad, it paid just $5 and over the following years received tens of thousands of dollars in state subsidies. In Arkansas, where prisoners were first leased in 1867, the penal system was operating at an annual loss of thousands of dollars by the early-1870s and Georgia was similarly indebted.[6]

The expedient early experiments in convict leasing were not, then, a panacea for the South's prison crisis, and neither were they the only innovations in post-Civil War southern penology. Several states pursued alternative policies while limiting or even prohibiting leasing agreements. Various southern states invested in penitentiaries. Virginia expanded its grand old prison building in Richmond in 1882, while Democratic administrations in the Carolinas began the construction of those states' first penitentiaries before the onset of congressional Reconstruction. South Carolina Governor William Orr was concerned that the penitentiary in Columbia should operate according to the latest penological thought. He based the institution's rules in part on recommendations in Theodore Dwight's influential 1867 *Report on Penitentiaries and Reformatories* and noted favorably that, unlike in most northern prisons, South Carolina convicts were not disciplined with the lash.[7] Amidst spiraling costs and accusations of corruption, the building work on the Carolina prisons continued over the next ten years under Republican administrations. Convicts worked first on penitentiary construction and then at manufacturing enterprises within the prison walls and these practices persisted even after "Redeemer" governments controlled by white supremacist Democrats introduced convict leasing in the mid-1870s. In 1882, 500 penitentiary inmates in South Carolina worked for three companies producing hosiery, leather goods, and shoes and in the same year the state established a prison farm and began working a further 200 prisoners on the Columbia canal. As in Virginia, the availability of alternative punishments in the Carolinas limited support for convict leasing, while powerful moderate political movements, which included African Americans in their ranks, acted as a bulwark against the complete privatization of the prison system. After an initial railroad building boom, local economic conditions also failed to generate the demand for forced labor that drove convict leasing's expansion in the Deep South.[8]

Although the Carolinas and Virginia stood on the edge of the southern penal mainstream, by the mid-1870s convict leasing was entrenched across most of the region and short contracts sweetened by state subsidies had been replaced by agreements that were long term and hugely profitable to the state and contractors alike. The change reflected the deepening financial crisis facing state governments as the American economy slid into depression, as well as the political upheavals of Redemption and the waning of federal efforts to secure equal rights and police racial violence. With white supremacist, one-party rule dominant, convict leasing expanded and by 1880 at least 5,000 convicts were leased across the southern states. Initially, most prisoners worked for railroad companies, but as the southern railroad boom slowed, agriculture and extractive industries promised the greatest financial returns from penal labor. In the Deep South, thousands of prisoners picked cotton, in Louisiana some also worked in sugar fields and on levee construction, and in Texas they herded cattle. Convicts were also employed at plantation labor and railroad work in Florida and Georgia, but over time they became concentrated in those states in naval stores production, phosphate and coal mining, as well as brick making. By 1906, Florida convicts produced 88,000 tons of phosphate and a combined 40,000 barrels of turpentine and resin. In Georgia, 862 convicts were leased to lumber camps where they cut and sawed 100 million feet of pine wood. A further 675 convicts spread across five camps mined 280,000 tons of coal and 36,000 tons of iron ore, while 238 convicts in two camps at Albany and Chattahoochee made 40,000,000 bricks.[9]

In Alabama and Tennessee, almost all convicts were leased to coal mining corporations, earning each state more than $100,000 a year by the mid-1880s. Boosted by cheap, forced labor, the coal industry boomed and in Alabama alone total output increased from 10,000 tons in 1872 to 400,000 tons in 1881 and 4 million tons in 1890. From 1880 to 1900, the combined output of the rich coal fields that stretched across Alabama, Georgia, and Tennessee rose by 500 percent, as growing conglomerates consolidated control of mining and related industries in part through the exploitation of convict labor. On the back of convict coal, Birmingham, Alabama, became the South's leading industrial center and home to some of the region's largest corporations such as Tennessee Coal and Iron (TCI) and Sloss Iron and Steel. TCI had expanded into Alabama in 1886 with the purchase of Pratt Coal and Coke and remained the state's principal lessee for the next 32 years, including after a takeover by US Steel in 1907.

Convict leasing was therefore integral to economic modernization in the South, attracting industrial investment to the region with the promise of reliable, cheap, and exploitable labor. In industries that relied heavily on convict workers, free laborers' wages fell and union influence was undermined as prisoners were used to cope with labor shortages and economic downturns and deployed as strike breakers. At the same time, however, leasing was also consistent with nationwide developments in penal administration through the late-nineteenth century that Rebecca McLennan has described as a "rationalization" of prison labor. As penal administrators sought to insure valuable contracts for prison workers against the vicissitudes of turbulent economic times that saw many small-scale contractors suffer bankruptcy, new agreements were drawn up with larger and more stable corporations that, across the nation, saw the total number of prisoners who worked during their incarceration increase from 6544 in 1873 to 45,277 in 1886. Corporate power was exerted most fully and devastatingly over prisoners' lives and working conditions in the South, but the dominance of private interests rather than state authorities was a feature of late-nineteenth century imprisonment nationwide.[10]

The economic benefits of convict leasing were underpinned in the South by racial ideology. There were always white convicts caught up in the system, but the overwhelming majority of prisoners were black and among leasing's primary justifications was the support it lent to the white supremacist social order. By 1880, inmates identified as "colored" accounted for 90 percent of all prisoners in Georgia, Mississippi, and South Carolina; 80 percent in Alabama; 72 percent in Virginia; and 67 percent in Tennessee. Among women prisoners, the percentage of African Americans was invariably even greater: in 1900, there were 68 black women and just two white women among more than 2000 prisoners leased in Georgia. Such figures were unsurprising to contemporary white southerners who read them as proof of innate black criminality and the predictable result of the abolition of slavery. In reality, however, the large black prison population was more specifically a product of engrained corruption and discrimination in the administration of justice, the introduction of long sentences for minor crimes, the criminalization of everyday black life, and the advantages of the penal system as a mechanism of labor control. In the cotton belt region of the Deep South during the period from Reconstruction to the 1910s, for example, rates of black imprisonment were related to fluctuations in cotton prices and economic cycles. When times were hard and cotton prices low, convict labor was used to discipline unemployed African Americans left beyond the more personalized control of a white employer or landowner. Convict labor also provided a cheap workforce that helped employers to survive economic downturns. Only after the Second World War, when Jim Crow and black disfranchisement laws were fully established and northward migration had reduced the supply of black labor in the South, weakening the demands of racial control, was there a decline in the correlation between economic conditions and rates of African American imprisonment and a higher proportion of white prisoners.[11]

Work, life, and death on the lease

In defending convict leasing before the Prison Congress in Atlanta in 1886, the Baptist preacher Dr. H. H. Tucker claimed that "the lessees are almost sure to be men of character, men who are known to be worthy of respect and confidence .... Such men know how to treat convicts humanely, and at the same time to utilize their labor to the best advantage."[12] This was the paternalistic, pro-slavery argument rehashed and it jarred with the evidence. In practice, convicts worked in scandalous conditions, suffered routine abuse and corporal punishment, and died at staggering rates from neglect, violence, and diseases including pneumonia and tuberculosis that were caused by poor diets, unsanitary living conditions, and a lack of medical care. In 1869, 92 of Alabama's 263 prisoners died. Twenty years later in the same state, one-third of 648 convict workers lost their lives over a two-year period at the Sloss-Sheffield mine in Coalsburg. Construction of the Greenwood and Augusta Railroad in South Carolina saw the deaths of 128 of 285 convicts between 1877 and 1880. The death rate was 15 percent in Tennessee in 1884 and 11 percent in Mississippi from 1880 to 1885, including, in one single year (1882), 126 deaths among 735 black prisoners (17 percent). Even for convicts who lived, survival could come at a horrific price. Theophile Chevalier, a black convict in Louisiana, lost both feet to frostbite-induced gangrene caused while working outdoors with no shoes; one foot rotted off, the other had to be amputated with a pen knife. No wonder that critics condemned leasing as worse than slavery; while slaves were valuable investments who could not be replaced without considerable cost to their owners, convicts were all too disposable: if one died, the state would provide another soon enough.

The work that convicts performed was unremittingly arduous. In coal mines, prisoners labored in dark, narrow, and poorly ventilated shafts, sometimes neck high in water, struggling to meet scarcely realistic targets of daily output while evading the many dangers of life underground, including outdated and unsafe equipment, falling rocks, and gas that could cause suffocation or explosions. In the turpentine camps of the north Florida pine forests, convicts spent winters cutting large gashes into virgin trees and attaching boxes to collect first gum and later resin that flowed from the wood. Through spring and summer new cuts had to be made, the resin collected into barrels and distilled into turpentine, and older trees felled for their timber. Elsewhere, the thousands of convicts employed on levee construction in Louisiana spent their days plowing and transporting earth or standing waist deep in swamps "delving in the black and noxious mud," while on farms and plantations across the South, backbreaking agricultural work from sunup to sundown could not but invoke the slave past. Women prisoners also performed hard manual labor, particularly fieldwork, but also railroad building and brick making, sometimes working alongside men in camps unsegregated by gender. As leasing arrangement matured, however, it became more common for women prisoners to be separated from men and set to work at domestic labor, hired out as servants in the homes of prison guards, or jailed in state penitentiaries.[13]

At the end of a day's labor, most convicts returned to rudimentary and unsanitary barracks. Among the worst conditions were those found along southern railroads where convicts slept in overcrowded cages on wheels that could be relocated as construction progressed. Similarly sparse arrangements persisted for decades in the form of box cars that held the convicts who built southern roads long into the twentieth century. In mining and turpentine regions, most convicts lived in some form of wooden shelter where they slept, often in chains, on hay-covered boards or filthy mattresses resting on iron cots. An Alabama warden was scathing in his critique of 14 prisons that he visited in 1882. They were, he wrote, "as filthy, as a rule, as dirt could make them, and both prisons and prisoners were infested with vermin .... They were poorly clothed and fed .... The sick were neglected, insomuch that no hospital had been provided, they being confined in the cells with the well convicts .... The prisons have no adequate water supply."[14]

In all convict industries, labor and subservience was compelled by the threat and routine practice of violence. A convict who fell short of a daily work quota or challenged a guard's authority might expect to be whipped, the many thousands who tried to escape were tracked by blood hounds and could be shot on sight, and women prisoners in particular faced the routine threat of sexual assault and the prospect of beatings if they resisted guards' advances. Reports of inhumane treatment of prisoners were rife from convict leasing's earliest years. In some cases, state authorities were so horrified by the conditions and abuses that were uncovered that they rebuked lessees and even revoked leasing contracts, albeit usually to little effect. Texas twice withdrew the lease, in 1867 and 1876; Governor Gordon of Georgia imposed a fine of $2500 on two penitentiary companies in 1887, and in the same year South Carolina returned 100 men to the state penitentiary who had suffered ill-treatment working on the Blackville and Newberry Railroad.[15] In most cases, however, there was little incentive for employers to mitigate conditions for a workforce that could resist but not withdraw its labor and had extremely limited political influence. In an era of sparse government, oversight of dispersed and often isolated convict camps was always difficult and in the case of the many thousands of convicts who were subleased, sometimes repeatedly, state authorities often had no idea even who was in custody and where they were held. What is more, corruption was rife across the system. A 1908 investigation into leasing in Georgia found evidence that prison officials, including the state warden and deputies, trafficked in convicts and received illegal payments from contractors whose treatment of prisoners they were supposed to regulate.[16]

Beginning in the 1890s, new leasing contracts included moves to increase state control over the treatment of southern convicts, though in practice these often proved little more than token gestures. In Georgia from 1899, only able-bodied men were leased and women, the infirm, and boys under the age of 15 were transferred to a new state penal farm in Milledgeville. Moreover, the state assumed responsibility for guarding, punishing, and providing medical care to convicts. There were similar developments in Florida, where a supervisor of state convicts was appointed in 1899 and in 1903 a Central Hospital for prisoners established at Ocala, Marion County. A state prison physician was appointed to inspect new prisoners (one-in-ten was found to be ill before they were even sent to a work camp) and tasked with visiting convict camps and transferring the sick and injured to the hospital. Ministers also monitored camp conditions and lessees were required to improve prisoner housing and hygiene. Convict mortality rates declined as a result, but when journalist Marc Goodnow visited a Florida turpentine camp in 1911 he still found the 200 prisoners sleeping on filthy mattresses, changing clothes only once a week, sharing just two bathtubs, and subject to discipline maintained by dogs, shotguns, and a fearsome leather strap.[17]

At some camps, efforts were made to persuade rather than coerce labor from convicts. Payments were offered for overwork and a task system operated that held out the possibility for convicts to shorten their standard six-day working week. Over the course of long sentences, some prisoners, notably in mining regions, acquired skills and remained in post after the expiry of their sentences, working for wages that compared favorably with those they might otherwise earn in the agricultural sector. The prospect of early release was also extended to prisoners. The novelist and outspoken critic of convict leasing George Washington Cable noted the unusually high number of pardons granted by southern governors in the early-1880s and claimed that most were issued "not because the prisoner has become so good, but because the prison is so bad." Recourse to clemency actually went hand in hand with the brutality, capriciousness, and discretion of the southern criminal justice system. It was a mechanism to keep discipline among convicts, perpetuate ideals of paternalistic race relations, and maintain a façade that justice was served in the South by mitigating the punishment of "deserving" prisoners. In contrast to appeals through the courts that were decided according to law and precedent, clemency was applied at the whim of political elites in ways that sustained the white supremacist racial order. Successful appeals typically required black convicts and their families to develop paternalistic relationships with white benefactors and conform to white expectations of their subordinate status. Clemency also gave the state leverage over released convicts. In Florida between 1889 and 1918, 1345 convicts were pardoned—11 percent of all those released from custody—most on the condition that they live "a sober, peaceable, law-abiding life" or face a return to custody.[18]

Whatever tactics of control were employed in southern convict camps, prisoners usually proved reluctant and inefficient workers. They resisted through work slowdowns, fighting back against guards, organizing strikes, setting fires, sabotaging machinery, and penning horrific accounts of their sufferings that were submitted in petitions to state governors or published in the press, fuelling public outrage. The demands of prisoners who refused to work at a coal mine near Atlanta in 1886, included better food, the dismissal of a whipping boss, and the abolition of corporal punishment. The "mutiny" was crushed, but contributed to new regulations on convict treatment imposed after an investigation by state authorities.[19] Other prisoners sought a more immediate end to their sufferings by running away. In Mississippi, 10 percent of convicts fled during the 1880s, and in Florida escapees accounted for up to 20 percent of all prisoners discharged from custody in the early-twentieth century. About half were recaptured, but the specter of violent and desperate felons roaming the southern countryside contributed significantly to calls for the state to take responsibility for more secure systems of punishment.[20]

Abolition and the limits of reform

The abolition of convict leasing occurred over a 40-year period from 1890 to 1928, as a result of deep-rooted changes in the political economy of the South, convict resistance, lower-class opposition to a practice that principally served elite interests, and persistent humanitarian criticisms. Change came first to Tennessee where, by 1890, all of the state's nearly 1500 inmates were leased to the Tennessee Coal, Iron, and Railroad Company (TCIR). About two-thirds of the prisoners were subleased, including 400 who worked in manufacturing at the state penitentiary, but there were sufficient convict miners to force down wages, discourage strikes, and challenge through association the proud identity of free mining communities. Driven by the growing strength of labor organizations such as the Knights of Labor and the United Mine Workers of America, tensions between free miners and the state mounted in Tennessee through the 1880s, and in October 1891 the miners rebelled, marching on the Briceville mine, wresting control of the convicts, and sending them by train to Knoxville. Similar incidents involving thousands of free miners occurred over the following months and into the summer of 1892, forcing the state to deploy troops to defend the collieries in a move that eroded the system's profitability. When the TCIR lease expired in 1896, it was not renewed and Tennessee's prisoners were removed to a new penitentiary in Nashville and a state-operated coal mine at Brushy Mountain.[21]

Lower-class protest also drove reform of convict leasing in Mississippi and Louisiana, but according to different dynamics. Since Reconstruction, the rural South had faced crippling economic circumstances and movements such as the Grangers, the Greenbackers, and the Farmer's Alliance agitated for the interests of small landowners and tenants. Alliance policies included limits on corporate expansion, a tax on land speculation, the opening of new lands for settlement, and an increase in the money supply to prevent falling prices for agricultural produce. Convict leasing was similarly condemned as a "special favor" to wealthy investors who secured cheap and disposable labor through corrupt political ties. In the 1890s, political elites in Mississippi and Louisiana acted to head off agrarian protests through state constitutional conventions that sought to unify Democrats around traditional and powerful conceptions of white supremacy and destroy black political power and the potential for interracial lower-class activism. The abolition of leasing consequently occurred alongside the introduction of property qualifications and literacy tests that disfranchised almost all African American citizens and many thousands of poor whites. In 1890, the Mississippi convention recommended that hiring convicts to corporations or individuals be prohibited, the state penitentiary in Jackson sold off to aid urban development, and a prison farm established. These measures took effect four years later and similar change came to Louisiana in 1901.

Advocates lauded the abolition of leasing in the language of penal reform and the southern tradition of paternalistic race relations, but it was politics that had driven the process and for most convicts, who continued to labor on plantations or at levee construction as they had done for decades, reform amounted to little more than a change in management.[22]

As the political winds that had sustained convict leasing began to turn, so too economic conditions that had once made penal labor so advantageous to lessees came to work against the system. In the 1890s, several long-term leases that had held the cost of convict workers artificially low since the 1870s finally expired. With demand for labor high and calls for greater regulation of prisoner treatment growing ever louder, the new agreements that were drawn up substantially eroded the comparative advantage of convict workers. The Macon *Telegraph* welcomed the end of Georgia's 20-year lease in 1899 on account of the opportunity it provided for the state to secure vast revenues that had hitherto "been reaped by the lessees" who had been paying under the odds for convicts for years. Overnight, annual state income from the lease increased five-fold to $125,000 and by 1904 the average price of a convict had doubled again to $225, a prohibitive cost for many contractors. Georgia would abandon the lease after newspaper exposés in the summer of 1908 revealed overwhelming evidence that the system was "barbarous, inhuman, and disgraceful," but leasing's demise by this point was already in train. In Arkansas, Colonel John M. Gracie did not wait for the state to act, but voluntarily abandoned the use of convict labor on his cotton plantation in 1909 after 23 profitable years, because of the cost of suits for damages brought against him by former convicts.[23]

Critical to the abolition of leasing was also the promotion of alternative forms of punishment. Across the Southeast, from Virginia to Georgia, the good roads movement called for state felons to be set to work modernizing the region's highway infrastructure to bolster economic development. County governments already used misdemeanor convicts on public works projects. In early-twentieth-century Georgia, around two-thirds of county prisoners worked on public roads, one-quarter were leased to turpentine and sawmill operators, and most of the rest went to farms (see Illustrations 4.1 and 4.2). In South Carolina, where leasing at the state level was always limited, there were 37 county convict camps in operation in 1905, each holding an average of 19 prisoners. In North Carolina in the same year, an average of 786 prisoners worked at 29 county

Illustration 4.1 Convicts and guard, Oglethorpe County, Georgia, May 1941. Courtesy of Library of Congress, Prints and Photographs Online, Farm Security Administration, Office of War Information Photograph Collection. <http://www.loc.gov/pictures/item/fsa1998007844/PP/>

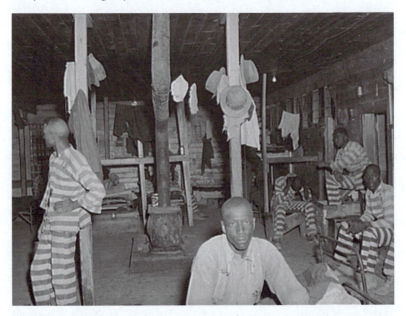

Illustration 4.2 At the convict camp in Greene County, Georgia, June 1941. Courtesy of Library of Congress, Prints and Photographs Online, Farm Security Administration, Office of War Information Photograph Collection. <http://www.loc.gov/pictures/item/fsa2000026294/PP/>

camps and even felony convicts remained under county control if sentenced to less than two years in prison.[24] Embracing central tenets of southern progressivism, good roads advocates outlined several advantages of assigning state convicts to county work camps. First, convict labor could serve as an efficient replacement for the long-standing and much abused practice of compelling local citizens to work for several days each year to maintain county roads. Second, it would eliminate the corruption and brutality that made leasing a counterproductive symbol of injustice and undermined African Americans' respect for the law in the interests of wealthy private individuals and corporations but at the expense of high rates of crime. While the pursuit of profit left leasing contractors unconcerned about reforming prisoners, a pressing issue given the frequency with which convicts escaped, it was believed that road labor regulated by county governments would serve to rehabilitate convicts' bodies and minds. Advocates maintained that county work camps were particularly appropriate for black convicts who were considered peculiarly suited to the rigors of outdoor labor under the hot southern sun. Such optimism soon dissipated, however, replaced by familiar charges of inhumanity, corruption, and inefficiency. A 1923 study of chain gangs in North Carolina found sanitary and living conditions scarcely better than under the lease and reported that even prisoners awaiting trial were routinely punished by flogging and days spent in unventilated and unlit dungeons for trivial acts of misconduct.[25]

If the chain gang was the new punishment of choice in the early-twentieth century Southeast, further west the state prison farm was the primary replacement for convict leasing. North Carolina and South Carolina had established the South's first prison farms in the early-1880s and their operations expanded rapidly. In the 1890s, farms were founded in Alabama, Georgia, and Virginia, and soon after the turn of the century Louisiana and Mississippi opened the South's most notorious penal plantations: Angola and Parchman. Both farms were located in inhospitable surroundings. Angola (see Illustration 4.3) was initially an 8000-acre site, later substantially expanded, and bordered on three sides by the Mississippi River.[26] Parchman Farm stretched by the early twentieth century across 20,000 acres. For most prisoners the work day consisted of arduous toil in one of 15 fields with little respite but the accompaniment of the repetitive call and response sounds of African- and slave-influenced work songs (see Illustration 4.4). Strung out in lines of up to a hundred

Illustration 4.3 Prison compound no. 1, Angola, Louisiana, July 1934. Courtesy of Library of Congress, Prints and Photographs Online, Lomax Collection. <http://www.loc.gov/pictures/item/2007660073/>

men, prisoners picked cotton from dawn until dusk under the watch of whip-wielding white drivers who patrolled on horseback. The men who toiled in the fields at Parchman were also surrounded by approximately 20 percent of their fellow convicts who were appointed to serve as "trustees." Armed and entitled to shoot-to-kill prisoners who attempted to escape, trustees enjoyed a privileged status. Invariably white, they received superior food, were spared the hard labor of field work, could move with some freedom around the plantation, and in some cases drew on connections with white officials in support of clemency appeals.[27] Similar methods of divide-and-rule were used to control prisoners in Louisiana, Arkansas, and Texas, where prisoners' dormitories were managed by "building tenders," convicts who held sway through violence that was unofficially sanctioned and often explicitly supported by guards. Brutality was commonplace, but even progressive penal reformers nonetheless endorsed prison farms as well suited to southern needs. After visiting Angola in 1906, Frederick H. Wines, of the National Prison Association, called the prison farm, an "ideal method of dealing with prisoners, especially Negro prisoners."[28] Four years later, Charles Richmond Henderson, President of the International Prison Congress, explained that southern penal labor was dictated by climate, the region's primarily agricultural economy, and "the presence of millions of negroes."[29] In the opinion of the *New York Times*, Parchman had solved the prison problem of the South: "The prison population menaces no trade, interferes with no skilled mechanic. It is self-supporting .... It turns out a class of good citizens, according to their humble station in life."[30] Mississippi state senator John R. McDowell agreed. Black convicts made "good farmers," he noted, adding that "few of them could be used at anything else."

Peonage

As state legislators moved to abolish convict leasing in the early-1900s, evidence of an even more pervasive form of forced labor began to reach a national audience. Peonage encompassed a range of connected legal and extra-legal practices that were most expansive in the Cotton Belt and turpentine lands of the Deep South where they entrapped indebted black laborers in the service of white employers. The debts on which the system rested stemmed from two main sources. First, they were incurred by tenant farmers and workers who were advanced payment or goods by the owners of the land they worked in exchange for future crop yields or labor. Second, they were incurred when courts levied fines and legal costs on black indigents for trivial misdemeanors. To avoid serving time on a chain gang or at a county work camp, convicts entered into contracts with whites who covered their financial liabilities in return for months or sometimes years of coerced labor. Once under contract, black laborers were subject to brutality and violence and bound by statutes that criminalized breach of contract and by law enforcement officers who entered into corrupt conspiracies with employers, made unjustified arrests to maintain a steady supply of forced laborers, and turned a blind eye to peons' sufferings.[31]

The legal basis of most black arrests in peonage cases were vagrancy statutes modeled on the black codes of Reconstruction that were enacted in every southern state except Tennessee between 1893 and 1909. Written in deliberately vague language to facilitate capricious enforcement, Alabama's 1903 law included as vagrants "any person wandering or strolling about in idleness, who is able to work, and has no property to support him; or any person leading an idle, immoral, profligate life, having no property to support him."[32] Misdemeanors and ordinance violations such as drunk and disorderly conduct were also subject to arbitrary enforcement by police officers and justices who arrested African Americans on scant pretext. In the convict leasing era, vagrants and other misdemeanants were often sent or subleased to the same private industries that employed state felons and many disappeared into an administrative no-man's land. At the Coalburg mine in Alabama, for example, there was not even a record of the charges against more than 500 of nearly 2,000 convict workers in 1895. In other circumstances, vagrants toiled on county or municipal work gangs. In 1904, this system was challenged in federal court when Henry Jamison was sentenced by a police magistrate in Macon, Georgia, to seven months on a chain gang for drunk and disorderly conduct. Though the offense violated a city ordinance rather than criminal law, there was little to distinguish Jamison's punishment from that of serious felony convicts. He wore iron leg manacles, dressed in striped convict clothing, and worked under the supervision of guards wielding guns and whips. Federal justice Emory Speer ruled that these conditions constituted "infamous punishment" and amounted to unconstitutional involuntary servitude as they were imposed by a single magistrate without the due process of a trial. On appeal the following year, however, the ruling was overturned.[33]

In the vast majority of peonage cases, convicts were handed over by sheriffs and constables to local employers with scarcely any legal process at all. Such was the practice in Central Alabama where Department of Justice investigations in 1903 uncovered an extensive and brutal network of human trafficking dominated by powerful landholders and corrupt law officers. Under a contract with the county, John Pace worked dozens of black convicts in his mines, sawmills, and fields, held them under armed guard in cells, and regularly inflicted corporal punishments.[34] To avoid the cost of paying fees for county convicts, Pace also received men directly from law officers and engaged in a nefarious arrangement with the nearby Cosby family in which James Kennedy, a justice of the peace and Pace employee, held sham hearings to provide indebted workers for the Cosbys, while justice William Cosby conducted similarly unregulated proceedings to send convicts to Pace on demand. Pace was among 18 men indicted for peonage in Alabama in the summer of 1903 but despite overwhelming evidence presented by the prosecution, only four men served short jail terms and in total just a few hundred dollars was levied in fines. Pace himself pleaded guilty and was sentenced to five years imprisonment, but he served not a day after first launching an appeal and then securing a presidential pardon from Theodore Roosevelt on grounds of ill health.[35]

Pace's involvement in convict labor continued and peonage thrived for decades largely unscathed either by ongoing Department of Justice investigations that were compromised by the refusal of all-white southern juries to convict, or by Supreme Court rulings that undermined the system's legal foundations. In *Bailey v. Alabama* (1911), the Court held that the criminalization of breach of contract violated the Thirteenth Amendment's prohibition against involuntary servitude. The case stemmed from early-1908, when Alonzo Bailey was arrested and sentenced to 136 days hard labor in lieu of a $30 fine plus costs for walking out on a year-long contract with the Riverside Company in Alabama after receiving a $15 advance. Three years later, in *Reynolds*, the Court went further and held that labor contracts amounted to an unconstitutional form of involuntary servitude when entered into for payment of fines and costs arising from criminal proceedings. Even so, in law professor Aziz Huq's assessment, neither *Bailey* nor *Reynolds* constituted a commitment by the Supreme Court to justice or the protection of black civil rights. Instead, they were designed in accordance with prevailing freedom of contract and laissez-faire jurisprudence that did not fundamentally challenge the white supremacist power structure.[36] In practice, moreover, the cases scarcely dented the South's peonage regime which survived the abolition of convict leasing and periodic revelations of horrendous brutality. Among the shocking events that briefly brought to light the all-too-normal conditions of peonage was the conviction in 1921 of John S. Williams, a white planter, and his black overseer, Clyde Manning, for the murder of eight African American men held as convict laborers on Williams' farm in Jasper County, Georgia. The killings were carried out to cover up evidence of peonage, murder, and endemic barbarity that was reported to federal agents in Atlanta by Gus Chapman, a former prisoner of Williams who had managed to escape. White Georgians rushed to declare the case a unique event, but Reverend John W. Ham was among those who recognized its typicality and, moreover, grasped the connections between peonage and the brutality that marked the rest of the Georgia penal system. In a sermon delivered several weeks after Williams' conviction, Ham argued, "We have nobody to blame but ourselves. For a century we have been practicing with legal sanction the very cruelties that we are now condemning in the individuals [Williams]."[37]

Deep-rooted economic and social changes in the South that were exploited by black workers would eventually weaken peonage, though the practice survived into the second half of the twentieth century. Mechanization undermined the system of sharecropping and the opening up of new job opportunities in southern and northern cities drew African Americans away from the Cotton Belt and enabled those who remained to negotiate for improved wages and weekly payments that facilitated the free movement of labor. By the late 1920s, groups including the National Association for the Advancement of Colored People (NAACP), the Communist Party, and the Southern Tenant Farmers' Union were also involved in organizing black laborers in strikes and other protests to secure citizenship rights, while the expanded role of the federal government in black life during the depression years of the 1930s also encouraged a massive increase in reports of peonage submitted by African Americans to the FBI.[38]

Penal reform in the twentieth century

The drawn out decline of convict leasing and peonage in the South beginning in the 1890s and the greater assertion of state control over convict labor in the form of chain gangs and prison farms was part of a nationwide shift from private to state regulation of imprisonment that had wide-ranging implications for the meaning and practice of punishment in the early-twentieth-century United States. New York was at the forefront of changes that eroded the centrality of labor to incarceration in most northern and western states by the 1930s. The state took over control of prison labor in 1894 in response to convict resistance and public outrage stirred by reports of brutal treatment by private contractors. Concerted opposition from powerful labor organizations and manufacturers quickly led to restrictions on the sale and transportation of convict-made goods that culminated amidst the mass unemployment of the 1930s in far-reaching congressional legislation. In states where prison labor was concentrated in manufacturing fields, convicts could still produce goods for use by internal state agencies, but demand was rarely sufficient to maintain full employment of the inmate population.

Where once forced labor had filled convicts' days, underpinned prison discipline, and generated revenues for the state that offset the costs of the penal system, constraints on convict labor "cast the penal arm of state government into a full-scale disciplinary, financial, and ideological crisis." The void left by the sidelining of convict labor was filled in most northern and western states by new disciplinary techniques and rationales for the purpose of punishment that represented an uneasy compromise among progressive penal reformers, politicians, state bureaucrats, prison administrators, and convicts themselves. Indeterminate sentencing and parole provided a mechanism to tailor punishment to the circumstances of individual convicts, offering early release to those who proved themselves rehabilitated or, more accurately in practice, abided by prison rules during their incarceration. Rather than isolating convicts from society and promoting an internal reformation of the soul through disciplined work and spiritual contemplation, parole also immersed criminals in the community with the aim of producing good citizens and efficient workers adapted to the demands of America's industrial economy. In this regard, parole increasingly represented an extension of convicts' experiences within prison walls. As convict labor declined, education and recreational programs were developed to maintain prison discipline and prepare prisoners for life on the outside. Innovations such as Thomas Osborne's Mutual Welfare League, for example, afforded convicts a stake and role in prison regulation comparable to the duties and responsibilities of free citizens. The expansion of juvenile reformatories, women's prisons, and asylums similarly represented a new concern with the classification of convicts that would allow for more targeted treatment of offenders.[39]

In the South, state use of convict labor survived in the form of chain gangs and prison farms, and what Progressive reformers called the "new penology" was adapted to the demands of the region's racial mores and political economy. Convict classification was used to entrench racial segregation and justify the restriction of education programs to white inmates. Juvenile facilities were similarly reserved for whites, and black youths were often condemned to work alongside adults in convict labor camps. Starved of state support, several early "colored" reformatories were established by black club women drawing principally on donations from within the black community. The Alabama Federation of Colored Women's Clubs opened a reformatory for African American boys in 1907 and in 1914 Virginia club women founded the Industrial School for Colored Girls outside Richmond. Such institutions were later administered by the state, though under separate and unequal conditions, and in Louisiana there was no reformatory for black juvenile offenders at all until the opening of the State Industrial School for Colored Youth in 1948, 44 years after similar facilities were provided for whites.[40]

Parole also developed according to distinct regional dynamics in the South. By the time of a US Department of Commerce investigation in 1938, only 28 percent of southern convicts were released under conditional parole compared with 77 percent across the rest of the nation.[41] Where parole did function in the South, it rarely operated according to the ambitions of penal reformers, but instead served to "maintain older economic relationships and traditional social ethics, habits and customs that underpinned forms of Southern authority."[42] G. Croft Williams, secretary of the State Board of Public Welfare in South Carolina, believed African American convicts were well suited to parole, claiming that "they are easily persuaded to obey, and they would not resent supervision."[43] In practice, black parolees had little choice: most were released to work for white employers who could return them to custody on any pretext. One white farmer in Alabama wrote bluntly to the Parole Board, "As I have a farm ... I am anxious to get some good, paroled convict to make and gather the crop. I would like to get some dependable middle age negro, who is trustworthy." The final decision to grant or deny parole rested with the governor and was often made on the basis of political considerations and without any investigation of the convict's circumstances. Moreover, upon release only a small minority of parolees were ever monitored by the parole board. Between 1935 and 1938, Alabama governor, Bibb Graves, granted 2194 paroles, but only 133 former prisoners were placed under parole board supervision.[44] Peter Taylor, an African American man paroled in Alabama in 1942 after serving 19 years for murder, described the system as a form of slavery that bore close resemblance to peonage. Taylor was paroled to Lamar King, a "Big Shot Political Farmer," who, Taylor alleged, had a total of 15 paroled men working on his land in Midway, Alabama, in a state of perpetual indebtedness that prohibited them from seeking alternative employment.[45] Probation in the South operated similarly. In the early-1920s, probation officers were employed in fewer than 10 percent of Georgia counties and courts across the state appointed volunteers who were "to aid the probationer" in abiding by the terms of early release, but in practice principally exploited convicts' labor.[46]

Commitment to penal reform was stymied in southern states by a racial ideology that conceived African Americans as scarcely capable of rehabilitation and underpinned strident opposition to investment in the penal system. Progressive reform organizations did develop in the region, but exercised only fleeting political influence. Historian Robert Perkinson has detailed cycles of reform and retrenchment that characterized Texas prison policy in the decades after the abolition of convict leasing. In the 1920s, for example, the National Committee on Prisons and Prison Labor conducted an "exhaustive" survey of prison conditions in Texas that prompted such innovations as prisoner education programs, training, and self-government, but fiscal and disciplinary crises, coupled with the intransigence of long-serving prison guards resistant to change, soon saw repressive measures of control reasserted. By the 1930s, Anglo and Mexican prisoners in Texas were engaging in widespread acts of self-mutilation in protest at the brutal conditions, although tellingly this practice was uncommon among African American convicts who seemingly were skeptical that anyone on the outside would even take notice if they severed their own limbs.[47]

In countless other ways, however, African American prisoners in the South did contest the conditions of their incarceration. Through ballads and the blues, black convicts forged a strong cultural identity. Work songs socialized prisoners in the rhythms and expectations of the chain gang and the prison farm (see illustration 4.4). They provided diversion, regulated the pace of repetitive labor tasks, and forged unity around collective expressions of the pains of prison life, the injustices of southern law enforcement, and hopes and longings for the future. This emotional form of release could serve the interests of prison guards through channeling frustrations into manageable forms of dissent, but work songs also bound convicts to a rich and powerful black cultural tradition of endurance and resistance amidst oppression. They were often adapted from old slave songs, and they resonated not only with the incarcerated, but also African Americans on the outside whose lives in the era of segregation were characterized by degrees of unfreedom, forced labor, and a parlous vulnerability to arbitrary arrest.[48]

African American prisoners identified also with civil rights activism. At risk of brutal punishment, they wrote letters to organizations such as the NAACP pleading for investigations into their sufferings. Black prisoners who reported abuses at Raiford prison farm in Florida, apologized that their letter was not typed and pleaded with the NAACP not to return it, "because it will get us in bad. You understand how it is here [sic]."[49] Another Florida convict wrote of guards inflicting beatings with a 3lb blackjack and locking convicts in a sweat-box the size of a telephone booth.[50] In 1946, three years after Georgia formally abolished the chain gang, Sylvester Turner reported an illegal convict camp in Scrivens County that held 31 black convicts who had been sentenced to the state penitentiary, but were

Illustration 4.4   Convicts singing in woodyard, Reed Camp, South Carolina, December 1934. Courtesy of Library of Congress, Prints and Photographs Online, Lomax Collection. <http://www.loc.gov/pictures/item/2007660142/>

sold off by the county sheriff and never passed into state custody.[51] When convicts escaped and fled to the North, civil rights organizations became involved in fighting extradition proceedings that saw the horrors of southern punishment laid bare in the northern press and courtrooms. In 1949, James J. Marshall removed his shirt and trousers in a New Jersey court to reveal "scars on his back, thighs and head" that had been inflicted by a prison guard in Georgia where he had been serving a 36-year term for robbery.[52] In 1958, Samuel Chambers told how he had fled from custody after a guard ordered him "to enter an Alabama pond known to be filled with poisonous snakes."[53] The political significance of such revelations had been apparent since at least the 1930s when the case of James Cunningham prompted a public clash over the standards of southern punishment between the governors of Georgia and Massachusetts. Cunningham had escaped from a Georgia chain gang in 1924, married in Cleveland and moved to Boston where he was arrested 13 years later for violating Massachusetts lottery laws and identified by his fingerprints as a fugitive. Georgia authorities demanded Cunningham's return, but NAACP representations of the cruelty of the Georgia chain gang persuaded Massachusetts Governor Charles Hurley against signing the extradition papers. Georgia's furious governor, Eurith Rivers, threatened in response to parole prisoners from his state and send them to Massachusetts.[54]

Convict resistance rarely assumed such explicitly politicized dimensions, but escapes were nonetheless also symptomatic of the fact that complete control over the prison population remained an elusive goal for penal authorities, in spite of fearful prison discipline. In practice, the changing regulations passed down from politicians to prison governors to guards were imposed haphazardly and shaped in practice by what historian Ethan Van Blue has characterized as "prisoners' covert networks and unofficial markets—from gambling to sex to violence and favors." From this perspective, though prisons were brutally repressive, they were also "in a constant state of confusion [and] disarray" and prisoners' lives were influenced in profound ways by their interactions with each other as well as their relations with guards and other representatives of the state.[55] The autobiography of Haywood Patterson, incarcerated at various Alabama prisons in the 1930s and 1940s, depicts a chaotic world in which prisoners traded in knives, drugs, sex, food, and clothing, gambled with dice and cards, and enticed strangers on the outside to send them money by posting lonely hearts adverts and fake stories in black newspapers. Patterson himself set up a store selling goods he purchased from the prison commissary and others that he acquired from outside, and like many inmates he used violence and money to keep another inmate as his "gal-boy."[56]

Southern prison farms and chain gangs proved resilient forms of punishment. They functioned largely unchanged in much of the region until the 1970s, serving as what David Oshinsky has called "a powerful link to the past—a place of racial discipline where blacks in striped clothing worked the cotton fields for the enrichment of others." In Alabama, the whip remained in use until 1962, convicts frequently spent days and nights in chains, food and housing conditions remained desperate, and each year dozens of men died from illnesses such as pneumonia and tuberculosis, as well as from violence perpetrated by guards and other prisoners. In Mississippi, the parole system was described in the late-1940s as like "human slavery" and on Parchman Farm the leather strap, known as "Black Annie," remained in use until 1964.[57] In South Carolina, state prisoners were still sent to county-run chain gangs in the 1960s, after every other state had abandoned the practice. Damning reports revealed unsanitary living conditions on the convict road camps, the absence of any system of classification to distinguish hardened felons from minor offenders, and a complete absence of recreational provisions and training programs.[58]

Amidst these conditions, convicts demonstrated their own resilience. Drawing on long-established traditions of resistance to incarceration, African American prisoners became influential participants in the civil rights and black power struggles of the 1960s and over the following decade they strived to bring the civil rights revolution to American cellblocks. In Alabama, Florida, Texas, and other southern states, black inmates filed lawsuits against segregation, overcrowding, mistreatment, and inadequate health care behind bars. The Supreme Court would eventually rule that prison conditions across the South—and much of the rest of the nation—were inhumane and unconstitutional and the result was the most far-reaching change to American punishment for a century. In keeping with almost all prison reforms over the previous century, however, the implications for prisoners themselves would include new forms of oppression as well as relief from old tortures, and they would be deeply conditioned by ideas about race.

5

Lynching and Law

Thus grew up a double system of justice, which erred on the white side by undue leniency and the practical immunity of red-handed criminals, and erred on the black side by undue severity, injustice, and lack of discrimination.
—W.E.B. Du Bois, *The Souls of Black Folk*, 1903

On August 14, 1936, Rainey Bethea was executed in Owensboro, Kentucky, for the rape of an elderly white woman. Bethea was also suspected of robbery and the woman's murder—both capital offenses in Kentucky—but he was charged only with rape, the one crime that carried a sentence of public hanging rather than electrocution behind prison walls. Bethea's arraignment had been a perfunctory event; there was little cross-examination and the jury decided on the sentence in less than five minutes. When he stepped onto the gallows, a crowd estimated at 10,000 looked on, jeering. Many had traveled from far afield—including reporters flown in from New York—filling the town's hotels. They "munched hot dogs and sipped pop" as Bethea prayed, and in the moments after his body fell souvenir hunters rushed forward to tear scraps of cloth from the mask that covered his face.[1]

The "picnic execution" of Rainey Bethea was the last public execution held in the United States. As such, it was an unusual event, but it was nonetheless symptomatic of how criminal justice was entangled with racial violence in Jim Crow America.[2] Bethea was killed by the state, but his final moments echoed those endured by victims of lynching. In the era from the end of Reconstruction until the 1960s, thousands of African Americans were lynched and hundreds more put to death by the state, but there was no clear and simple dividing

113

line between the law and the mob. Confessions were beaten out of defendants by police officers, all-white juries condemned black defendants in courtrooms surrounded by crowds baying for blood, and judges passed death sentences that were hastily enacted for fear that the mob would otherwise inflict summary punishment. Outside of the courtroom, black communities were also denied the police protection afforded to white neighborhoods and both black-on-black and white-on-black crime was neglected by law enforcement officers. The toleration of violent and discriminatory judicial practices, often on the grounds that they served to combat mob rule, was testament to the pernicious impact of lynching on American legal culture. This influence reflected that lynching itself, though inherently a demonstration of lawlessness, was in practice closely related to criminal proceedings administered by the state and popularly understood as a form of justice. Lynching parties held mock investigations and deliberated over appropriate punishments, routinely seized their victims from courtrooms and jail cells (sometimes with the connivance of officers of the law), and explained their killings as a more righteous response to crime than the state could or would provide.

This chapter traces the connected histories of racial violence and law enforcement in the South during the era of segregation from the 1880s to the 1940s. In the early years of this period, white southerners developed a powerful pro-lynching ideology based around the perceived sexual threat that black men posed to white women and the slowness and uncertainty of achieving justice through the legal system. African American campaigners and civil rights organizations persistently attacked this narrative, revealing it as a shroud for white supremacist politics of racial domination and labor control. Coupled with social and economic changes in the South and the threat of federal action against mob rule, this agitation contributed to a stark decline in the frequency of lynching. By the 1930s, African Americans accused of rape and murder were invariably prosecuted through southern courts rather than subject to mob violence, but less publicized and individual acts of racial violence persisted without sanction, and equal justice for African Americans before the law remained a distant prospect while white supremacy continued to structure American society.

Lynching and its advocates

The origins of the term lynching date to the Revolutionary era—in legend to a Virginia judge, Charles Lynch, whose vigilante activities against the British during the War of Independence were subsequently deemed justifiable by the state legislature on account of the "imminence of danger."[3] The meaning and practice of lynching, however, evolved over time. Lynching in the antebellum era was associated particularly with western frontier towns while in the southern slave states mobs frequently targeted whites, particularly abolitionists, as well as black slaves. In the post-Reconstruction era lynching occurred more frequently than ever before, for the first time African Americans became the primary victims, torture became a common part of lynch mobs' work, and killings were increasingly concentrated in the South. A conference of anti-lynching organizations in 1940 proposed that a lynching was an illegal killing conducted by a group "under the pretext of service to justice, race, or tradition," but even this broad definition scarcely reflected the varied incidents to which the term was (and was not) applied.[4] From the 1890s, the most spectacular lynchings were highly ceremonial affairs conducted before huge crowds, sometimes numbering in the thousands, and often involving brutal and prolonged torture. More commonly, however, lynchings were perpetrated by secretive terrorist groups, small private mobs who killed by cover of night, and posses of men working openly alongside officers of the law. By contrast, mob killings that occurred in the midst of race riots were rarely designated as lynchings at all, however death arrived.[5]

Lynching statistics were collected from the early-1880s by the *Chicago Tribune* and in later years also by Booker T. Washington's Tuskegee Institute and the National Association for the Advancement of Colored People. The production of detailed statistical evidence would prove integral to the anti-lynching struggle, but the figures were conservative, due to imperfect sources (mostly white newspaper reports), mobs' efforts to cover their tracks, and uncertainty over how to define the crime. Available records nonetheless serve as a valuable guide to the scale of lynching in Jim Crow America. At least 4743 people were lynched between 1882 and 1968 and 3446 (73 percent) of the dead were black. After 1900, African Americans comprised more than 90 percent of lynch mob victims, though viewed in the aggregate, the lynching of black men and women (who were targeted in approximately 2 percent of lynchings) peaked in the 1890s when there was a lynching about once every three days somewhere in the United States. The decline that followed was slow and inconsistent through the 1930s. The average number of African Americans annually killed by lynch mobs fell from 111 in the 1890s, to 80 in the 1900s, 57 in the 1910s, and 28 in the 1920s. After twenty people were killed by mobs in 1935, the number of recorded lynchings never again rose above eight in a calendar year and in 1952 the United States experienced its first year without a lynching since records began. Mobs continued to strike intermittently over the following decades, however, and secretive, unreported lynchings, persisted with much greater frequency.[6]

Lynching was a national phenomenon, but in the segregation era it was concentrated particularly in the former slave states and it was typical of some parts of the region more than others. Lynching occurred most often in the cotton plantation lands of the Black Belt from Georgia across to Louisiana, a pattern that was a product of socioeconomic conditions in the region. Sharecropping, single crop agriculture, and a large black labor force fostered exploitative labor relations and violent forms of social control among white landholders sensitive to any evidence of black economic or social progress.[7] Analyzing lynching at the county level, Stewart Tolnay and E. M. Beck argue more specifically that mob violence occurred mostly in plantation regions with majority black populations, large numbers of landless white farmers, and limited free land, conditions which fuelled intense economic competition across the color line that readily sparked into violence, particularly in times of falling cotton prices and economic crisis.[8] Edward Ayers offers a different interpretation, noting that rates of lynching relative to population were lower in the Black Belt and Piedmont regions than elsewhere in the South, such as along the Gulf Plain and in the cotton uplands, and mountain regions. Ayers argues that lynching flourished in these isolated rural areas primarily because of the absence of law enforcement officers and a large influx of transient black workers which caused "fear and insecurity" among local whites. By contrast, in the Black Belt, a highly personal form of racial control reigned, based on "intimacy" between deeply rooted black and white populations bound together by "paternalism and racial etiquette."[9] White supremacy was still underpinned by violence, but it most often flared between individuals, as personal ties across the racial divide and conservative white elites' desire for order and stability discouraged more general lawlessness.[10]

Numbers and patterns of lynching alone, however, tell an incomplete story. Many Americans lived in places that never experienced a lynching, but much of the terror of the crime was that it might occur at any time and in any place. Moreover, beginning in the 1890s spectacular and grotesque "public torture lynchings" became commodified as mass entertainment, attracting participants and curious voyeurs from far beyond the localities where they occurred and generating press reports that horrified and titillated audiences nationwide. The first such lynching occurred in Paris, Texas, in 1893. Schools were dismissed by order of the mayor, whisky stores closed, and thousands of people traveled from far and wide by train, wagon, and on horseback to witness the killing of Henry Smith, an African American alleged child murderer. The crowd stood witness and cheered as Smith was transported through the streets of Paris on a float, placed upon a scaffold scrawled with the word "justice," tortured with red hot irons by the dead child's male relatives for almost an hour, and then set alight. In such cases, the mob's work did not cease even when death finally came. Corpses were mutilated, ears, fingers, and limbs taken as macabre souvenirs, and photographs snapped to be published in newspapers and sent as postcards, spreading the message of the lynching far and wide. African Americans suffered other forms of racial violence more frequently than lynching during the Jim Crow era, but lynching's shocking brutality and overt public display of white supremacy made it a uniquely powerful form and symbol of oppression.[11]

The audacity of the men, women, and children who posed for posterity alongside the strange fruit of their labors was chilling evidence that they acted without fear of legal sanction and with complete faith that what they had done was just. In sociologist David Garland's assessment, such public torture lynchings were "political theater," a form of criminal punishment that carried a host of social meanings. They echoed archaic forms of punishment—deliberately so—for by denying alleged black criminals a day in court, lynch mobs perpetuated notions of black inferiority and inhumanity, denied African American claims to citizenship rights, and identified the regulation of black criminality as a matter for white society, as it had been under slavery, rather than the law.[12] Interpreting the cultural roots of lynching in a far broader context, Jacqueline Goldsby argues that the practice was also an expression of an aggressive and modern America that was elsewhere evident in the form of imperial expansion in the Caribbean and the Philippines, the extermination of Indian populations in the West, and the unprecedented scale and efficiency of killing in the Civil War and the First World War. The narratives of bestial black savagery that were strengthened by lynchings supported American expansion by reaffirming and giving meaning to claims about the superiority of "white" civilization. Furthermore, lynching made plain that contrary to segregation laws that defined African Americans as "separate but equal" citizens, in reality the Jim Crow system was more particularly about the supremacy of the white race. As Historian Grace Hale has argued, in a rapidly changing society where technological change, new patterns of consumption, black autonomy, and class distinctions among whites increasingly threatened to erode the racial divide, it was significant that "Only whites ... could experience the 'amusement' of a black man burned. Only African Americans could be extralegally and publicly tortured and killed."[13]

In practice, pro-lynching advocates explained lynching very differently. Drawing on popular caricatures of the sexually aggressive and uncontrollable black male and invoking American traditions of personal vengeance and limited state authority, segregation-era southern mobs claimed that lynch law was necessary primarily to protect white women from the sexual advances of black men. Philip Alexander Bruce, a southern historian writing in the early-twentieth century, argued that black men found "something strangely alluring and seductive ... in the appearance of the white woman; they are aroused and stimulated by its foreignness to their experience of sexual pleasures, and it moves them to gratify their lust at any cost and in spite of any obstacle."[14] Writing in the *North American Review* in 1904, Thomas Nelson Page, a Virginian, argued that lynching was primarily a response to rape and that any form of legal process for rapists was inappropriate. Even if the accused were convicted in court, in Page's view the white female victim was dishonored by having to recount her ordeal in public. What is more, Page believed that the opportunity to preach from the gallows made even the death penalty little deterrent to many black criminals. The law was also attacked as a cumbersome and insufficiently fearsome mechanism of justice. Reflecting popular hostility toward centralized state authority that took particular hold in the southern states where slavery had sanctified white male autonomy, the Georgia Bar Association in 1893 identified "a distrust, and a constantly growing distrust, in the promptness and efficiency of the law," as a further catalyst of mob activity.[15]

Pro-lynching arguments were repeated time and again in newspaper reports of mob killings, helping to unify white society in support of lynching and in common cause against the rhetorical "black criminal," but in reality they were disingenuous fictions. The white-dominated legal system dispatched black men to the gallows with alacrity and rape was not even the alleged cause of most lynchings, which were instigated more often by accusations of murder and also sparked by a host of noncapital "offenses." In just a single year in the 1890s, these included counterfeiting, arson, flogging a white boy, political activity, race prejudice, insulting a white woman, and burglary. In 1890, eight black prisoners accused of murder were taken from a prison in

Charleston by a mob of hundreds, tied-up, and shot dead. Arkansas mobs lynched a black man with small pox in 1894, a man accused of hog stealing in 1898, and, in 1907, a black bartender for fighting with a white man. A lynching the following year in Alabama was prompted by an alleged assault on a white woman, and the black press regularly reported incidents in which mobs acknowledged they had killed the wrong person altogether. Black women were targeted, too. In Georgia, Mary Turner was burned alive after she threatened to institute legal proceedings against the mob that had lynched her husband; her unborn child was cut from her womb and crushed to death.[16]

Rather than failing to check black criminality, southern criminal law conspired to facilitate mob rule. Anti-lynching statutes—the earliest dating to the 1890s—were enacted across at least 15 states by the 1930s, but were rarely enforced. An investigation in 1933 by James Chadbourn for the Southern Commission on the Study of Lynching found that prosecutions had been instigated in relation to only 12 lynchings since 1900 and just 67 people out of the thousands who had participated in the mobs had been convicted.[17] The problems of enforcement were readily apparent in North Carolina in the wake of the 1906 lynching of J. V. Johnson, a white man, in the town of Wadesboro. The case marked the first time that a serious effort was made to enforce the state's 1893 anti-lynching law. The press led condemnation of Johnson's killers and Governor Robert B. Glenn promised resources to ensure a vigorous prosecution, but a jury of local white men returned unanimous not-guilty verdicts against the first two men charged with the lynching and in one case they did not even leave the courtroom to deliberate. In response, the "disgusted" presiding judge chose to strike the remaining cases from the docket rather than sit through a repeat of the farcical proceedings.[18] Away from the courtroom, law enforcement personnel likewise assisted in lynching as often as they strived to bring a mob to justice. Hundreds of lynching victims were seized from police custody, courtrooms, or jail cells. Sometimes the mob did have to overpower police, a sheriff, or jailer, but on other occasions jail doors were deliberately unlocked or left unguarded.

The anti-lynching movement

Though lynching reflected the power of the mob in an era of white supremacy and barely checked violence, African Americans and their allies persistently challenged the rhetoric and ideology that supported mob rule. In 1883, Frederick Douglass condemned the rape myth and

called for interracial cooperation with white Republican allies to protect black constitutional rights, but black commitment to the party of
Lincoln was sorely tested as the Supreme Court constrained the scope
of the Fourteenth Amendment after Reconstruction, annual rates of
lynching increased, and national politicians demonstrated little interest in stemming the violence. In 1887, T. Thomas Fortune, editor of the
New York Age, rejected any reliance on mainstream political parties.
Instead, he argued that African Americans should "take hold of this
problem ourselves" and pushed the formation of the Afro-American
League, one of the earliest national civil rights organizations, to agitate
for federal intervention against state authorities that failed to protect
African Americans from white violence. Others had less faith still in
national political responses to lynching. In mid-1890s' Virginia, John
Mitchell of the *Richmond Planet* worked with local white politicians—
notably Governor Charles T. O'Ferrall, who opposed lynching as a form
of lawlessness—to combat mob activity. While the political winds blew
fair, Mitchell achieved considerable success. There were few lynchings
in Virginia during O'Ferrall's four-year term, but opposition to mob rule
had shallow roots and the situation reversed once O'Ferrall left office.[19]

Black leaders also advocated armed self-defense in the face of mob
violence. "Meet force with force," advised John Edward Bruce in 1899,
though black individuals and communities needed little encouragement.
African Americans in Clarksville, Tennessee, were suspected of burning
the town's business district in 1880 in protest against a lynching and the
fatal shooting of a colored man by a police officer. Reporting the incident, the *Chicago Conservator*, a black newspaper, regretted "the necessity" of black lawlessness, "but not the act." It hoped that the example
of Clarksville would inspire other black communities "from Virginia to
Texas" and warned southern whites "that they need not expect ... one-
sided scenes of butchery in the future." In 1892, hundreds of African
Americans assembled to protect the jail in Jacksonville, Florida, where
Benjamin Reed was held on suspicion of the murder of Frank Burrows, a
white man. The black men, "armed to the very teeth," questioned whites
in the area and pointed loaded pistols at any who approached the jail.
Several militia companies were called out to protect the jail and the black
crowd eventually dispersed without bloodshed. Across the South, lynching was least common where African Americans comprised a majority
of the population, an indication that white mobs were discouraged when
the balance of power was against them.[20]

Grassroots anti-lynching tactics, including armed self-defense and
economic boycotts of white businesses, were endorsed by Ida B. Wells

(see Illustration 5.1), the most prominent anti-lynching campaigner of the 1890s. Born a slave in Mississippi in July 1862, Wells moved to Memphis, Tennessee, in the mid-1880s and became a renowned race activist. By 1889, she was the co-owner and editor of a newspaper called the *Free Speech* and had a national reputation for her bold statements on issues including the poor quality of African American education and the expansion of segregation laws. Following the 1892 murders of three black businessmen in Memphis, Wells dedicated herself to exposing the fallacies of pro-lynching rhetoric. She later recalled that the killings in Memphis "opened my eyes to what lynching really was. An excuse to get rid of Negroes who were acquiring wealth and property and thus keep the race terrorized and 'keep the nigger down.'" In a series of newspaper editorials, articles, and pamphlets that combined powerful accounts of lynchings with detailed statistical evidence, Wells unmasked the pro-lynching argument that mob rule was a response to inherent black criminality, particularly the rape of white women, and the inefficiency of the criminal justice system.[21]

IDA B. WELLS.

Illustration 5.1   Ida B. Wells, head and shoulders portrait, 1891. Courtesy of Library of Congress, Prints and Photographs Online, Miscellaneous Items. <http://www.loc.gov/pictures/item/93505758/>

Wells also generated international publicity for the anti-lynching cause, undertaking two tours of Britain in 1893 and 1894 that forced the issue onto the national agenda, engaging the concern of the northern US press and white middle classes. Yet through the early-twentieth century, Wells's uncompromising denunciations of lynching not only met with fierce resistance from southern white supremacists, but were also contested by more moderate black critiques of lynching that were constrained by a pragmatic recognition of the power of white supremacy and a middle-class commitment to the politics of respectability and racial uplift. Socially conservative black news-papers condemned black criminality in the same breath as lynching, implicitly accepting the pro-lynching assumption that victims were guilty of the crimes that mobs charged. Even Mary Church Terrell, head of the National Association of Colored Women and an outspo-ken opponent of lynching, tended to accept this premise, which fitted with her negative views of the immorality of the black poor. Other African American commentators supported tough law enforcement as an antidote to lynching, even though black defendants had little more chance of justice within the legal system than at the hands of the mob. When William Bloxham, newly elected Governor of Florida, called for castration as an antidote to lynching in cases of rape and attempted rape, an African American newspaper in Indianapolis endorsed the proposal as a "severe" but justified way to uphold "the moral code".[22]

In the 1910s, the National Association for the Advancement of Colored People (NAACP) emerged as a new and powerful force in the anti-lynching movement. Founded in 1909, to defend the rights, forward the causes, and challenge the "systematic persecution" of African Americans, the NAACP stood at the forefront of campaigns against lynching through the first half of the twentieth century. The leading figures in the early NAACP were mostly white men and women, relatively wealthy, well educated, with family backgrounds rooted in abolitionism and personal experience in many areas of the progressive movement. Within a decade, however, African Americans were at the forefront of the NAACP's work and constituted more than 90 percent of the Association's rank and file members. The intensification of NAACP anti-lynching activism was led by two of the Association's most prominent new black leaders: the lawyer and writer James Weldon Johnson, appointed field secretary in 1916, and Walter White, whose work with the local Atlanta chapter of the NAACP to improve education provisions for African Americans led to his employment as assistant secretary at the Association's national office in New York in 1918. Both men later headed the NAACP as executive secretary.[23]

The NAACP's anti-lynching work included the carrying out of detailed investigations into mob killings. These were often conducted personally, and at great personal risk, by Walter White whose light skin color enabled him to pass as white and secure evidence from both the perpetrators as well as the victims of racial violence. White's reports drew on and gave voice to long-standing opposition to lynching in local black communities[24] and, in keeping with the work of Ida B. Wells, they challenged the stories that whites told to justify mob rule. In addition, however, the NAACP also adopted more explicitly political tactics and goals, including establishing mass participation political campaigns that aimed to promote passage of federal anti-lynching legislation to overcome the failure and sometimes outright refusal of southern courts to prosecute mob participants. Proposed federal anti-lynching laws aimed to circumvent the corrosive influence of local sympathies for lynching parties on the administration of justice by creating new crimes under the Fourteenth Amendment that could be prosecuted in federal rather than state courts. In 1920, Congressman Leonidas C. Dyer, a Republican who represented a majority black area of East St. Louis, introduced a bill—developed in conjunction with the NAACP—that targeted all parties who enacted or facilitated a lynching: minimum five-year jail terms were proposed for mob participants; law enforcement officers who failed to take reasonable steps to prevent a lynching faced up to five years in jail and a fine of $5000, and counties where lynchings occurred were required to pay up to $10,000 compensation to the victim's family, a measure that aimed to undermine the widespread tolerance of lynching in southern white communities.[25]

On January 26, 1922, the Dyer bill passed the House of Representatives by a vote of 230 to 119, but southern Democrats attacked the legislation using time-honored arguments. Finis J. Garrett of Tennessee called it "a bill to encourage rape," and others shared his view that it would leave southern women defenseless against black rapists. Southern politicians also declared the bill unconstitutional, arguing that lynching was simply murder, and murder was a crime for which state judicial systems were already responsible. With the tacit support of some Republicans, Democrats eventually used the filibuster to condemn the Dyer Bill to defeat in the Senate. Driven by persistent NAACP agitation and protest against lynching (see Illustration 5.2), further anti-lynching legislation was proposed in every Congress except one until

Illustration 5.2 NAACP members protest against lynching outside a crime conference in Washington, D.C., December 11, 1934. Courtesy of Bettmann/Corbis

1948 and twice more, in 1934 and 1940, it won approval in the House, but died in the upper chamber. On each occasion, southern Democrats led the opposition, sometimes using familiar arguments about the failure of federal intervention during Reconstruction and the threat of black criminality, but also pointing to the declining frequency of lynching as evidence that the South was capable of putting its own house in order. By this point, southern elites were less concerned that a federal anti-lynching law would undermine mob rule than that it could serve as a precedent for further national legislation on other civil rights issues.[26]

For all that white southerners defended lynching, there was also a tradition of white anti-lynching activity in the South that dated back to the 1890s. The earliest opposition came from conservative elites concerned to uphold the rule of law, retain local control of race relations, and attract external investment to the region. When hundreds of thousands of African Americans left the South in the 1910s in search of new opportunities and greater personal security in the urban North, moderating the most extreme racial violence became even more important for southern white landholders dependent on cheap and pliant black labor. A long-term shift in elite attitudes toward mob rule was evident in Tampa, Florida. In the early decades of the twentieth century, cigar makers in Tampa used vigilantism as a form of labor control. Vigilance committees were established to break strikes and run leading union men out of town and in this context lynching had widespread support. In 1903, for example, two black men accused, but not prosecuted, in separate incidents of sexual assaults on white girls were castrated and one hanged in the city. When a lynching was threatened in 1927, by contrast, 500 national guardsmen were called out to prevent violence as municipal leaders strived to promote Tampa as an orderly and law-abiding place to prospective new businesses and investors. By the 1930s, amidst the economic turmoil of the Great Depression and after the cigar industry had reached an accommodation with the unions under pressure from the federal government, lynching persisted but mostly in the form of secretive attacks. Mob rule was condemned in the press and prosecutions were brought against vigilante leaders, as well as law officers who failed to protect prisoners in their custody.[27]

There were other signs of changing attitudes toward lynching in the 1920s' South. Shortly before leaving office in 1921, Georgia governor Hugh M. Dorsey published an exposé of 135 cases of lynching, peonage, and other crimes against African Americans. He proposed measures to combat mob rule, including forming a state constabulary and drawing jurors for lynching trials from beyond the vicinity of the crimes. Dorsey's analysis of racial violence sparked outrage and was damned by his successor, Thomas Hardwick, as a "slander on the people" of Georgia, but elsewhere in the South other administrations were more willing to use force against white vigilantes. In 1920, as a mob attempted to storm a North Carolina jail holding three African American men suspected of raping a white woman, one white man in the crowd was shot dead by the National Guard that had been deployed to protect the prisoners. Five years later, five people were shot and dozens injured as officers used fire hoses, guns, and tear bombs to defend a jail in Dallas from a mob of more than 2,000 people seeking to lynch two African American murder suspects. Equally significant, southern-based reform movements began to promote changes in cultural attitudes toward lynching. The Commission on Interracial Cooperation (CIC), formed of progressive black and white southerners following a series of race riots in 1919, worked with local authorities to prevent mob violence and prosecute lynching parties under state legislation. In 1930, the Texas-born suffragist leader Jessie Daniel Ames founded the Association of Southern Women for the Prevention of Lynching (ASWPL). An all-white CIC offshoot, the women of the ASWPL investigated and denounced racial violence perpetrated in their name and used their moral authority under southern gender conventions to commit police officers and sheriffs to uphold the law against mob rule.[28]

Legal lynchings

From the mid-1930s, there was a precipitous decline in the frequency of recorded lynchings. In particular, the era of spectacular public lynchings was at an end, but in many respects the practice had largely served its purpose for white supremacists by this point. Reports of torturous mob killings had long-since assumed a standardized narrative form that made them almost interchangeable and along with the circulation of lynching's material culture of postcards, sound recordings of the victim's dying moments, and body parts and ropes taken as souvenirs from the scenes of the crime, they had become so deeply embedded in the American imagination that, in Hale's analysis, "Whites could now consume a lynching without consuming a black man," and amidst growing criticism of the practice both within and beyond the South, it was increasingly advantageous to do so.[29]

Reflecting these developments, the black newspaper the *New York Amsterdam News* commented in early-1934 that a new federal anti-lynching bill then pending before Congress was less urgently required than some alternative federal intervention to protect African American from "lynchings" perpetrated "by a judge and jury," which it called an "ordinary occurrence south of the Mason-Dixon Line."[30] Like other civil rights activists, the *Amsterdam News* recognized that without reform of the criminal justice system any decline in annual rates of lynching constituted hollow progress for black Americans. Across the nation, the specter of mob rule was deployed to justify a form of law enforcement against African Americans that amounted to little more than "legal lynching." Amidst forced confessions, segregated courtrooms, local mobs threatening violence, all-white juries, and inadequate legal counsel, justice for black defendants was reduced to farce. In one especially egregious Kentucky case in July 1906, Allen Mathis, charged with raping a white woman, stepped into court, pleaded guilty, was sentenced to death, and executed all within an hour, as local officials sped through the proceedings to prevent a lynching.[31] Miscarriages of justice were inevitable and sometimes explicit. In South Carolina, Ben Bess served 13 years of a 30-year sentence for rape before the white woman he allegedly attacked confessed on her death bed that she had fabricated the charge and the governor issued a pardon. In Knoxville, Tennessee, Maurice Mays survived an attempted lynching before he was convicted and executed in 1922 for the murder of Bertie Lindsey, a white woman. Five years later Sadie Mendell, also white, confessed that she had committed the crime.[32]

Racism imbued all aspects of southern law enforcement. Segregated courtroom facilities—including even the Bibles on which witnesses took their oaths—signaled black inferiority, compromising the standing of all African Americans involved in legal proceedings. This was particularly significant for black attorneys, whose numbers in the South were always small due to the paucity of black law schools in the region. They invariably faced a hopeless task to win the trust of white jurors and in some communities were prohibited even from entering the halls of justice. More routinely, black attorneys were subject to derogatory remarks and violent threats as they argued their cases. Black witnesses and defendants also met with racist comments. Prosecuting a black woman defendant, one attorney told a jury, "she is a negro: look at her skin. If she is not a negro, I don't want you to convict her." In another case, the prosecuting attorney advised the jury that "[y]ou must deal with a negro in the light of the fact that he is a negro, and applying your experience and common sense." The guilty verdicts in these two cases were overturned on appeal, but this was not always the case. In another incident, the prosecutor declared to the jury, "[i]t is just such impudent and sassy negroes as the defendant is shown by the evidence to be causing trouble in this county."[33] When the defense objected to this comment the judge overruled the complaint, yet the case was never taken before a higher court. The message to the jury was clear: all African Americans were criminals and therefore the defendant had to be convicted, for were he found innocent then blacks in the local community would likely become more impudent still toward whites. Irrespective of the evidence, white racial supremacy demanded a conviction.

Throughout the first half of the twentieth century, African Americans were almost entirely excluded from southern juries. In 1879, the US Supreme Court's decision in *Strauder v. West Virginia* protected African Americans' constitutional right to jury service, but over the following years black jurors became less common in the South than had been the case during Reconstruction. In 1910, a correspondent from Georgia reported there was "Not a blooming one [Negro juror], and not likely to be." In the same year, a parish official in Louisiana reported there had been as many black jurors as white in the late-1890s but, since the state's new constitution in 1898 had excluded most Blacks from voting, integrated juries had become rare. Similarly, in one Arkansas county, African Americans had often comprised a majority on trial juries until 1894, but not a single black juryman had served since. By the mid-1930s, little had changed. In 1937, the NAACP collated information on rates of black jury service from branches across the South. M. H. Martin reported that in 20 years of practicing law in Okfuskee County, Oklahoma, he had "never known a Negro to be called for jury service." In Kansas City, Missouri, African Americans did serve on criminal juries, but never on the grand jury, which decided which cases went to trial. In Lake Charles, Louisiana, there had been only two African Americans on a grand jury since 1896.[34] In all southern communities, white officials gave similar explanations that black jurors were excluded due to illiteracy, incompetence, and because their moral character was "not what it should be."[35]

The significance of white-dominated criminal trial proceedings was reflected in the thousands of African Americans condemned to labor on southern chain gangs and prison farms, but it was even more readily apparent in the grim business of southern death chambers where African Americans were routinely executed more frequently than whites. This racial disparity was most explicit in cases of rape. In the 11 states of the former Confederacy, African Americans were 361 of the 400 rape convicts hanged, electrocuted, or gassed between 1890 and 1945 and 48 of the 49 men executed for attempted rape.[36] Across all categories of capital crime in these states over the same period, 2592 African Americans were put to death, accounting for 75 percent of all executions. The peak decades for executions of African Americans in the South were the 1930s and 1940s. This was a period when the number of lynchings declined markedly, but the death penalty was more than a replacement for murder by mobs. For most of the first-half of the twentieth century, the two practices were mutually reinforcing, with executions sometimes encouraging vigilantism and the prospect of mob rule spurring state-sponsored killings. At the same time, however, there was a correlation between urban-industrial development and recourse to the formalized execution processes of the state. In Tennessee, for example, executions were typically carried out by mobs in rural northwestern counties, but by the state in cities such as Memphis. Likewise, in Kentucky, lynching was disproportionately concentrated in the rural west of the state, while execution was the more common fate for murderers and rapists in central regions around the cities of Louisville and Lexington. These in-state variations echoed nationwide trends over a longer period. When lynching was at its peak in the South in the 1890s, capital punishment had already developed as a "highly racialized mechanism" in the heavily urbanized Northeast driven by a broader commitment to due process, public order, and centralized state power among middle-class and business communities who were fearful of unchecked mob violence.[37]

Contesting Jim Crow justice

White domination of law enforcement persisted into the civil rights era of the 1960s and beyond, but the tradition of anti-lynching activism also survived in the form of challenges to the discrimination and violence of criminal justice proceedings involving African Americans. Protests against the conviction of black defendants in unjust trials and racial disparities in the enforcement of the death penalty were multi-faceted and had diverse roots. They involved black newspapers, black and white attorneys, civil rights organizations, including the NAACP and the American Civil Liberties Union, and groups with links to the Communist Party, such as the International Labor Defense (ILD) and the Civil Rights Congress (CRC). In the short term, these activists only rarely achieved anything approaching justice for individual defendants, but their work contributed to long-term processes of legal change that historian Glenda Gilmore has characterized as, an "evolution of injustice: from lynching to a mob-dominated trial to a perfunctory trial."[38]

In the first half of the twentieth century, the NAACP argued the cases of hundreds of African Americans facing criminal prosecution and won a series of major victories for black defendants in the US Supreme Court. The Association took up its first criminal case in 1910. Three years earlier, Pink Franklin, a black farm laborer, had been sentenced to death for the murder of Constable Henry Valentine in South Carolina. The killing had occurred in the middle of the night when Valentine and his deputy entered Franklin's house and attempted to arrest him for contract fraud that was allegedly committed when Franklin left the property of his white employer and failed to repay an advance he had received. After the case was unsuccessfully appealed to the US Supreme Court on the grounds that African Americans were excluded from the trial jury, the NAACP mobilized prominent white South Carolinians, as well as President Taft and Booker T. Washington, to persuade Coleman Blease, the newly elected governor of South Carolina, to commute Franklin's capital sentence to life imprisonment. In 1919, following further NAACP agitation, Franklin was paroled.[39]

In 1911, the NAACP established a five-man national committee to direct its legal work. Based in New York, the committee was at first mostly comprised of wealthy, white attorneys from the Empire State who donated their time *pro bono* to progressive causes, but in later years the NAACP's legal work was taken over by some of the leading black attorneys in America. Constrained by limited resources, the committee initially fought reactively against particularly egregious miscarriages of justice, but following a model pioneered in civil rights litigation of the 1890s it also sought out test cases that had broad implications for African Americans' legal status and might lead to high-profile Supreme Court hearings that would generate publicity and support for the fledgling organization. This approach produced important early victories, including *Guinn v. United States* (1915) in which the Supreme Court ruled unconstitutional the grandfather clauses that were used in several southern states to enfranchise illiterate whites who otherwise would have lost the right to vote on account of literacy tests that were intended to exclude black voters. In 1917, *Buchanan v. Warley* saw the Court strike down residential segregation ordinances, but there were defeats as well, notably in early jury discrimination cases.[40]

The NAACP scored its first major legal victory in the field of criminal justice in 1923. After decades in which the Supreme Court had, with rare exceptions, refused to intervene in state-level criminal procedures, in *Moore v. Dempsey* it held for the first time that state law enforcement had violated defendants' rights as secured under the due process clause of the Fourteenth Amendment to the Constitution. Specifically, the Court upheld a defendant's right to a trial free of mob influence. The case concerned death sentences passed on 12 African Americans charged with murder for their part in a 1919 race riot in Philips County, Arkansas, in which around 10 whites and more than 200 African Americans were killed. Mob influence on southern court proceedings involving black defendants was not new, but several factors were conducive to the groundbreaking ruling. At a time of widespread anti-lynching activism, including pressure for federal legislation, the extreme circumstances of the Philips County case called loudly for redress. Also significant was the recent appointment to the Supreme Court of new, activist justices, as well as the growing resources and experience that the NAACP brought to the case at the national level and the strength of local organizing and campaigning among black communities in Arkansas.[41]

Over the following decades, criminal procedure litigation became a staple of civil rights protest and a series of US Supreme Court rulings established a defendant's right to effective counsel in capital cases (*Powell v. Alabama* (1932)), prohibited the exclusion of African Americans from jury selection (*Norris v. Alabama* (1935)), and extended federal oversight to cases of coerced confessions (*Brown* v. Mississippi (1936)). *Powell* and *Norris* stemmed from one of America's most infamous criminal cases: the prosecution of nine African American boys and young men, aged from 12 to 20, on charges of raping two white women on board a freight train in northeastern Alabama in March 1931. The case originated when several white men who had been traveling on the train reported to a station master in the small town of Stevenson that they had been attacked and thrown from their carriage by a group of African Americans. When the train arrived at its next destination, Paint Rock, two stops down the line, it was met by a sheriff and a posse of armed white locals who had been hastily deputized for the occasion. The nine defendants were found on board in a carriage along with Ruby Bates and Victoria Price who would later testify in court that they had been raped by up to six of the youngsters while others pinned them down and held knives to their throats. News of the affair spread quickly and by the time the accused had been moved to a jail cell in the nearby town of Scottsboro a threatening mob had gathered. There was no lynching that night in Scottsboro, but the atmosphere of mob rule persisted when the accused were put on trial less than a week later. The prosecution evidence was thin and inconsistent, but this proved inconsequential. With a large crowd surrounding the courthouse and demanding a conviction and the defendants shoddily represented by a white attorney from Tennessee who was retained by local black ministers but admitted he had not prepared a case and was unfamiliar with Alabama law, guilty verdicts were returned against eight of the accused and all were sentenced to death. On account of his age, the prosecution did not request the death penalty for 12-year-old Roy Wright, though seven members of the jury called for his execution nonetheless and the judge was eventually forced to declare a mistrial in Wright's case. Though just one year older, at 13, Eugene Williams was left to face the gallows.[42] (See Illustration 5.3.)

Illustration 5.3   The Scottsboro defendants with one of their attorneys, Samuel Leibowitz, 1932. Courtesy of Bettmann/Corbis

An appeal against the Scottsboro death sentences was immediately launched by the ILD, a communist organization founded in 1925 that had been building support among Alabama's black poor since 1929 when the Communist International had made the rights of black workers in the South a policy priority. ILD activists had worked first in mining regions around Birmingham, but in the early-1930s they began to organize unions in the Cotton Belt where the Depression had exacerbated the already desperate poverty of black tenant farmers and they saw in the Scottsboro case an opportunity to extend their appeal among this new constituency. This approach contrasted with the initial response of the NAACP to the case. The Association's nearest local branch in Chattanooga had folded the previous year and its national leaders were reluctant to represent the Scottsboro nine for fear that association with convicted rapists could harm their hard-won and fragile connections with moderate whites. As the case evolved into a national cause célèbre and the injustice of the verdicts became apparent during April 1931, the NAACP did attempt to take charge of the defense, but after months of bitter conflict with the ILD the Association withdrew from the case in early-1932 and it was the

ILD attorneys who successfully argued before the Supreme Court in *Powell* that the condemned youths had received such inadequate legal counsel that it amounted to a violation of their right to a fair trial.[43]

Among the many issues that divided the NAACP and the ILD was the latter's commitment to fomenting popular protests in support of the ongoing struggle in the courts. Marches, rallies, economic boycotts, and strikes were organized in support of the Scottsboro boys in Europe, Latin America, Africa, and Asia, as well as across the United States. Building on existing ILD campaigns comparing American lynching to fascist and anti-labor violence in Europe and Western colonialism in Africa and Asia, the international Scottsboro protests aimed to build class sympathies that transcended national boundaries. Ada Wright, mother of Scottsboro defendants Andy and Roy Wright, traveled with ILD representatives across 16 European countries addressing hundreds of thousands of protestors as far afield as Moscow. Outside the US consulate in Dresden, German Communists protesting Scottsboro condemned "American murder and imperialism" and declared themselves "[f]or the brotherhood of black and white young proletarians!"[44] Within the United States, similar leftwing mobilization met with police repression. In July 1931, police broke up a Scottsboro protest meeting at Camp Hill, Alabama, causing rioting that left one man dead and led to several lynchings in subsequent days and dozens of arrests. Further afield, in Fort Lauderdale, Florida, white authorities reported finding communist literature in the "negro section" of town that was intended "to stir unrest and dissatisfaction" over the Scottsboro verdicts, while in January 1932, police in Pittsburgh broke up an ILD meeting that had attracted an audience of 400, mainly African American men and women, to demand the Scottsboro boys' release. In November of the same year, police used tear gas to remove 100 ILD protestors from the Capitol Plaza on the day the Supreme Court issued its ruling in *Powell*. NAACP leaders considered these protests a cynical attempt to spread communism that would alienate potential white sympathizers and reaffirm the commitment of the Alabama authorities to move ahead with the executions, yet this critique proved out of step with the views of many African Americans, including NAACP members who were increasingly sympathetic to leftist politics during the early years of the Depression. Moreover, in practice popular agitation—both at home and abroad—played a significant role in influencing the Supreme Court to hear the case on appeal.[45]

After the first Scottsboro conviction was overturned, the cases returned to the Alabama courts where they played out through a series of further trials that continued even after Ruby Bates admitted that the charges were false. First in the dock, Haywood Patterson was convicted and sentenced to death by a jury, only for Judge James Horton to break with southern racial protocol and overrule the verdict due to the unreliability of the prosecution case, which was now dependent solely on the entirely discredited testimony of Victoria Price. After Horton withdrew from the case, his local reputation and political career in ruins, Patterson and Clarence Norris were tried and condemned once more. Patterson's lawyer, a Jewish New Yorker named Samuel Leibowitz who was vilified in the southern white press, described the verdict as "an act of bigots" and a new wave of protests was sparked with Ruby Bates herself among 3,000 demonstrators who marched on the White House in support of the ILD's unsuccessful request for a meeting with President Roosevelt to discuss the case. Legal appeals were launched again, and in 1935 the Supreme Court overturned the convictions for a second time on account of the willful exclusion of African American jurors. But still the case dragged on. With the state of Alabama reeling from the costs and controversy of the prosecutions, by 1937 charges had been dropped against six of the original accused, but at the fourth time of asking convictions stood against the three other defendants who were eventually spared the electric chair but served several more years in prison for a crime they did not commit.[46]

Even in the early-1930s, Scottsboro seemed to mark a turning point in the African American history of crime and punishment. Writing in the NAACP magazine, *The Crisis*, in 1933, Harry H. Jones of the West Virginia bar concluded that both the US Supreme Court and state appellate courts were "more fairly disposed toward colored people" than at any time in the past.[47] Despite the Supreme Court's interventions and the saturated media coverage and international condemnation of events in Scottsboro, however, over the following two decades there was little evidence of real change in the administration of criminal law in the South and it became apparent that there were limits both to the Supreme Court's capacity to enforce its rulings and its willingness to interfere in the work of state criminal courts. In some southern jurisdictions, steps were taken to include African Americans on juries, but mostly violations of constitutional protections persisted. In 1939, for example, the Court overturned a black-on-white murder conviction in St. John's Parish, Louisiana, where not a single African American juror had been selected between 1896 and 1935 and only one had served in 1936 as a token gesture immediately following *Norris*. Even so, over the next 18 years in another Louisiana parish where African Americans were one-third of the population, just a single black juror sat on the grand jury alongside a total of 431 whites.[48]

Historian Michael Klarman argues that the Supreme Court's criminal due process decisions may have had a negative impact on the fate of black defendants by providing a veil of rhetorical legitimacy to trials that continued to operate in the service of white supremacy as authorities learned to administer discriminatory justice in ways amenable to the Court.[49] Certainly, there is evidence that the Supreme Court was satisfied by even limited progress toward procedural fairness. In *Akins v. Texas* (1945), for example, the Court rejected an appeal based on the exclusion of African Americans from the trial jury, reasoning that there had been one black juror on the panel and although this was far below the proportion eligible there was no evidence of "purposeful limitation ... by race." Similarly in *Oklahoma v. Lyons*, the court upheld a conviction based on an alleged coerced confession. W. D. Lyons claimed that he was threatened and beaten by police for 11 days following his arrest for the murder of Elmer Rogers and his family and confessed when he could stand no more torture. The case was appealed by the NAACP, whose lawyers drew on a series of unanimous precedents dating back to *Brown v. Mississippi* (1936) in which three black sharecroppers had been sentenced to death for murdering their white landlord based solely on their own confessions extracted under torture. In *Chambers v. Florida* (1940), the Court had expanded the definition of coerced confessions to include psychological abuse and intimidation as well as physical violence, but in *Lyons* a divided court affirmed the conviction in a ruling that can be read as evidence that justices were increasingly concerned that the expansion of federal intervention into state criminal proceedings had gone too far. Lyons suffered brutal treatment at the hands of the police, but his fate was distinct from the "legal lynchings" of earlier cases: he was afforded a proper defense—led by NAACP chief counsel Thurgood Marshall—in a trial that took place more than a year after his arrest, and he was sentenced to life imprisonment rather than death. Though Lyons might have suffered abuse, justices skeptical of federal intrusion on states' rights could still make a case that his trial was fair.[50]

Seven years later, the Supreme Court again rejected a Virginia death penalty appeal, this time in the case of seven African Americans convicted of raping Ruby Floyd, a white woman, in Martinsville. Chief Justice Huggins of the Virginia Supreme Court of Appeals would later argue that the trial court was "extremely careful to avoid" racial prejudice influencing the outcome of the case, and the proceedings were undoubtedly relatively fair by the standards of the time: the accused men were afforded a competent defense, for example, and African Americans were included in the jury pool, although all were dismissed for cause or by peremptory challenges. Nonetheless, on appeal the NAACP did not question the probity of the trial proceedings, but instead argued that the convicts had been denied equal protection of the law on the grounds that the state of Virginia had executed 45 African Americans for rape since 1908, but not a single white man. No appellate court would hear the case, however, an indication that judicial reform of criminal trial proceedings was restricted to process rather than substance.[51]

In 1952, the Tuskegee Institute recorded America's first year without a lynching since records began 70 years earlier. Writing in *The Crisis*, sociologist Marguerite Cartwright was unimpressed. She argued that the statistic reflected only "a shift in the plane of violence" and an overly narrow definition of what lynching was. The "old-fashioned, messy and rather crude" methods of the mob had given way to new techniques, including bombings and legal lynchings, while other long-practiced forms of racial violence persisted, including executions, police shootings, and urban riots. These practices demonstrated that justice for African Americans could not be secured through court rulings alone. Its causes were social and political, as well as legal, and entangled with African Americans' subordinate economic and social status, as well as the denial of civil rights.

The reluctance of appellate courts to address the structural factors that impeded African Americans' access to justice was evident in the trial of Odell Waller, an African American laborer charged in Pittsylvania County, Virginia, in 1940 with the murder of Oscar Davis, a white tenant farmer. That Waller shot and fatally wounded Davis was not in doubt, but while the prosecution charged premeditated murder, the defense argued that Waller acted in self-defense when Davis reached for a gun.[52] An all-white jury returned a verdict of guilty and Waller was sentenced to death. As at Scottsboro, the defense was organized by a communist organization, the Chicago-based Revolutionary Workers' League. In appealing for a new trial the defense team focused on Virginia's jury selection process, which excluded poorer citizens who did not pay the state poll tax and consequently did not appear on voter registration lists. The Supreme Court refused to hear the case and Odell Waller was eventually executed on July 2, 1942. Reflecting the views of the workers' organizations that had led his defense, Waller went to his death viewing American justice as a form of class oppression. He declared in a dying statement, written in his cell on the eve of his execution that "The penitentiary all over the United states are full of people ho [who] was pore tried to work have something couldnt does [do] that maid [made] them steel an rob[.] [*sic*]"[53] Decades of agitation had discouraged lynching and placed limits on abuses of due process in criminal prosecutions, but broader social change would be required to address the underlying structural factors that supported white racial violence and limited the scope and significance of African Americans' due process rights.

6

Crime, Policing, and Urbanization

A movement to demand negro Police Captains, and the same health protection as white people get, was started yesterday afternoon at a public meeting of negroes in Liberty Hall, on 138th Street, between Seventh and Lenox Avenues.... The meeting was held to protest the arrest of Richard B. Moore, negro labor leader..."

New York Times, September 27, 1926.

In April 1942, ten months into a minimum three-year sentence for grand larceny, Janice Monica outlined her life story in a letter to the National Association for the Advancement of Colored People (NAACP) written from her cell in the New York state prison for women at Bedford Hills. Born in Chattanooga, Tennessee, Monica had moved to New York in 1938 at the age of 19 and worked as a domestic servant. Despite her conviction, she did not "feel at all criminal" and believed her life would have taken a different course, "had my circumstances on the outside been different." In prison, she explored these circumstances through creative and political writing, including a novel, *Native Girl*, inspired by Richard Wright's *Native Son*, about "the average southern, Negro girl who goes to a metropolis to make good." Looking to the future, Monica did not want to return to "the conditions" she had "tried to elude" in Tennessee, and nor did she want to continue with the drudgery of domestic work in New York. Instead, she had learned to type and taken a Red Cross First Aid course at Bedford Hills and hoped the NAACP might help find her a position that would satisfy the parole board requirements for early release.[1]

Janice Monica was one of millions of African Americans who migrated from the South to the urban centers of the Northeast and

Midwest in the first half of the twentieth century. For many black migrants, America's sprawling northern metropolises appeared as places of opportunity that promised liberation from the violent subordination of the Jim Crow South and particularly the brutal and capricious grasp of peonage, convict leasing, and lynching. Monica remained convinced of this promise even in prison, and the training opportunities she was afforded at Bedford Hills were examples of meaningful differences between African American experiences of crime and punishment in the North and South. There was, however, no clear-cut regional divide. The conditions and context of urban black life above the Mason-Dixon Line generated high rates of crime and African Americans frequently experienced discrimination in the courts from judges and jurors and violence on the streets at the hands of mobs and police officers. Moreover, these practices informed new cultural associations between race and criminality that were powerful precisely because they were not rooted in such overt white supremacist ideology as characterized the rhetoric of crime and punishment in the South. Through the first half of the twentieth century, northern black communities were, nonetheless, increasingly assertive in contesting and challenging racial violence and discriminatory law enforcement and by the 1930s a powerful connection had been forged between issues of crime and punishment and civil rights activism.

The top of the world

On the eve of the Civil War, African Americans comprised less than 2 percent of the population of the northern United States. About 130,000 lived in the mid-Atlantic states of Pennsylvania, New Jersey, and New York, another 25,000 in New England, and some 66,000 more made their homes in more recently settled communities in the Midwest. A majority of the northern black population resided in the region's booming cities, but few African Americans benefited from the economic opportunities that drove America's urban-industrial expansion in the Gilded Age. Black workers rarely broke into manufacturing occupations and most scraped by on meager incomes from menial employment. Black women overwhelmingly worked in domestic service and the laundry business, and men as unskilled laborers, dockworkers, railroad porters, and messengers, occupations that offered fewer rewards than the industrial jobs that provided opportunities for social advancement for the millions of white immigrants who entered the United States in the decades after Reconstruction, mostly from southern and eastern Europe.

By 1910, the northern black population had grown to around 1 million, but still 90 percent of African Americans lived in the South. Over the next decade, however, as many as half a million southern blacks headed north, driven by the violence, discrimination, and poverty of the rural South and drawn by new opportunities for industrial work, education, and social mobility that were opened up by the First World War. Where previously black workers had mostly been excluded from industrial occupations, they were now sought after due to the voracious labor demands of the wartime economy, the military draft of 1917, and the collapse of European immigration as a result of the war and restrictive new legislation enacted by Congress. Though the promise of well-paid work and social advancement quickly proved illusory for many, rates of black migration from the South thereafter increased each decade until the 1950s, through the crisis of the boll weevil and soil exhaustion in the rural South of the 1920s, the Great Depression that shattered the northern economy in the 1930s, and the Second World War that drove up industrial labor demand once more in the 1940s. Between 1910 and 1930, the total black population of America's five largest industrial cities—Chicago, Cleveland, Detroit, New York, and Philadelphia—increased from 234,460 to 973,173, encompassing 8.2 percent of the nation's entire African American population.[2] By 1940, when a sizeable black population had also developed in western cities such as Los Angeles, 24 percent of African Americans lived outside the southern states of whom more than 90 percent were concentrated in urban areas.[3]

Population growth combined with residential segregation led to the consolidation and expansion of black-majority urban neighborhoods in the early-twentieth century. The Black Belt in Chicago, Black Bottom in Detroit, Philadelphia's Seventh Ward, and Harlem in New York were home to vibrant black communities that by the 1920s supported a sizeable and dynamic black middle class and in some cities were characterized by growing ethnic diversity as a result of migration from Jamaica, Puerto Rico, and other parts of the Caribbean. Churches, businesses, social clubs, and civil rights organizations sat at the heart of black community life providing mutual support and a basis for political activism. New York was home to the headquarters of the NAACP and Marcus Garvey's Universal Negro Improvement Association, which boasted 800 branches and, by Garvey's own estimation, six million members in the early-1920s, attracted by an empowering and dignifying message of pan-African Black Nationalism. The Chicago *Defender* and the *New York Age* were among leading black newspapers that debated and advocated on race issues and contested what invariably was derogatory reporting of African American crime and punishment in the white press. Hailing the contribution of African American troops who had represented their country in the killing fields of Europe during the First World War, the *Defender* in 1919 described "the Negro who went across the seas" as "altogether a new man, with new ideas, new hopes, new aspirations and new desires." Writing in the NAACP magazine, *The Crisis*, W. E. B. Du Bois similarly envisaged a reinvigorated fight for racial equality on account of black wartime experiences, while related sentiments were evident in 1920s' Harlem, which became the fulcrum of an urban black cultural and literary renaissance promoting the image of a race-proud, confident and assertive "New Negro," far removed from the stereotypes of black inferiority and subordination promulgated in the Jim Crow South.[4]

For the majority of African Americans, the promises of black life in the North were significantly compromised by the realities of everyday life during the first half of the twentieth century. Civil rights legislation in support of racial equality was enacted in many northern states in the late-nineteenth century, but segregation was common in public accommodations through the early-twentieth century and even black laborers who secured industrial work typically found themselves confined to the most menial and dangerous parts of production lines that were strictly segregated by race. Moreover, the very real opportunities for black autonomy in the North and the development of strong families and communities could not hide that most urban black neighborhoods were racked by interrelated social problems, including poverty and crime, as well as overcrowding and residential segregation that contributed to a persistent deterioration in housing conditions and spiraling rates of disease and death.[5] Exploitative realtors imposed high rents that often forced several families to live in single apartments or take in lodgers, with one NAACP report on Detroit concluding that "75% of the Negro homes have so many lodgers that they are really hotels." In the wider community, a lack of parks, playgrounds, and recreation centers drove children and young adults "into the streets or to questionable places of amusement" and when prosperous blacks tried to move out of the ghetto to predominantly white neighborhoods, they faced vicious retaliation in the form of burning crosses, mob violence, and bombs hurled into their properties. These attacks were symptomatic of burgeoning racial tensions in northern cities that on other occasions led to lynchings and erupted into race riots that not only left hundreds dead, caused thousands to flee their homes, and destroyed property, but also revealed the limits of municipal law enforcement protection for black communities. In the first years of the twentieth century, rioting occurred in the Tenderloin and San Juan Hill in New York, in small towns in Indiana and Ohio, and in 1908 in Springfield, Illinois. In the following weeks, police were repeatedly called out to prevent riots in Chicago, St. Louis, and smaller Midwest towns. The onset of mass migration and the return of black troops from European battlefields a decade later led to more widespread rioting between 1917 and 1921 in communities across the country from Connecticut to Nebraska to Arizona, with the most serious clashes occurring in East St. Louis in 1917, Chicago in 1919 and Tulsa, Oklahoma, in 1921.[6]

Race, crime, and community

In 1899, W. E. B. Du Bois published *The Philadelphia Negro*, a groundbreaking historical and sociological study of the largest urban black community north of the Mason-Dixon Line. His research found that African Americans had comprised 4 percent of the Philadelphia population in 1896, but accounted for 9 percent of arrests and 22 percent of the most serious recorded crimes. Comparable disparities were found across the northern states. A survey of penitentiaries in the 1890 census revealed that there were five times as many black prisoners as white in New York relative to population, six times as many in Pennsylvania, seven times as many in Indiana, eight times as many in Michigan, Minnesota, and Ohio, and nine times as many in Illinois.[7] In Du Bois' view, such figures partly resulted from the fact that African Americans were "arrested for less cause and given longer sentences than whites," but he was nonetheless persuaded that high rates of black imprisonment in the North also reflected disproportionate levels of black criminality.[8] Du Bois proposed a wide-ranging explanation of black crime as a consequence of the legacy of slavery, rapid social changes brought about by emancipation, the upheavals of migration from the South, unfamiliar and intolerable urban living conditions, and white "oppression and ridicule" that limited opportunities for black economic progress and social uplift. Specifically, Du Bois attributed most black crime to "a distinct class of habitual criminals," who included substantial numbers of young, male migrants from the South whom Du Bois was anxious should not be confused with the law-abiding black majority. Monroe Work, an African American sociologist, offered a similar analysis, explaining high rates of black crime in Chicago as a product of the "transitional state" of black life in the city and poor economic conditions.[9]

In focusing on social environment as the root cause of crime, the analyses of Du Bois and Work contested the emerging and influential arguments of white social scientists led by Frederick Hoffman, a German-born actuary, who, in his *Race Traits and Tendencies of the American Negro* (1896), interpreted racial disparities in northern prison commitments as evidence that black crime was a product of inherent racial inferiority. Coincident with the entrenchment of white dominance in the South through disfranchisement and lynching, and the Supreme Court's endorsement of segregation in *Plessy v. Ferguson*, Hoffman's interpretation lent the legitimacy of social science research to American racism and reinforced popular social-Darwinist theories of hereditary criminality.[10]

The reality of turn-of-the-century black crime in northern American cities contrasted both with Hoffman's identification of the inherent and intractable black criminal and Du Bois's depiction of a distinct black criminal class. While large numbers of whites benefited from the economic opportunities of industrialization, many African Americans became trapped in cycles of poverty, instability, discrimination, and frustrated political ambitions, conditions which encouraged violence, theft, and vice. As historian Kali Gross has argued of high rates of crime among black women in Philadelphia, the real causes were "a volatile mix of systemic bias, abject poverty, and obstructed dreams" that reflected the stark disjuncture between migrants' high expectations of racial tolerance and social and economic advancement and the reality they encountered in the North of persistent discrimination and limited employment opportunities. Although black female convicts were often portrayed in the white northern press as fearsome and bestial characters, therefore, in practice their offenses were usually sporadic and opportunistic and rooted in the conditions of their everyday lives. To a far greater degree than among white women, for example, black women were compelled by necessity to work outside the home where they commonly faced exploitative conditions that presented opportunities and incentives to commit crime. Black women were sometimes also able to take advantage of white racism as a cover for criminal activity, for example by robbing white men who they lured into vice districts with promises of exotic black sexuality, or securing domestic jobs to gain access to valuable possessions in white households.[11]

The roots and practice of black violent crimes were similarly complex. While the black community was small in the late nineteenth century, encounters with whites were common in the poor, industrial neighborhoods where most African Americans lived and a combination of poverty, liquor, and the bravado of white gangs could readily lead to interracial clashes.[12] Most black violent crime, however, was intraracial, though in form there was little that was distinctive about assaults and homicides within black communities. They mostly involved young men fighting and sometimes killing each other, often in disreputable nightspots, and commonly over perceived slights to their masculinity. In scale, however, violent crimes involving African Americans occurred with disproportionate frequency. In Chicago from 1890 to 1920, African Americans were only 2.3 percent of the population, but "made up 14 percent of killers and 15 percent of homicide victims."[13] Likewise, in late-nineteenth-century Philadelphia, homicide rates fell across the city as a whole, but increased among African Americans due to a variety of factors that included municipal policies concentrating disorder in black neighborhoods, high rates of black handgun ownership caused by fear of white assault, overcrowding, and "frustrations felt as white foreigners moved up and past them."[14] Harrowing personal experiences and structural racism were likewise a cause of domestic violence within black families. Black women charged with murdering or assaulting a husband or partner were often found in court to have personal histories of abuse, emotional damage, trauma, and frustration, though juries usually were unsympathetic; in Chicago, conviction rates for black women charged with killing their husbands were nearly four times higher than for white women. Historian Jeffrey Adler argues that black men in Chicago who beat and murdered their wives were in part also responding to the constraints of northern black life, taking desperate measures "to exert control over their private lives" in compensation for their powerlessness outside the home.[15]

As well as sites of frequent violence, black districts in northern cities also developed in the first decades of the twentieth century as centers of prostitution, gambling, and drunkenness, not only among residents, but also whites in search of illicit pleasures. Poverty and a lack of legitimate work led many African Americans into illegal trades, but municipal politics and progressive reform movements were the main reasons for the zoning of vice in predominantly black neighbourhoods. During the 1910s, vice commissions, women's refuges, and municipal police authorities worked with considerable success to purge prostitution from reputable, white communities, but they paid less attention to black women involved in the trade. A series of vice raids in Philadelphia in 1912, for example, saw arrest rates rise in white neighborhoods by 20 percent, but decline in black areas of the city by 10 percent.[16] In the same year, the Chicago chief of police "warned prostitutes" that they would not be disturbed by his officers if they restricted their business to an area that housed the largest proportion of the city's black population, churches, and social institutions.[17] In New York City, the Committee of Fourteen— a self-appointed vice-commission formed in 1905—investigated conditions in black-owned hotels, restaurants, and saloons primarily in an attempt to police interracial sexual encounters. Although civil rights laws in New York stringently prohibited segregation, where the Committee found evidence of white women socializing alongside African Americans, it required the proprietors to sign promissory notes committing to maintain segregated facilities and threatened to remove critical support for the premises' liquor licenses if its undercover investigators found that proprietors were failing to comply.[18] Even the work of more liberal reform organizations, such as the interracial National League for the Protection of Colored Women (NLPCW) was restricted by a racial ideology that considered black women inherently immoral not on account of race, but their experiences in slavery. From this starting point, the NLPCW conceived the "solution" to black women's criminality to be moral regeneration and the organization consequently failed to confront the structural social and economic causes that limited black women's horizons and left many dependent on vice to supplement limited wages from unstable legitimate employment.[19]

By the 1920s, prostitution was firmly entrenched in northern black neighborhoods and new developments during the years of Prohibition only strengthened the connection. As the liquor business was forced underground by the Volstead Act, legal parts of the sex industry expanded in the 1920s to become an important element of urban nightlife. Nude modeling and commercial dance halls where male patrons paid 10 cents a ticket for a "taxi dance" offered relatively lucrative and safe work for young white women. Black women were excluded from these businesses, however, and their already disproportionate involvement in prostitution was consequently exacerbated. In particular, black women became concentrated in dangerous and poorly paid street prostitution where they were especially vulnerable to police harassment and arrest. In New York City, these circumstances contributed to black women accounting for 54 percent of all women arrested by 1939.[20] Equally significant, these developments perpetuated ideas of African Americans as a uniquely threatening criminal class even as essentialist readings of race and crime as rooted in culture and biology were increasingly challenged by sociologists, liberal white reformers, and black racial uplift organizations. As historian Marcy Sacks argues, through concentrating vice and crime in urban areas largely populated by African Americans reformers and the police, "molded black neighborhoods to conform to popularly held stereotypes about blacks." At the same time, through dedicating resources to the social uplift and integration of immigrant white women, Progressives over time eroded the significance of ethnicity in discussions of white crime.[21]

Cultural constructions of black criminality in the northern states were apparent in relation to other criminal justice policies, which, on their face, appeared racially neutral. In 1910, for example, Congress passed the Mann Act, also known as the White Slave Traffic Act, which criminalized the transportation of women across state lines for "immoral purposes." Kevin Mumford argues that through this legislation, "antivice reformers constructed a racialized subject worthy of uplift—the white slave [prostitute]—and in the process erased the black prostitute."[22] The enforcement of the Mann Act further contributed to cultural constructions of white victimhood, most notably through the sensational prosecution of the world heavyweight boxing champion Jack Johnson. One of the most famous and controversial black men of the early-twentieth century, Johnson earned public opprobrium for defeating a succession of white challengers to his title and he scandalized the nation with a string of affairs and marriages with white women (see Illustration 6.1). In 1912, Johnson began a relationship with Lucille Cameron, a young white woman whose mother attempted to undermine the union by accusing Johnson of kidnapping her daughter. The prosecution collapsed when Lucille refused to cooperate with the case, but shortly afterwards an anonymous tip led the Justice Department to Belle Schreiber, a prostitute and spurned former lover of Johnson, who eagerly provided incriminating testimony that he had given her money to travel across state lines from Pittsburgh to Chicago where she established a brothel. Based largely on Schreiber's evidence, Johnson was convicted and sentenced to a year in prison, though with an appeal pending against the sentence

Illustration 6.1   Jack Johnson and his wife, Etta, 1910. Courtesy of Library of Congress: American cartoon print filing series. <http://www.loc.gov/pictures/item/2011649815/>

he fled the country and did not serve the term until returning to the United States in 1920. US District Attorney Harry Parkin acknowledged that the legal pursuit of Johnson might have amounted to persecution, but he justified the government's case on the grounds that Johnson was "the foremost example of the evil in permitting the intermarriage of whites and blacks" and his conviction was necessary "to teach others that the law must be respected."[23]

As the Mann Act "decriminalized" white women involved in prostitution, so in the late-1920s the introduction of mandatory life-without-parole sentences for fourth-time felony offenders in New York promoted sympathetic cultural constructions of white criminality. Advocates of this legislation, known as the Baumes Law, claimed that it would bolster the capacity of the criminal justice system to fight the violent gangsters who ran the illegal liquor trade during Prohibition, but in practice it mostly trapped small-time offenders convicted of repeat nonviolent property crimes. These prisoners included African Americans, but as critics moved to condemn the lifetime imprisonment of petty criminals, the archetypal victim of the legislation they presented to the public was implicitly white. In contrast to the perception of African American convicts as innately criminal, debates on why whites were in prison became centered on the severity of law enforcement. Within six years, sympathetic portrayals of harshly treated white criminals led to repeal of the Baumes Law's most punitive measures, juries "refusing to convict white defendants," and the introduction of new programs to rehabilitate white prisoners who were seen as deserving of state support, but which discriminated against black inmates.[24]

As white northerners neglected black criminality and offenders as undeserving and irredeemable, the black community assumed a central role in preventing crime and supporting black offenders during and after their encounters with the legal system. Organizations such as the NLPCW, YMCA and YWCA branches, the National Urban League, and the Negro Fellowship League promoted moral reform and racial uplift, provided practical support for black migrants in northern cities, supported men and women on probation and parole, and in some cases represented black men on trial and in prison. African Americans who found themselves embroiled in the criminal justice system also sought aid through informal community contacts. When black prisoners became eligible for parole, for example, they invariably turned first to relatives, friends, and former employers to find the jobs and accommodation that were a prerequisite for early release. During four years that Roger Walker spent on probation in early-1930s New York, he lodged in 14 different residences and often depended on roommates for financial support, particularly while in-between the nine jobs he held at various times. Walker's relationships were forged during leisure time spent on the streets and in "speakeasies, billiard halls and movie theatres," but others depended on more structured ties, including bonds formed in churches and social clubs.[25]

By the 1930s, the appointment of hundreds of black men and women to positions in the administration of northern law enforcement increasingly institutionalized community influence over the fate of black offenders in prison and following their release from custody. Justifying the appointment of Samuel Battle as the first African American to serve on the New York City Parole Commission in 1941, for example, Mayor Fiorello LaGuardia cited a perceived black crime wave and argued that Battle, a veteran police officer, "has been in close touch with the problem for many years … knows all the children in Harlem from the time of their birth and has been very active in social work[.]" Black commentators concurred on the importance of Battle's community ties. John Newton Greggs, a black attorney, argued that "a colored man has a more intimate knowledge of the problems of his people, than those of the other race."[26] Black influence, however, did not make for a racially egalitarian penal system. Black parole officers were usually prevented from supervising whites, and parole board decision-making was heavily influenced by race, notably in the case of hundreds of black convicts who were paroled to the southern states where northern parole board members believed they would be most effectively rehabilitated. Reflecting a persistent white conviction that African Americans were unsuited to city life, New York's Parole Board commissioner described one black female applicant for early release in 1932 as "not the type of Colored person who can stand the North.[27]

Trial and punishment

On December 17, 1875, New York witnessed a triple execution. William Ellis, William Thompson, and Charles Weston, all African Americans, were hanged for the murder of Abraham Weissburg, a white peddler. All three men had confessed to the crime, which the judge at their trial called "one of the most horrible, revolting and atrocious … ever committed in this country." Three days after the executions, however, in a sermon delivered at the Fleet Street Colored

Methodist Church in Brooklyn Reverend Dr. I. N. Gloucester criticized the court proceedings. The condemned men had not been legally tried and convicted, Gloucester argued, as they had been denied a jury of their peers. "Colored men," Gloucester concluded, "ought to be tried by colored jurors."[28] Some six decades later, when the novelist Richard Wright published *Native Son*, he offered a depiction of the criminal trial of a black defendant in Chicago that indicated little had changed. In Wright's imagining, which was heavily based on the execution of 18-year-old Robert Nixon for the murder of five white women in 1938, Bigger Thomas is portrayed as a "maddened ape" and a "treacherous beast" by the state prosecutor in court proceedings held "in an atmosphere of mob hysteria and race hate" that lead to his execution.[29]

Race mattered in the northern criminal justice system during the early-twentieth century, though rarely so consistently or overtly as in the South. In 1944, Swedish sociologist Gunnar Myrdal concluded in his monumental study of race relations, *An American Dilemma*, that, "for the most part, Negroes enjoy equitable justice," a situation he attributed principally to black political influence in the North and a commitment among whites in the region to "impartial" justice, "regardless of race, creed or color." In a study of murder prosecutions in late-nineteenth-century Philadelphia, Roger Lane similarly found that "justice was surprisingly color-blind." In cases involving killers who acted alone, whites were, in fact, more likely to be convicted for the murder of blacks than vice-versa, although this pattern was marginally reversed in the overall statistics. Lane further noted that the vast majority of black defendants were prosecuted for crimes against victims of the same race and that, overall, "black Philadelphians did not complain about the justice system so much as use it, and did not complain about the cops so much as take over the arrest process on their own." Similar patterns prevailed in juvenile courts, with 56 percent of children "committed at the request of parents, relatives, guardians, or friends." In a study of murder cases in nineteenth-century New York, Eric Monkkonen agreed that African Americans were no more likely than whites to be convicted, but he did find that race became a prominent factor at later stages of the judicial process with black defendants convicted of murder six times more likely than whites to be sentenced to death.[30]

To the extent that African Americans were disadvantaged in northern courtrooms as defendants, several contemporary commentators argued that it was mostly on account of their marginal social and economic status. In Myrdal's assessment, poverty and a lack of education were far more significant barriers to equal justice for African Americans than race. As the Chicago *Defender* explained in 1914, "Afro-American people are too often unable to protect themselves against the prejudice of the jury room because of their poverty and want of influential friends".[31] Clarence Darrow, the most prominent defense attorney in the nation, agreed, arguing that disproportionate rates of black convictions, imprisonment, and execution, were due to African Americans' "inability to defend themselves, to their poverty, and to the deep prejudice that everywhere blocks their way."[32] Compounding this situation in the view of the New York branch of the NAACP was the small number of black public defenders available to represent African American defendants in court. In a report submitted to the New York Legal Aid Society, the NAACP argued that white attorneys, who earned little from criminal trials, too often persuaded black defendants to plead guilty in return for a shortened sentence so as to expedite the case.[33] This was part of a wider malaise at the earliest stages of the northern judicial process that reflected both class and racial discrimination against black defendants. As evident in the frequent complaints of black convicts, justice was also undermined by arbitrary arrests by the police and the imposition of fines by magistrates that lengthened the prison terms of impoverished black defendants who were unable to pay.[34]

As in the southern states, lynching and the law of the mob had an insidious impact on the administration of criminal justice in northern cities. The lynching of African Americans occurred far less frequently above the Mason-Dixon Line than in the South, but there were at least 123 cases recorded in the northern states outside of New England from the 1880s to the 1930s. The highest concentrations were in the Upper Midwest, with dozens of cases in Illinois, but relative to population African Americans were as likely to be lynched even in Pennsylvania as in South Carolina or Alabama and attempted lynchings averted by police intervention or black community resistance were even more common.[35] The proceedings of these northern lynchings invariably mimicked the grim rituals that were so common in the South. Robert Jackson was seized from jail in 1892 and hanged before a crowd of more than one thousand people in Port Jarvis, New York, for the alleged rape of a young white girl, and in 1903 George White was lynched in Wilmington, Delaware, for the rape and murder of Helen Bishop, also white.[36] In August 1911, Zachariah Walker was dragged from a hospital bed in Coatesville,

Pennsylvania, and burned at the stake in front of thousands after allegedly shooting dead a white police officer before attempting suicide. Similar mass mobs gathered to lynch three black men in Duluth, Minnesota, in 1920 and ten years later in Marion, Indiana.[37]

Invariably quick to condemn the murderous acts, northern politicians routinely promised that lynch mobs would face justice, but their words usually rang hollow. Illinois was among the northern states that adopted an anti-lynching law and under its provisions the Alexander County sheriff, Frank Davis, was dismissed in 1909 after a mob lynched one William James, but mob participants were rarely prosecuted and all-white juries invariably refused to convict those who were. Two days after an 1894 lynching in Stroudsburg, Pennsylvania, a coroner's jury ruled that Richard Puryear "came to his death by being hung by persons unknown," and a grand jury soon concurred that it was "impossible to fix the responsibility."[38] Likewise, within a few months of the Coatesville lynching, the District Attorney had dropped all of the indictments concerning the case, "declaring it impossible to get a conviction." Judge Butler, presiding, called the developments "a public calamity to law and order" in Pennsylvania and the black newspaper the Pittsburgh *Courier* agreed. "It is one thing to arrest," noted a sardonic editorial, "it is another to bring to trial, another to convict, and still another to execute." In Duluth, three white police officers served short sentences for rioting in connection with the 1920 lynching, but no one was convicted of murder.[39]

The influence of lynching on northern law enforcement went far beyond the injustices suffered by individual mob victims. During Reconstruction, William Howard, a black man charged with raping a young German girl in Rochester, New York, claimed he was forced to confess when the District Attorney threatened to turn him over to the large, angry crowd that was attempting to break into the jail where he was held. One reporter for the *New York Sun* suspected that the case would have to be reopened or that Howard would be pardoned, but neither happened and Howard later died in jail following a fight.[40] In a comparable case, when three African American men were accused of the robbery and assault of Mrs. Charles Biddle in Mount Holly, New Jersey, in 1904, the date of their trial was kept secret to guard against mob violence. A company of state guardsmen was called in to maintain order but on the day that the defendants arrived by train from Camden a crowd of 500 people massed outside the courthouse and rumors of lynching were rife. All three were said to be "shaken with fear" as they pleaded guilty in accordance with the advice of their assigned defense attorney. Albert Schafer similarly waived a trial for fear he would be lynched and admitted assaulting a ten-year-old girl, while George Washington "was the picture of abject terror" as he passed up the right to an examination on charges of attempting to rape a young French woman in Suffolk County, New York, despite strongly protesting his innocence. In the days before Washington's scheduled court appearance, he was beaten while in police custody by the husband of his alleged victim and threatened by a mob of up to 70 men who "battered down" the outer door of the prison where he was held.[41]

Lynching also influenced public discourse on issues of race, crime, and punishment, encouraging toleration for tough law enforcement measures against black offenders. In many cases, the decision making of police officers, prosecutors, judges, and jurors was influenced by popular notions of justice that held deep sway in criminal court-rooms and could supersede a concern for strict adherence to due process. In the 1888 trial of Zepyhr Davis, a young black man convicted in Chicago of murdering an Irish American girl, Maggie Gaughan, the judge waived away defense concerns that prospective jurors had already formed an opinion on the case and summarily dismissed medical testimony introduced by Davis's attorneys to mount an insanity defense. Both decisions were consistent with white public opinion on the case expressed in the city's newspapers, which scarcely doubted that Davis was guilty. The press was broadly sympathetic to efforts to lynch Davis before he was arrested and reporters depicted him as "brutish" and "barely human" during his trial and railed against the possibility that legal technicalities might impair the law's capacity to administer what they considered to be "justice."[42]

In other cases, northern judges invoked similar arguments as lynch mobs to justify imposing harsh punishments on black defendants. In 1893, New Jersey Supreme Court justice Charles Garrison, refused to spare the life of John Hill, a 17-year-old African American sentenced to hang for murder, on the grounds that "if the penalty of death should be set aside, many a person belonging to the same race in this community ... might be inspired to commit the same crime." Four murders had recently been committed by African Americans in the county and, to Garrison's mind, "imprisonment does not seem to terrify them in the least".[43] Thirty years later, in sentencing John Henry, a black laborer from Florida, to between 22 and 27 years for the attempted rape of a white girl in New Jersey, Judge J. Edward Knight declared the accused was, "fortunate [his crimes] occurred in the North and not in the South." Knight apologized for the inflammatory remarks, but the NAACP dismissed the gesture amidst allegations that Knight had also discouraged a black woman, Willa Hempfield, from filing a rape complaint against the son of a fellow judge.[44] Such rhetoric was part of the racialization of northern criminal punishment. In historian Janice Barrow's assessment, executions "offered a way in which white residents could discipline and intimidate outsiders, criminals, recent immigrants, and other groups perceived as socially dangerous" while guarding against the lawlessness of the mob.[45] In this manner, Gross argues that the specter of "literal lynchings in the South enabled [northern] judges to enact their own legal 'lynchings' with impunity."[46] Indeed, even black commentators, fearful that lynching might become more widespread in the North, were pressed to express support for hard-line law enforcement policies that embraced the rhetoric of inherent black criminality. Commenting on the case of three black men found guilty of assaulting a white woman in New Jersey, for example, the Philadelphia *Defender* argued that "surgical operation" should be a part of the punishment, as it would "terrorize these unnatural brutes" far more even than lynching.[47]

The manner in which limited financial resources, inadequate legal advice, and racial discrimination combined to impair black defendants' access to justice in northern courtrooms was apparent in a high-profile case in the 1920s that resulted in a rare black legal victory. Born into humble surroundings in Florida, Ossian Sweet had graduated from Howard University and was a successful physician in Detroit by September 1925 when he moved his family into a new home in a formerly all-white area of the city. Sweet considered the property commensurate with his professional status, but the purchase brought him into conflict with whites who were intent on maintaining residential segregation in the city. Through the summer months of 1925, Detroit mobs, sometimes numbering in the thousands, had forced several prominent black families to abandon attempts to move into all-white neighborhoods and when the Sweets took up residence in their new home they, too, were met by baying crowds. On September 9, with a mob throwing rocks at the house, shots were fired from inside, a white man, Leon Breiner, was killed, and Sweet, his wife, and nine other African Americans defending the property were charged with murder.[48]

The black community rallied in support of Ossian Sweet and his co-defendants. When the case first came up for a preliminary hearing, 500 black Detroiters gathered at the courthouse, details of the affair were carried in the black press across the nation, and when news of the prosecutions reached James Weldon Johnson of the NAACP, he quickly decided that the respectable, successful, and middle-class Sweet would provide the ideal test-case to challenge the racial violence that underpinned residential segregation. Johnson threw the weight of the NAACP's National Legal Committee behind the defense and retained Clarence Darrow to argue the case. At trial, the key issue was whether the accused were justified in acting in self-defense. The prosecution sought to downplay the size and threat of the mob outside the Sweet house on the night of the shooting and Darrow later recalled that "fifty or seventy-five" white persons perjured themselves testifying to that effect despite clear evidence to the contrary. "[T]hese people were almost all members of churches," Darrow sorrowfully recalled, "and in the ordinary matters of life were truthful and kind. Their fear that their property would be injured, together with their racial feeling, justified them in their testimony." A first jury failed to agree on a

Illustration 6.2 Sign advocating residential segregation at the Sojourner Truth Housing Project, Detroit, Michigan, 1942. Courtesy of Library of Congress, Prints and Photographs Online, Farm Security Administration, Office of War Information Photograph Collection. <http://www.loc.gov/pictures/item/owi2001018484/PP/>

Illustration 6.3 Police and African Americans at the Sojourner Truth Housing Project, Detroit, Michigan, 1942. Courtesy of Library of Congress, Prints and Photographs Online, Farm Security Administration, Office of War Information Photograph Collection. <http://www.loc.gov/pictures/item/owi2001018470/PP/>

Note: Nearly 20 years after the Ossien Sweet case, the police and National Guard were required to protect the project's first black residents from white segregationists.

verdict even though, in Walter White's opinion, "the State's case fell down completely," but when the case came up for trial a second time, the jury did vote for acquittal. Critical to the outcome was jury selection, as Darrow and his colleagues worked meticulously through 198 potential jurors to create a panel, "most likely to sympathize with the defense's case." Far more effectively than in the first trial, the defense also tore apart the prosecution witnesses on cross-examination. The result was one of the NAACP's most stunning legal victories, but for all that it rested on Darrow's renowned courtroom acumen it revealed the hopeless odds that the majority of black defendants faced in court.[49] Residential segregation, moreover, persisted and racial conflict over housing remained a common cause of violence in several northern cities, including Detroit. In 1942, nearly twenty years after the Ossien Sweet case, federal authorities were forced to deploy more than one thousand police officers and National Guardsmen to protect black residents in Detroit's new Sojourner Truth Housing Project following violent white protests (see illustrations 6.2 and 6.3).

Policing and protest

Throughout the first half of the twentieth century, damning assessments of police brutality, corruption, and neglect of black neighborhoods were a staple concern of black politics and protest. In 1930, writing in the *Chicago Daily News*, Ida Wells Barnett attacked a city culture that tolerated police shootings of African Americans. Referring to several incidents in which police officers had fatally shot African Americans—including a 16-year-old boy whose house was stormed by 100 officers armed with tear gas and machine guns— Wells observed that there had been no convictions, no "condemnation editorially by our molders of public sentiment, no aroused public conscience, no rewards offered for the arrest and punishment of the murderers, and nobody in authority [had] condemned the inefficiency, the outrageous conduct of the police".[50]

Little had changed for decades. In 1900, white police in New York had joined a mob numbering in the thousands in tearing through the Tenderloin district attacking black residents on the night of a wake held for Robert Thorpe, a plainclothes officer fatally injured in a clash with an African American man who was attempting to prevent Thorpe from arresting his wife for soliciting. Five years later, New York police used brawls between blacks and whites in San Juan Hill to justify another violent crackdown. In raids on saloons and pool halls, African Americans were indiscriminately attacked, at least one man shot and killed, and dozens arrested and subjected to violent beatings at police station houses. Black community leaders alleged the police brutality was revenge for the murder conviction of a white officer for shooting a black suspect in the back the previous year. White authorities denied the charge, but failed to convince thousands of black New Yorkers who organized protests against the police's actions in a revealing example of the centrality of law enforcement issues to the development of race conscious politics. After the 1900 Tenderloin riot, a Citizens Protective League was established by black professionals and attracted 5,000 members in pursuit of legal redress. The League downplayed the racial dimension of the riot, instead condemning police brutality as a product of corruption and immorality on the force, but by 1905 a Colored Citizens Protection League formed after the rioting in San Juan Hill identified police abuse as the product of explicitly racial discrimination.[51]

Racial conflicts over policing were also central to the race riots of the late-1910s. In East St. Louis, the 1917 riot followed weeks of white thuggery and harassment of black residents that went unchecked by a police force that instead had concentrated its resources on a "high-profile" crackdown against "notorious colored crooks." The spark for the riot occurred when dozens of black residents returned fire on a white gang and, in an ensuing chase, killed two detectives in an unmarked police car. This example of armed self-defense reflected the growing strength and assertiveness of northern black communities that historian Malcolm McLaughlin argues stemmed from the political and cultural autonomy that had built up over years in the black ghetto of Denverside, the "physical proximity" of ghetto residents that encouraged collective action, and a long tradition of black neighborhood patrols that compensated for police neglect.[52] There was similar evidence of support for armed self-defense among black communities in other riot-torn cities. After two black families were attacked by white neighbors in Philadelphia in 1918, the city's leading black newspaper, the *Tribune*, wrote, "[w]e favor peace but we say to the colored people of the Pine Street war-zone, stand your ground like men." Walter White of the NAACP expressed similar sentiments in praising the black men who fought during the Chicago riot to protect "their lives and liberty," while Claude McKay's 1919 poem "If We Must Die" captured the spirit of armed black resistance, calling on black men to "face the murderous, cowardly pack/Pressed to the wall, dying, but fighting back."[53]

That urban black residents did not trust the police to protect their lives and property in the midst of race riots was due to the fact that northern policing was routinely characterized by discrimination and violence toward black citizens. In Chicago, the 1919 riot commission concluded that the police share "the general public opinion that Negroes 'are more criminal than whites.'" Blacks in the city were taken into custody and brought before the Chicago Identification Bureau twice as frequently as whites, who officers considered easier to recognize and more likely to challenge unwarranted arrest. Black men on probation or parole in Chicago were likewise "interrogated," "arrested," and "molested" more often than whites, "even while on legitimate business."[54] In Detroit, African American men were more than twice as likely to be arrested as whites and black women were seven times more likely to be arrested than white women. When a 1926 survey in Philadelphia similarly found that African Americans accounted for less than 4 percent of the city population, but more than 20 percent of arrests, Anna Thompson, a social worker in the city, blamed discriminatory policing rooted in racial prejudice. Nearly 20 years later, senior white officers continued to attribute black criminality in part to "heredity" and "African ancestry."[55] Once in jail, African Americans were often held in custody for days before being given access to a lawyer and during that time they might be subjected to all manners of threats and beatings.[56] In New York in 1921, Luther Boddy, a black teenager, testified to several occasions when he was beaten in police custody, including once by seven officers armed with a broomstick wrapped in a rubber hose. Boddy was eventually executed for the murder of two police officers in an escape attempt. Recalling the case a decade later, the New York *Amsterdam News* concluded that "the law made Luther Boddy a killer."[57]

The persistence of northern police prejudice and violence into the mid-twentieth century was accompanied by continuing black resistance, which became increasingly strident during the 1930s. The most marked expression of black hostility toward the police occurred in March 1935 when rioting broke out in Harlem. The riot exploded on the back of rumors that police officers had beaten—and possibly murdered—a black youth suspected of shoplifting. Sixty-four people were injured in the violence and a black high school student—Lloyd Hobbs—was shot dead by a police patrolman. The violence was distinct from previous northern race riots. It was instigated by African Americans and principally targeted white property, though as the night wore on rioters also attacked the businesses of prosperous blacks, possibly reflecting communist influences. The underlying causes of the riot were the social and economic conditions of black life in Harlem and the failure of municipal authorities to address poverty, segregation, injustice, and, most of all, police brutality, through political channels. As a mayoral commission established to investigate the riot concluded, however, "[p]olice aggressions and brutalities more than any other factor weld the people together for mass action against those responsible for their ills."[58]

In the following years, the commission's assessment proved prescient as African Americans continued to respond to police brutality through community protest movements. NAACP branches handled a litany of complaints, but there was also widespread grassroots organizing around law enforcement issues. A community meeting in

Brooklyn in 1937 detailed a series of fatal police shootings that had gone unpunished and outlined three principle complaints against the police: "(1) The illegal imprisonment of our people; (2) The infringement of our personal rights in our homes; (3) The creation of much unnecessary expenses to our group." In Amityville, New York, Mary Nowell, was involved in founding a Citizens Defense Committee to investigate police brutality in the area and wrote to the NAACP attorney, Charles Houston, to enquire how the organization might go about constituting itself as a branch of the Association. In Suffolk County, New York, protest leaflets circulated urging black residents to exercise their voting power to remove from office local officials who failed to address police violence. Recognizing increasing black voting strength, the NAACP sought to ensure adequate police protection for black residents through political channels. It was at the Association's urging, for example, that Police Commissioner Grover Whalen detailed an officer to guard the new house of T. S. Edwards in Jamaica, New York, after the windows were smashed and threats were made that the property would be "blown up" if Edwards did not leave the previously all-white neighborhood.[59]

Communist organizations, which emerged as a political force among northern blacks in the early-1930s, were also involved in protests against discriminatory and violent law enforcement. The Communist Party attracted support among the black poor through uncompromising criticisms and direct action campaigns in protest at housing conditions, police brutality, and unemployment, but most of all its organizing work in black communities gained traction from the involvement of the International Labor Defense in the Scottsboro case and the defense of Angelo Herndon, a black communist convicted of insurrection for organizing workers in Georgia in 1932. Herndon and Ada Wright, mother of two of the Scottsboro boys, were among speakers who appeared at communist rallies in Harlem that connected the injustices of the Deep South with the everyday violent discrimination of New York policing. A march in honor of Wright in 1934 ended with thousands in the crowd fighting police and led to a peaceful protest of black and white workers against police brutality the following week.[60] Communist influence was also evident in 1935 when the Young Liberators and the Young Communist League distributed leaflets on the night of the Harlem riot encouraging black and white working-class unity in the face of police violence. Although white politicians and the press initially blamed communist agitators for instigating the violence, the riot investigating committee eventually conceded that communists deserved "more credit than any other element in Harlem for preventing a physical conflict between whites and blacks." In addition, the prominence that Communists gave to police discrimination also contributed to the NAACP giving a higher priority to the issue to avoid being outflanked as it had been at Scottsboro.[61]

In the rapidly expanding northern cities of the first half of the twentieth century, racial violence, discriminatory law enforcement, and ideologies of black criminality assumed distinctive forms that in many ways paralleled contemporary developments in the South, but were a product of specifically northern social-economic conditions, race relations, and the experiences of African American urban community development and migration. These factors also shaped patterns of black crime and the capacity of black communities and civil rights associations to engage with the causes of crime through reform organizations, support defendants and offenders caught up in criminal justice proceedings, and organize resistance to white violence and discrimination. Viewed over the long term, it is nonetheless difficult to find evidence of significant progress toward racial equality in northern law enforcement prior to the Second World War. On the contrary, cultural attitudes evolved in ways that maintained a strong connection between African Americans and crime that transcended growing challenges to theories of criminality as rooted in inherent biological or cultural traits. Moreover, racial disparities in criminal justice statistics proved impervious to reform efforts that concentrated on securing equality of judicial processes rather than addressing structural factors such as poverty and the zoning of crime in black neighborhoods that disproportionately brought African Americans into contact with the police and the courts.

Part Three

Civil Rights and Beyond

7

The Black Freedom Struggle

[T]here was a policeman ... who was pacing the aisle ... behind us, where we were seated, with his club in his hand, just sort of knocking it in his hand .... And you had the feeling that he didn't know what the hell to do.
> —Franklin McCain recalls the 1960 Greensboro sit-in.[1]

At the Democratic Party Convention in June 1964, Fannie Lou Hamer, a former sharecropper from Mississippi, recounted the racist brutality of southern law enforcement to a national audience. She told of her first attempt to register to vote in 1962 and the white plantation owner who evicted her on learning of the application. She told of the 16 bullets fired into the house of friends where she slept days later. And she told of the day in June, 1963, when she was arrested in Montgomery County, when two black prisoners at the county jail were ordered to beat her until they were exhausted, and when she was sexually assaulted by a state highway patrolman. Suffering partial blindness, kidney damage, serious leg injuries, and bruising across her body, Hamer was still in jail three days later when Byron de la Beckwith, a member of the White Citizens' Council, an organization committed to the preservation of white supremacy, assassinated Medgar Evers, the National Association for the Advancement of Colored People's (NAACP) Mississippi field secretary.

Fannie Lou Hamer's testimony and the murder of Medgar Evers bear powerful witness to the intimate connections between the long history of the civil rights movement, racial violence, and abusive law enforcement. Throughout the twentieth century, American criminal justice worked alongside racist vigilante movements to suppress black

165

political activism. From Marcus Garvey, the Jamaican-born founder of the United Negro Improvement Association, imprisoned and later deported on federal mail fraud charges in the 1920s, to Martin Luther King, jailed repeatedly for participating in nonviolent civil rights protests in the 1950s and 1960s, there were few prominent black leaders whose work did not provoke the attentions of the police or result in periods of incarceration. Likewise, hundreds of thousands of rank-and-file protestors confronted violence, arrest, and imprisonment when they joined civil rights organizations, participated in bus boycotts and marches, and brought legal cases challenging segregation. Yet, the encounters of black political activists with law enforcement officers, white vigilantes, and the criminal justice system were always far more than narratives of violence, discrimination, and oppression. They were also a central means by which black freedom fighters advanced their cause and never more so than in the decades after the Second World War when the civil rights movement reached its zenith.

Spanning nearly three decades from the mid-1940s to the early-1970s, this chapter traces several related developments that reshaped the relationship between African American political activism, law, violence, and the criminal justice system. First, it explores the powerful political, cultural, and economic forces that slowly changed the dynamics of race relations in the South in the aftermath of the Second World War in ways conducive to profound reforms in the administration of law enforcement, the prosecution and outcomes of criminal trials, and government responses to racial violence and discrimination. Second, it examines how civil rights protestors used varied tactics of litigation, mass nonviolent protests, and armed self-defense to confront the discrimination and oppression of American criminal law and to advance a broader struggle for racial equality in the 1950s and 1960s. These civil rights campaigns built on long traditions of black activism that had persistently challenged the strictures of segregation since the nineteenth century, but in many respects they also marked new departures in the form and purpose of black engagement with the police and the courts. Third, the chapter looks at the more radical critiques of American law enforcement put forward by black nationalists from Malcolm X to the Black Panther Party which met with a fierce criminal justice response from the federal government. At a time in the late-1960s when Supreme Court rulings and civil rights legislation had initiated wide-ranging reforms in American criminal justice and punishment, this response demonstrated that the scope of change would be confined within a relatively narrow ideological framework.

Race and criminal justice after the Second World War

In the years after the Second World War, the criminal justice system remained a bastion of white supremacy. In 1948, anti-miscegenation laws were still in force in 30 states, mostly in the South and the West, and racial segregation was entrenched in law in all of the southern states and by common practice—often backed by police complicity—across much of the rest of the nation. In the South, African Americans were routinely excluded from trial juries, sentenced disproportionately to brutal prison farms and chain gangs, and subject to white racial violence that was rarely restricted by either local or federal officials. For elderly Americans in 1950, the criminal justice system would, on the surface, have appeared to have changed little for generations. Nonetheless, as historian Gail O'Brien argues, there is an "intrinsic link between political arrangements and criminal justice components," and in the 1940s and 1950s powerful forces were reframing the context in which issues of African American crime and punishment played out.[2]

First, within the South, the rural black population plummeted. Only 2 percent of African Americans lived on farms by 1969, undermining the systems of sharecropping and peonage that white landholders and county sheriffs had exploited since Reconstruction. The South's growing urban black populations faced different law enforcement challenges, including police brutality, rioting, and pervasive segregation laws, but they also benefited from strong community institutions headed by churches, labor organizations, and NAACP branches. Second, black troops returned from war in Europe and the Pacific with a renewed determination to fight at home for the rights and ideals they had helped to secure overseas. Third, the place of civil rights in national politics was reformulated by the expansion of federal power instigated by the New Deal legislation of the 1930s, a more activist Supreme Court, and growing presidential concern for civil rights issues. This was in part a product of the Cold War and independence movements in Africa and Asia that gave domestic race issues in the United States an unprecedented diplomatic salience. In conjunction with these developments, engrained practices of southern law enforcement and racial violence began to shift in the 1940s. African American protest and resistance forced the appointment of black police officers in the South for the first time since Reconstruction, federal lynching investigations intensified, and a small number of criminal trial juries returned unexpected verdicts favorable to black defendants and victims of crime at the expense of whites.[3]

Following a lead set by Baltimore, Maryland, in 1937, most major cities in the South appointed black police during the 1940s: Miami in 1944, Richmond in 1946, Dallas in 1947, and Memphis and Nashville in 1948, by which time 279 African Americans were employed as police officers in 54 southern cities and Mississippi and Louisiana were the only states with no black officers at all. Municipal leaders justified these appointments to an invariably hostile white public as an effective means to combat criminality in segregated black neighborhoods. In Macon, Georgia, a black auxiliary police platoon appointed for purposes of civilian defense won praise from Chief of Police, Robert L. Miller, for improving law and order at "Negro 'jook' joints and other troublesome spots." In Miami, five black officers appointed in 1944 were expected to pay quickly for themselves by reducing fights and shootings in black districts. In deference to southern racial mores, police departments also imposed limits on the powers and prestige of the first black officers, who often did not wear uniforms, patrolled only in black neighborhoods, were prohibited from arresting whites, and excluded from benefits such as pensions and disability payments.[4]

The real driving force behind black police appointments in the 1940s, however, was African American community protest and political influence. In several cities, police brutality served as a catalyst for civil rights groups to demand black officers. In Nashville, for example, the Interdenominational Alliance and the NAACP Legal Defense Fund formed an interracial Community Council on Human Relations after police rioted through the city's black business district in April 1943 throwing tear gas into crowds, beating shoppers and traders, and firing guns into the air. By late-summer, the Council had secured the appointment of black military policemen to replace white officers in the district. The following year, the Supreme Court ruled in *Smith v. Allwright* that white-only primary elections were unconstitutional. Thousands of African Americans registered to vote in Democratic primaries for the first time and police reform was high on their list of political priorities. In Savannah, Georgia, an intensive voter registration drive increased the black electorate from 800 to 20,000 by 1947, and African American leaders were able to secure a campaign promise from mayoral candidate John G. Kennedy that black officers would be appointed under his administration. Following Kennedy's election, six African Americans were sworn into the force in a public ceremony in May 1947. In New Orleans, Mayor Morrison, elected in 1950 with a majority of just 4,000 votes, similarly moved to appoint black officers after the number of registered black voters doubled to

26,000 in just two years. He acted under pressure from civil rights organizations such as the Citizens Committee on Negro Police and after legal proceedings were instigated against the city by Carlton Pecot, a black police candidate who scored highly in civil service exams but was passed over for appointment in favor of less qualified whites.[5]

Factors that facilitated the appointment of black police officers in the South also brought about limited changes to the prosecution of black suspects and the protection of African Americans from white violence in courts of law. The number of African Americans executed in the Upper South fell from 154 in the 1940s to 47 in the 1950s and in the Deep South declined from 319 to 179 over the same period. Change was particularly notable in prosecutions involving rape and other sexual offenses that struck at the heart of white supremacist ideology. Across the South as a whole, executions of black men for rape declined from 161 in the 1940s to 81 in the 1950s. A detailed study of post-war Virginia similarly found a growing reluctance to bring capital rape prosecutions against black men involved in consensual relationships with white women and the imposition of "little or no punishment" at all against nearly half of 59 black men charged with serious sexual offenses against white women between 1946 and 1960. These changes were indicative of the growing strength of black civil rights protests, but also reflected cultural changes, including more liberal sexual attitudes that caused jurors to be more skeptical of white women who claimed they had been raped by black men in order to cover up illicit interracial relationships.[6]

The late-1950s also witnessed some of the first convictions in the South of white men accused of sexual assaults on black women. In 1959, four white men were convicted in Tallahassee, Florida, for the rape of Betty Jean Owens, a young African American woman they had abducted at gunpoint and raped repeatedly over several hours. The verdict was delivered with a recommendation for mercy that ensured the men would not be executed. This was in contrast to the fate of many black men convicted of comparable crimes, but still the case was a landmark victory that, in Danielle McGuire's analysis, "fractured the philosophical and political foundations of white supremacy by challenging the relationship between sexual domination and racial inequality."[7] In speaking out against her assailants, Owens followed in a long tradition of black women testifying against white rapists, and by participating in mass meetings and prayer vigils to campaign for justice, black students at Florida A&M University similarly built on years of activism in defense of black womanhood. The unusual verdict also reflected local factors, such as Florida's dependence on northern tourism, the lower-class status of the accused, and a politically active local black middle-class, but the wider resonance of the Owens case was nonetheless apparent over the following months as three more white men were convicted of sexual attacks on black women and girls in the South. They included Fred Davis who was sentenced to death by a jury in Burton, South Carolina, though his life was eventually spared.[8]

Global affairs and international diplomacy gave an additional dimension to a series of interracial rape cases during the 1950s that attracted worldwide notoriety and protests. In 1958, for example, thousands of petitioners from around the world joined with American businessmen and Secretary of State John Dulles in calling on Alabama Governor Jim Folsom to spare the life of African American convict Jimmy Wilson. Found guilty by an all-white jury of robbery in the trivial sum of $1.95, Wilson was sentenced to death after his alleged white, female victim made unsubstantiated allegations on the witness stand that he had attempted to rape her. Amidst intense international scrutiny, Folsom granted clemency, but the Cold War context was not always conducive to African American struggles against criminal injustice. Notably, the strength of domestic anticommunism undercut the work of radical and leftist organizations that had taken a lead in protecting black defendants since the 1930s. This was apparent when the communist-aligned Civil Rights Congress (CRC) represented Willie McGee, a black sharecropper charged in late-1940s Mississippi with raping Wiletta Hawkins, a white woman. After McGee was tried three times and sentenced to death, the CRC retained Bella Abzug, a white attorney from New York, to lead the appeal. Rather than highlighting the very real abuses of due process that had marked McGee's trial, Abzug constructed an innovative and radical defense based on the claim that McGee and Hawkins had been involved in a consensual relationship. Abzug aimed to expose that southern rape laws were not principally concerned with the protection of white women, as their advocates claimed, but rather were used to police racial boundaries and prevent legitimate interracial relationships. This was a profound challenge to ideas about race and gender that were at the heart of white supremacy in the South. It emanated from Abzug's involvement in leftist feminist movements and contrasted starkly with the liberal, race-based strategies of NAACP litigation that secured incremental procedural gains for black defendants but left much of the underlying ideology of white supremacy uncontested. In the context of

Cold War civil rights, however, Abzug's position was unsustainable. CRC protestors who marched in support of McGee in Jackson were arrested, Abzug herself was subject to FBI surveillance and threats of violence, and neither the courts nor the state governor would take up the case. Despite global outrage, McGee went to his death on May 8, 1951. By 1956, the CRC was defunct, crippled by internal divisions and financial weakness brought on by years of state persecution.[9]

The ambivalent history of African Americans and the criminal justice system in the decade after the Second World War was echoed in developments in racial violence in the same period. In part driven by the growing vigor with which the Department of Justice and the FBI investigated lynchings, there was a decline in the recorded numbers of African Americans lynched from 31 in the 1940s to 6 in the 1950s. Notable wartime prosecutions were brought against an Atlanta detective, W. F. Sutherland, for torturing a burglary suspect into confessing in 1940 and three Georgia lawmen, including Sheriff Mack Screws, for murdering a black prisoner in 1943. As in the wake of the First World War, however, the return of African American troops from military service coincided with what President Truman called the "[i]ntentional misuse of police authority" and "several of the most abhorrent instances of mob vengeance in the history of the nation." In February 1946, after four police officers were wounded by African Americans in clashes following an attempted lynching in Columbia, Tennessee, state highway patrolmen stormed through the city's black business district destroying property, beating and arresting residents, two of whom were later killed in custody. Later in the year, two black farmers and their wives were shot dead by a lynch mob in Monroe, Georgia; Isaac Woodard, a war veteran, was beaten and permanently blinded in a South Carolina jail after he was arrested following an argument with a white bus driver; and a total of six African Americans were shot dead by police in separate incidents in Atlanta. The following year, 21 men accused of lynching Willie Earle were acquitted by an all-white jury in Greenville, South Carolina. In response to these incidents, Truman established the President's Committee on Civil Rights in December 1946 and advocated a stronger role for the federal government in the protection of civil rights, declaring, "[w]e cannot, any longer, await the growth of a will to action in the slowest state or the most backward community."[10]

In practice, federal anti-lynching rhetoric, recommendations, and investigations did little to secure justice in the 1950s' South when either white law officers or private citizens murdered African Americans.

In 1951, a Florida sheriff, Willis McCall, shot two black men, one fatally, after the US Supreme Court overturned their conviction for raping a white woman, and boasted to his boss, "I got rid of them; killed the sons of bitches." McCall was never charged and served a further five terms as sheriff until 1972. In 1955, the year after the US Supreme Court ruled in *Brown v. Board of Education* that racial segregation in American schools was "inherently unequal" and unconstitutional, three more racially motivated murders went unpunished in Mississippi. White killers gunned down Reverend George Lee in May 1955, and Lamar Smith, in front of a courthouse, in early-August after both men had worked on black voter registration campaigns. Later the same month, a young black boy from Chicago named Emmett Till traveled South to visit his cousins in the small rural town of Money. Three nights after he allegedly wolf-whistled at a white woman—Carolyn Bryant—in a grocery store, Till was seized from his great-uncle's house and driven away. He was beaten and tortured over several hours, shot dead, and his body dumped in the Tallahatchie river where it was found floating several days later. Carolyn's husband, Roy Bryant, and his half-brother, J. W. Milam, were identified as Till's killers and prosecuted for murder. They would later confess their guilt to a journalist from *Life* magazine, but in court they were swiftly acquitted after defense attorney John C. Whitten made an explicit appeal to racial prejudice in his closing statement to the all-white jury (see Illustration 7.1): "Every last Anglo-Saxon one of you," Whitten declared, "has the courage to free these men."[11]

The murder of Emmett Till and the failure to convict his killers caused widespread condemnation of Mississippi criminal justice that was fueled by the insistence of Till's mother that her son's casket remain open during his funeral. Along with the killers' acquittal, pictures of the mangled state of the boy's corpse prompted huge rallies in cities including Chicago, New York, and Washington and led to demands for the US attorney general to investigate the case. The demonstrations occurred at a critical juncture in civil rights history. The *Brown* decision had been a stunning victory for the NAACP that was at once a culmination of years of activism and litigation at grassroots and national levels, an inspiration to further civil rights campaigns, and a legal landmark that reversed the Supreme Court's support for segregation that had stood for 60 years since *Plessy v. Ferguson*. At the same time, however, *Brown* also initiated a backlash among white southerners committed to preserving whites-only schools. What became known as "massive resistance" to integration

Illustration 7.1 Jury for the Emmett Till trial, Sumner, Mississippi, September 21, 1955. Emmett Till Jury. Courtesy of Bettmann/Corbis

was led by the White Citizens' Council, a grassroots organization that had hundreds of thousands of members at its peak in the late-1950s. Proclaiming a commitment to middle-class respectability, law, and public order that contrasted with the crude violence of the Klan, citizens' councils advocated political and legal measures to uphold states' rights and prevent desegregation. As the NAACP fought legal battles across the South to force implementation of *Brown* on defiant local school boards, southern politicians responded with hard-line pro-segregation policies including hundreds of new laws to impede integration and attack the NAACP, which was outlawed in several states and saw its membership halve in the South by the end of the decade in the wake of forced publication of its membership lists that facilitated economic and political intimidation, police harassment, and vigilante attacks.[12]

It was in this context that Governor James P. Coleman established the Mississippi Sovereignty Commission as an investigative unit that relied on detectives and a vast network of black and white informants to police race relations through the monitoring, harassment, and arrest of civil rights activists. This was a sophisticated new style of southern policing that Coleman intended not only to prevent school desegregation, but also to spare his state a repeat of the national scrutiny provoked by the crude injustice of the Emmett Till case. When the brutal lynching of Mack Charles Parker in 1959 revealed the limits of Coleman's reforms, the Governor went further, inviting the FBI to investigate and calling on other southern states to address mob violence in order to preserve states' rights and white supremacy. This approach contrasted with the actions of Arkansas Governor Orval Faubus who two years earlier had provoked a direct confrontation with the federal government when he called out the state National Guard to prevent the enrollment of black children at Little Rock Central High School. The troops were stood down after negotiations with Washington, but a white mob was allowed to form at the school that "caused so much disruption that school officials withdrew the black students for their own safety." With Arkansas in direct violation of *Brown v. Board of Education*, President Eisenhower was forced to send in federal troops to secure desegregation, but contrary to Coleman's fears such intervention from Washington was rare even when violence accompanied the integration of educational institutions in other communities. Collectively, these events demonstrated that while traditional forms of southern law enforcement had been destabilized by pressures from many different directions by the late-1950s, only the most limited of reforms had occurred and the role of the criminal justice system in support of the white supremacist regime remained fundamentally intact. That situation would change dramatically over the following decade.[13]

The civil rights movement and southern policing

In February 1956, several weeks into a boycott of local buses by African Americans in Montgomery, Alabama, police arrested dozens of the protest's leaders using a rarely invoked 1921 state law that prohibited conspiracies against businesses "without a just cause or legal excuse." Among those taken into custody was Rosa Parks, a middle-class black woman and long-term civil rights activist whose arrest the previous December for refusing to give up her seat to a white passenger had sparked the boycott. Also detained was the Reverend Martin Luther King, a young Baptist pastor who had become the national face of the boycott, and the Reverend Ralph Abernathy of the city's

First Baptist Church, who warned that the authorities had made a mistake: "This mass arrest has put us together," he declared, "and right now the bus protest is 99 percent effective."[14]

For a further nine months, thousands of African Americans in Montgomery refused to travel the buses and at the same time lawyers for the Mississippi Improvement Association (MIA)—the umbrella organization leading the boycott—challenged Alabama's bus segregation laws in the courts. Through this period, whites responded with diverse tactics, spanning from law enforcement mechanisms to vigilantism. Black cab drivers who gave cheap rides to the boycotters were arrested, "for trivial or nonexistent traffic violations," police failed to investigate bombings that targeted black churches and the homes of movement leaders, and city officials sued the MIA for operating what they claimed was an illegal car pool system to transport African Americans. After the US Supreme Court ruled in November 1956 that segregation on Montgomery's buses was unconstitutional (*Browder v. Gayle*), black passengers in the city were assaulted and shot at, bombing campaigns intensified, and local juries acquitted two white men who admitted to a role in the violence.[15]

The bus boycott in Montgomery was not the first mass civil rights protest against segregation, but it marked a new phase in the struggle by providing a successful model of collective, nonviolent direct action and securing a major victory against Jim Crow in the courts. It was also representative of a shift in the role of crime and punishment in civil rights protests that would reach full fruition in the 1960s. Rather than seeking to redress injustice in specific criminal cases in line with NAACP policy since the 1910s, civil rights activism in the 1950s and 1960s confronted the foundations of southern law enforcement as as an integral part of the broader struggle for transformative social and political change in black life. This did not mean abandoning legal strategies, but rather incorporating litigation and criminal defense alongside nonviolent direct action campaigns of civil disobedience and, in many parts of the South, armed self-defense. On the streets and in the courts, therefore, criminal justice became the primary terrain on which the campaigns of the civil rights movement were fought.[16]

In the first half of the 1960s, hundreds of thousands of civil rights activists participated in protests that aimed to translate the promise of *Brown* into meaningful desegregation and equal civil rights in all aspects of black life. In February 1960, four black college students in Greensboro, North Carolina, sat at a Woolworths lunch counter reserved for white customers and refused to leave when they were denied service. Over the following weeks, the young men were joined in their protest by hundreds of their peers and as news of the affair spread rapidly across the South, similar demonstrations were inspired in hundreds of different communities. By April 1960, as many as 70,000 students had participated in lunch counter sit-ins and nearly 3,000 had been arrested, most for trespassing and unlawful assembly. The sit-ins prompted the formation of the Student Non-Violent Coordinating Committee (SNCC), an organization that marked a newly "dynamic, youthful, radical, and aggressive brand of activism" that many in the black middle-class initially considered a dangerous departure from the legal strategy of the NAACP Legal Defense Fund (LDF). The LDF pursued litigation against segregated public facilities and transportation, but at this time still considered racial discrimination by private actors to be beyond the reach of the Fourteenth Amendment's equal protection clause, as it had been since Reconstruction. The students were dismissive of this distinction between public and private discrimination, but more importantly they had learned from ongoing white resistance to the implementation of *Brown* that even if federal law was on their side, judicial rulings from Washington meant little without active support for racial change on the ground in local communities.[17]

This point was driven home the following year. In 1961, the Campaign for Racial Equality (CORE) organized "Freedom Rides" designed to enforce the desegregation of interstate bus travel in accordance with the recent Supreme Court ruling in *Boynton v. Virginia* (1960). After an initial group of 13 CORE activists set off from Washington DC, a total of 400 people participated at some stage in the Freedom Rides, traveling through some of the most dangerous parts of the South toward New Orleans. The first bus to arrive in Anniston, Alabama, had its tires slashed and was bombed and riders on the second bus were assaulted by a white mob. The riders were beaten again by Klansmen when they arrived at Birmingham bus station after the city police chief deliberately withheld protection. SNCC activists continued the Freedom Rides, first in Montgomery, where they were surrounded by an angry white crowd while taking shelter at the First Baptist Church, and then in Mississippi where 328 Freedom Riders were arrested in Jackson and imprisoned in the county jail and later at Parchman Farm. National media attention protected the young activists from the extreme brutality for which Parchman was notorious, but still they were subjected to sleep deprivation, extreme temperatures, solitary confinement in "the hole," and, for women prisoners, sexual humiliation at the hands of male guards.[18]

The jailed Freedom Riders joined thousands of other civil rights protestors imprisoned in the early-1960s as SNCC adopted a policy of "jail no bail." On a practical level, refusing to pay fines and bail costs lifted a financial burden from the black community while increasing the cost to southern authorities (and white taxpayers) of fighting the civil rights movement through expensive criminal prosecutions and mass imprisonment. It also helped to reformulate African Americans' relationship with southern law enforcement. John Lewis, a leading figure in SNCC, recalled that his mother had, "made no distinction between being jailed for drunkenness and being jailed for civil rights," but the protests challenged such perceptions, transforming imprisonment into "a badge of honor" for civil rights workers. Jailed students also provided a focal point for rallies and demonstrations and an inspirational model of redemptive suffering and refusal to be cowed by what SNCC's Diane Nash called an "evil" and unjust court system. Finally, the experience of imprisonment unified black and white campaigners from diverse backgrounds across the nation and gave movement participants time to debate and develop ideas, helping to bridge tactical and philosophical differences among them.[19]

As civil rights campaigns intensified in the early-1960s, so too did the criminal justice responses of white authorities. In 1963 alone, over 20,000 arrests were made as a result of demonstrations in 115 cities, though events were not uniform across the South. In some communities, the demands of white business elites for the preservation of law and order outweighed the influence of violent white supremacists, and police officers were able to employ a variety of nonviolent tactics that often proved effective in containing civil unrest. In 1961 in Atlanta, for example, downtown business leaders had helped to promote a negotiated settlement for partial integration supervised by the police. Similarly, during protests in Albany, Georgia, the following year Chief of Police Laurie Pritchett succeeded in limiting national media coverage and preventing immediate desegregation by maintaining a dialogue with the demonstrators, making orderly arrests, and ensuring civil treatment for those in custody.[20]

These tactics were facilitated by local courts that upheld the use of injunctions, trespass, and breach of the peace charges to police civil rights demonstrations. Southern judges invariably sided with prosecutors in civil rights trespassing trials and set unreasonable bail costs to keep protestors in jail when defense lawyers appealed the convictions to federal courts. In the wake of renewed demonstrations by SNCC in Atlanta beginning in 1963, for example, judge Durwood Pye set bail at $4500 for Prathia Hall, a young black student from Philadelphia, charged with trespassing, $15,000 for a white woman, Mardon Walker, who was prosecuted after she entered a segregated restaurant with a group of African Americans, and $20,000 for a 67-year-old black minister who attempted to enter a white church. These judgments had a far-reaching impact. Walker's treatment in particular met with outrage among white liberals in the North who decried it as "jungle justice" and a federal court eventually reduced Hall's bond to $1,000 and ruled that persons charged with misdemeanors should not be held to more than $5,000 security. Locally, Pye's discriminatory judgments also temporarily united Atlanta's black community that for many years had been fractured along tactical and generational lines between students involved in direct action and older residents committed to the litigation strategies of the LDF. Yet from the white perspective, Pye's approach worked, at least in the short term, as SNCC turned its attention away from the city before the 1964 Civil Rights Act made segregation unconstitutional and the Supreme Court's rulings in *Hamm v. Rock Hill* (1964) and *Lupper v. Arkansas* (1964) abated the convictions and pending prosecutions of all civil rights activists charged with criminal trespass.[21]

In other parts of the South, civil rights demonstrators met with more traditional southern police repression and mob rule. In Danville, Virginia, for example, Police Chief E. G. McCain ordered fire hoses turned on a crowd of 150 people who gathered at the city jail to protest the arrest of 38 civil rights demonstrators. He also deputized a white posse, which attacked the protestors with table legs, injuring dozens. More than 100 people were arrested (see Illustration 7.2) and many of the women in custody were forced by police to submit to humiliating pelvic examinations "to check for venereal disease." Sam Shirah, a white folk singer from Alabama, was among those taken into custody. He was beaten by police, jailed with white Virginians at the city work farm who beat him some more, and fined $50 for vagrancy.[22] Such aggressive forms of policing were once again facilitated by local courts. In March 1963, Golden A. Frinks, a local movement leader in Edenton, North Carolina, was jailed on a contempt-of-court charge filed shortly after he had secured a warrant against the local police chief for striking him during a protest. Civil rights activists contrasted this treatment with the fate of two white men who had recently killed

Illustration 7.2 Segregation protestors at jail, Birmingham, Alabama, May 5, 1963. Courtesy of Bettmann/Corbis

African Americans in the area. No charges at all were brought against one of the men who crashed his car into a black pedestrian, while the other was released on bail despite facing charges of second-degree murder.[23]

Dramatic scenes of peaceful civil rights protestors confronted by violent white mobs and police officers gave powerful weight to the argument of civil rights activists that their cause was morally right. As Martin Luther King wrote in a letter from his jail cell amidst the most significant demonstrations of 1963 in Birmingham, Alabama, southern law was, "unjust … out of harmony with the moral law … not rooted in eternal or natural law," and degrading of human personality.[24] Movement leaders denied courting police brutality, but the success of the key civil rights campaigns in Birmingham and in Selma two years later was heavily dependent on the sympathy for the cause that was generated among whites when the police resorted to force. When Americans saw images of officers in Birmingham confronting school-age demonstrators with police dogs, water hoses, and tear gas, and hundreds of marchers on a bridge in Selma beaten as they prayed on what became known as Bloody Sunday, "these seemed not to be legitimate law enforcement techniques, but an unjust effort to eliminate the expression of opposition."[25] In the public mind, Birmingham's bigoted, firebrand police chief, Eugene "Bull" Connor and Dallas County Sheriff Jim Clark were the embodiment of violent southern law enforcement, though it is important to recognize that these individuals were also symptomatic of their local communities. The brutal tactics they employed reflected their dependence on a white supremacist electorate that expected violent law enforcement and official toleration of vigilantism against African Americans.[26]

Armed self-defense

For all the police brutality and courtroom discrimination that met civil rights campaigns in southern towns and cities, it was in rural areas of the Deep South, where law enforcement was scarce, that activists faced the most murderous violence. Among the dead in the early-1960s was Herbert Lee, who worked on voter-registration projects in Mississippi and was killed in 1961. A black witness to the crime, Louis Allen, was threatened, jailed, and eventually assassinated three years later. NAACP field secretary, Medgar Evers, was shot dead in his home in June 1963, and the following year, when hundreds of SNCC activists worked on voter-registration campaigns in Mississippi as part of Freedom Summer, Klansmen killed two black hitchhikers in Meadville and three civil rights activists in Philadelphia. There were also more than 1000 arrests of civil rights workers in Mississippi in 1964, 25 shootings, dozens of bombings, and countless assaults. In Alabama, William Moore, a white postman from Baltimore, was murdered in 1963 as he marched to deliver a letter against segregation to the governor and later the same year four young black girls died when segregationists bombed a Birmingham church that was used for civil rights meetings. Two years later, Jimmie Jackson died at the hands of state troopers as he protected his grandparents on a civil rights march and James Reed, Viola Liuzzo, and Jonathan Daniels, all white northerners, were killed in separate incidents by the Klan for their involvement in civil rights activities.[27]

These crimes received little attention from the police or the courts. Instead, as civil rights lawyer Fred L. Banks, Jr. later recalled, Mississippi judges in such cases acted as, "the unrobed Klan—or the Klan in Black robes instead of white sheets."[28] Nor was justice in these cases served by the federal government. The FBI was fully aware of the threat to civil rights workers in the Deep South, and used informants and undercover agents to monitor some Klansmen, but they held mostly to a strict separation of state and federal powers, warning SNCC recruits bound for Mississippi in the Freedom Summer of 1964 that "[t]here is no federal police force—the responsibility for protection is that of the local police." Persistent Justice Department investigations supported by innovative legal arguments led to convictions of the Klan killers of civil rights worker Viola Liuzzo in a federal court in 1965, and in 1967 guilty verdicts were returned against seven of 18 men charged in connection with the 1964 triple murder of civil rights workers in Mississippi, but these cases were exceptions, not least because all but one of the victims involved were white.[29]

Local people in the Deep South had long lived with extreme racial violence and readily perceived the dangers and limitations of nonviolent activism in their communities. A tradition of armed self-defense ran deep in the rural black society of the Deep South. It drew on a strong sense of masculine honor among black men whose commitment to the protection of their families and communities, with arms if necessary, alienated many from the nonviolent philosophy of the mainstream civil rights movement. It also traced a lineage to slave rebels, Reconstruction-era black militias, and the crowds that protected black men and women from lynch mobs. In time, the absence of local police protection and the limited powers of federal authorities would similarly convince SNCC and CORE civil rights workers to tolerate and later embrace armed self-defense as imperative to the survival and success of their work. Yet armed self-defense in the civil rights era was not just a legacy of the past that stood in opposition to the nonviolent struggle. It was also evidence of, "a new sense of entitlement and a new combativeness in the black consciousness" that developed in tandem with the philosophy and achievements of the broader civil rights movement. In historian Christopher Strain's assessment, armed self-defense was an assertion of African Americans' constitutional right to self-protection and, "an essential part of the struggle for citizenship itself."[30]

Among the earliest and most prominent advocates of militant black activism in the civil rights era was Robert Williams, president of the Union County, North Carolina, branch of the NAACP. In the late-1950s, Williams experienced Klan rallies led by police patrol cars and he witnessed the exoneration in local courts of a white defendant who threw a black maid down a staircase and another who attempted to rape a black woman and offered in defense only that "[h]e was just drunk and having a little fun." Williams concluded that "Negroes *must* protect themselves," declaring in 1959 that if the courts would not provide protection then African Americans "must meet violence with violence." The NAACP suspended Williams for these views and he was later expelled after a concerted campaign to discredit him within the organization. Two years later, he fled the United States while under FBI investigation for allegedly kidnapping a white couple he had sought to protect from an angry black crowd after they inadvertently drove into Monroe's black neighborhood while police downtown were attacking civil rights protestors. Williams' message, however, resonated widely even in his absence, as he broadcast a weekly radio program from Havana, Cuba, from 1962 until 1965.[31]

During this period, black communities increasingly fought back against white violence. From 1963 to 1965, black protestors fought running battles with police and Klansmen during civil rights demonstrations in cities across the South, from Cambridge, Maryland, to St. Augustine, Charleston, and Natchez. In the rural Deep South, armed self-defense took more organized forms. The most substantial militant black political group in the region was established by local black men in the Louisiana mill town of Jonesboro in 1964 to protect CORE activists involved in voter registration activities who were the targets of threats and harassment from white gangs. As CORE's work expanded into school desegregation, the Klan became active in Jonesboro—with the support of the police—and violence and arrests of civil rights demonstrators mounted. In response, local African American men began to provide security for the civil rights workers and by the fall they had organized as the Deacons for Defense and Justice. During 1965 and 1966, the Deacons not only protected CORE workers, but also became "a symbol of a sea change in black consciousness" through their direct confrontations with white power. In March 1965, for example, four Deacons armed with shotguns prevented police in Jonesboro from turning water hoses on school children who were boycotting their classes, and in July of the same year, in Bogalusa, Henry Austin, one of the youngest of the Deacons at 21 years of age, shot at a white mob that attacked a black teenager, Hattie Mae Hill, as she participated in a Voters League march on city hall. One man was injured in the shooting, but survived, and with racial tensions high Austin was released on bail and returned a hero to the black community. More significantly, to prevent further clashes that white authorities feared could descend into race war, the Justice Department filed suits to enforce the 1964 Civil Rights Act in Bogalusa, destroying the Klan, requiring the police to protect black citizens, and desegregating public facilities. Further successes accrued through 1966, as the Deacons incorporated 21 chapters and gained hundreds of members across Louisiana and Mississippi.[32]

Armed self-defense also characterized the black freedom struggle in Lowndes County, Alabama. Among the most racially repressive societies in the nation, public civil rights protests did not begin in Lowndes until early-1965 when SNCC activists, led by Stokely Carmichael, sought to mobilize the black community through voter registration campaigns and the organization of the Lowndes County Freedom Organization (LCFO), an independent black political party. White vigilantes responded with endemic violence, forcing activists to travel in armed convoys and barricade their homes against nightriders. In contrast to the Deacons in Louisiana, armed defense in Lowndes was not formalized in a paramilitary organization, but practiced as required in response to the equally diffused and uncoordinated nature of white terrorism in a county where racial violence was so pervasive that it did not require organized Klan activity. When black voters cast their ballots in the LCFO nomination elections on May 3, 1966, for example, SNCC field secretaries kept watch for white attacks and one elderly man, recalling racial violence of the past, promised that, "We gonna protect our friends this time." Speaking earlier that year, Stokely Carmichael admitted he had simply "stopped telling people they should remain nonviolent. This would be tantamount to suicide in the Black Belt counties where whites are shooting at Negroes and it would cost me the respect of the people." By the summer of 1966, Carmichael's position had shifted further, and both CORE and SNCC had jettisoned their former commitments to nonviolence. In June, when Carmichael was released from jail after being arrested for the 27th time, he declared a new approach toward American law enforcement consistent with the self-defense traditions of the Deep South: "I ain't going to jail no more," Carmichael told a rally in Greenwood, Alabama.[33]

Black Power

On July 18, 1964, rioting broke out in Harlem after CORE-led demonstrations against the fatal police shooting of James Powell, a black teenager, by an off-duty police officer led to confrontations with police and a series of arrests. Late in the evening, a police tactical patrol force charged into a crowd of around 1000 African Americans and the ensuing violence was followed by six days of sporadic clashes resulting in hundreds of injuries and one fatality (see Illustrations 7.3 and 7.4).[34]

Illustration 7.3 African Americans demonstrate against the killing of James Powell in Harlem, July 1964. Courtesy of Library of Congress, Prints and Photographs Online, New York World-Telegram and the Sun Newspaper Photograph Collection. < http://www.loc.gov/pictures/item/2006689552/>

Within days, further rioting had broken out in Rochester, New York, and in August riots also struck Jersey City and Philadelphia. Clashes in these cities, however, were small in scale compared to the rioting that engulfed Watts and South Central Los Angeles the following summer, just days after President Lyndon Johnson signed into law the Voting Rights Act striking down the discriminatory barriers to voter registration that had denied generations of black Americans the franchise. The initial violence in Los Angeles was again sparked by an encounter with the police. After Marquette Frye, an African American youth, was pulled-over on suspicion of drink driving, blows were exchanged between white officers, Frye, and his mother, who had arrived at the scene along with a growing crowd of African Americans who began to hurl abuse and missiles at officers. Six days later, up to 10,000 people had been involved in the worst urban violence in America since the Detroit riot of 1943. Thirty-four people were dead, more than 4000

Illustration 7.4 Policeman confronts African American men during violence in Harlem, July 1964. Courtesy of Library of Congress, Prints and Photographs Online, New York World-Telegram and the Sun Newspaper Photograph Collection. <http://www.loc.gov/pictures/item/2006689554/>

arrested, and property damage was estimated at $40 million across 46 square miles of the city.[35]

Coming at a moment when the southern civil rights movement appeared to have achieved the key objectives of desegregation and equal rights, the events in Los Angeles shocked America, but scenes of burning cities became commonplace over subsequent summers. Forty-one major civil disturbances were recorded in 1967 with the worst violence in Detroit and Newark where a total of 68 people were killed. In April 1968, the assassination of Martin Luther King sparked riots in more than 100 cities, including major disturbances in Baltimore, Chicago, and Washington, DC, where nearly 14,000 federal troops were deployed to restore order and enforce curfews. Collectively, these riots were distinct from most of the violent civil disorder stemming from racial conflict in earlier eras. Rather than whites, the violence was instigated by African Americans—mostly young, black men—and their principal targets were property and symbolic representations of white power. The National Advisory Commission on Civil Disorders (the Kerner Commission), established by President Johnson in the summer of 1967 to investigate the riots identified a complex array of interconnected causes that reflected America's deep racial divisions: "Our nation is moving toward two societies," the report concluded, "one black, one white—separate and unequal." This inequality was manifest in the entrenched economic deprivation of inner-city black neighborhoods, though it was relative destitution as much as absolute poverty that underlay the violence. As postwar American prosperity and the judicial and legislative successes of the civil rights movement failed to translate into black economic progress and improved race relations, frustration had built in urban communities creating a "disturbed social atmosphere" in which "tension-heightening incidents"—commonly involving the police—created explosive circumstances out of "a reservoir of underlying grievances" including housing segregation, unemployment, and poverty.[36]

In investigating law enforcement specifically, the Kerner Commission drew attention to long-standing black complaints that police neglected their responsibilities for crime control in black communities, tolerated "illegal activities like drug addiction, prostitution, and street violence," and used excessive force, illegal searches, and discrimination against African American citizens.[37] These were not new accusations. Though attracting considerably less national recognition than the racially motivated murders perpetrated by Klansmen and the police in the South, the racist police brutality that had marked northern and western cities earlier in the century had persisted in the years after the Second World War. In New York, for example, 46 unarmed African Americans had been killed by police between 1947 and 1952 alone.[38]

Rioting was only one response to the police violence, discriminatory justice, segregation, and limited social and economic opportunities that characterized black life in the urban ghettos of the 1960s, and it was far from the most common. As in earlier times, black antipathy toward the criminal justice system was also evident in organized forms of political activism. Much had changed, however, from the popular front protests of the Depression years and the Second World War, and even from the southern civil rights activism of the early-1960s when confrontations with police were used as a tactic to challenge segregation and secure black voting rights. By the mid-1960s issues of law enforcement in northern communities increasingly sat at the heart of new revolutionary Black Nationalist programs for racial change.

For the young, radical, and articulate spokespersons of the Black Power movement, the brutality and injustice of American policing was a central preoccupation of the black freedom struggle in and of itself. In the assessment of SNCC's Julius Lester, writing in 1968, "the American black man has never known law and order except as an instrument of oppression .... It exists for that purpose."[39] H. Rap Brown, one-time chair of SNCC, similarly declared, "justice is a joke in this country, and it stinks of its hypocrisy." These comments were heavily influenced by the ideas and example of Malcolm X. In the aftermath of the fatal shooting of two Muslim men in Los Angeles in 1962, Malcolm, then a minister and the leading spokesman for the Nation of Islam, had called for "an immediate end" to police brutality and warned black Americans that "A black man can't get justice in the court system of America .... The only way you get justice is when you make justice for yourself." Malcolm had acted on this premise in the past. In 1957, he gathered an estimated 800 followers outside a police precinct house in Harlem after Hinton Johnson, a fellow black Muslim, was viciously beaten by police. Fearful of the angry crowd, police chiefs hastily agreed to Malcolm's demand that the incident be fully investigated and Johnson eventually won a record $70,000 in damages.[40]

In Oakland, California, Malcolm's message was one of the inspirations for Huey Newton and Bobby Seale when they founded the Black Panther Party in 1966. Taking its name from the symbol of the Lowndes County Freedom Organization, the Black Panther Party combined revolutionary aims with practical, grassroots activity in support of black communities. Although widely attacked by mainstream white America as a violent and criminal organization, the Party built strong bonds with local black communities through pragmatic responses to social problems and a proud and militant image and ideology. At its height in 1969, the Black Panthers had more than 2000 members, offices across the country, and provided services including medical care and free breakfasts for children. These figures probably understate support for the Party. In 1970, 25 percent of African Americans told pollsters they had "a great respect for the Black Panther Party," and shortly after police shootings of Black Panthers in Omaha in 1970, 80 percent of black respondents said the incident "had made them feel that Blacks 'should stand together.'"[41] In New Orleans, where a Black Panther Party branch was based in the Desire projects, one of the most deprived areas of the city, attempts by 300 police to evict the Panthers from their headquarters were resisted by more than 2000 residents who forced the police to retreat.[42]

Law enforcement provided the overriding focus of the Black Panthers' early activism. Describing the police as "an occupying army in the black community that enforced the larger society's illegitimate rule," Newton and Seale's Ten Point Program of party policy included three demands concerning policing, criminal trials, and punishment: first, an "immediate end to police brutality and murder of black people"; second, "freedom for all black men held in federal, state, county and city prisons and jails", and third, the convening of all-black juries to sit in judgment on black defendants consistent with the constitutional right to a trial by one's peers. These policies were more than rhetoric. In October 1966, Newton and Seale began surveillance of police patrols in black neighborhoods in Oakland to combat police brutality in the city, and the following year they led armed demonstrations to the California state legislature in Sacramento against proposed restrictions on carrying loaded firearms that they claimed would leave black communities defenseless against police violence. Reflecting considerable divisions within the black community, Roy Wilkins of the NAACP feared, quite to the contrary, "that proclaimed protective violence is as likely to encourage counter-violence as it is to discourage violent persecution."[43]

Throughout the late-1960s, the Black Panther Party's development was almost inseparable from its repeated clashes with law enforcement authorities. In October 1967, Huey Newton was arrested following a gunfight in Oakland in which one police officer was killed and another wounded. On trial for murder, Newton was eventually convicted on a lesser charge and served a short prison term. The case was critical to the Party's growth. In court, the defense presented Newton as, "a selfless political prisoner," and representative of the dispossessed black working class, and on the outside a campaign to "Free Huey," orchestrated by the Party's minister of information, Eldridge Cleaver, helped give the Panthers an international profile, expanded its reach within black communities, and generated support among students and the New Left. It also attracted the attention of the FBI, however, which in August 1967 launched an extensive counterintelligence program against Black Nationalist "hate groups," that it defined broadly to include organizations as diverse as the Southern Christian Leadership Conference, CORE, SNCC, the Deacons for Defense and Justice, the Nation of Islam, and the Revolutionary Action Movement. In conjunction with local police departments, the FBI's aim was to "expose, disrupt, misdirect, discredit, or otherwise neutralize" these organizations, in order "to counter their propensity for violence and civil disorder." A model for this work was provided by FBI agents in Philadelphia, where SNCC and the Revolutionary Action Movement were, "virtually destroyed" by a joint undercover operation involving the city police department's Civil Disobedience Unit that repeatedly arrested the associates of "a known Negro extremist" for minor offenses until they could no longer make bail.[44]

By 1968, the US government was involved in what SNCC activist Cleveland Sellers called "a systematic attempt to intimidate the black liberation struggle,"[45] and the Black Panther Party, described by J. Edgar Hoover as the most dangerous organization in America, was the primary target. Over the next two years, dozens of Black Panther Party members were killed and arrested in police operations. Two were shot dead by police at a student meeting on the UCLA campus in support of the university's new Black Studies center.[46] Police raided the New York City Black Panther Party offices in April 1969 and indicted 21 Panthers on conspiracy and possession charges, all of whom were eventually acquitted in 1971. In Chicago, the Panthers engaged in a series of shootouts with officers in 1969 that culminated in a police raid purportedly in search of illegal weapons, in which two Party leaders were shot dead, including Fred Hampton who was killed in his bed. On a single day in 1970, bombings in Omaha, Columbus, and Minneapolis were attributed to Black Panthers, leading to widespread arrests and eventually to life sentences for some of the alleged participants. In both New Orleans and New York, Black Panthers were held to $100,000 bail, a figure so far in excess of the normal bail limits that Bobby Seale described it as violating the defendants' constitutional rights.[47] Huey Newton's attorney, Charles Garry, slammed the police treatment of the Panthers as unprecedented persecution and criticized the judges who refused to stand up "against the onslaught of the police state[,]" declaring that "most of them are frightened, and most of them are racists."[48] Although several Black Panthers were freed by the courts due to the weakness of the prosecution case against them, others received lengthy prison terms, joining fellow black radicals, such as Martin Sostre in New York and three members of the Alabama Black Liberation Front, as victims of what one study calls "FBI-engineered convictions."[49]

The Black Panther Party's uncompromising critique of American criminal justice and the incarceration of so many of its leaders helped to attract recruits from within the black prison population. The Black Panthers argued that poor people's crimes against the rich were heroic and positive assertions of black masculinity, challenges to stereotypes of black docility, and a rejection of "white-dominated workplaces" that were "racially humiliating for blacks."[50] From this perspective, convicts were, "potential revolutionaries who would be transformed into political activists through participation in political-education classes and survival programs." In recruiting prisoners, the Black Panthers also tapped into an ongoing prisoners' rights movement that identified prisoners alongside other "victimized minorities" who were struggling to redefine their citizenship status in American society in the postwar decades. Since the 1950s, Black Muslim prisoners had been at the forefront of campaigns against racial and religious discrimination and had won notable victories before the Supreme Court, including in *Cooper v. Pate* (1964), a case that extended to prisoners the constitutional right to contest their treatment in federal courts. Further cases secured prisoners' rights to literary materials and restricted state interference in correspondence between inmates and their attorneys, measures that would facilitate the spread of radical political thought on America's cell blocks.[51]

It was in this context that George Jackson joined the Black Panther Party while incarcerated at San Quentin penitentiary in California. Convicted in 1961 for armed robbery, Jackson received an indeterminate sentence of one year to life that was extended first due to infractions of prison rules and subsequently by his emergence as a revolutionary. During years in solitary confinement he read widely on economics, military affairs, radical literature, and political philosophy and he wrote extensively on issues of colonialism, violence, and revolutionary politics, connecting American imperialism and overseas interventions in the Philippines, the Caribbean, and Vietnam to the domestic systems of capitalist control that maintained the subordination of black Americans. In a letter to his lawyer, Fay Stender, in April 1970, Jackson compared San Quentin to the Nazi concentration camps at Dachau and Buchenwald and described the heightened consciousness of black prisoners he had witnessed during the ten years of his incarceration. "There are still some blacks here who consider themselves criminals," Jackson began, "but not many ... with the time and incentive that these brothers have to read, study, and think, you will find no class or category more aware, more embittered, desperate, or dedicated to the ultimate remedy—revolution."[52]

In 1971, after Jackson had been charged with the murder of a prison guard, he was shot dead during an alleged escape attempt that many of his supporters considered a setup consistent with the objectives of the FBI's war on black America. Responses to the shooting at Attica penitentiary in New York made evident the national influence of Jackson's writings on American convicts. The day after Jackson died, Attica inmates staged a hunger strike over breakfast and days later hundreds occupied the prison's hospital area to protest against inadequate standards of health care. Black Panthers at Attica had previously debated radical politics with black Muslims, the Puerto Rican activists of the Young Lords, and white radicals, but it was only in tribute to Jackson that these disparate groups came together in coordinated activism. Two weeks later, convicts at Attica took 42 prison officers and civilians hostage in an uprising that ended five days later when state police retook the prison by force in an operation that left 43 prisoners and hostages dead. Among the prisoners' demands to end the siege was transportation to a nonimperialist country.[53]

Across the United States in the 1950s and 1960s, African Americans engaged with the institutions of American law enforcement in diverse ways as part of the wider struggle for black freedom. They courted arrest and imprisonment through nonviolent demonstrations, found protection in armed self-defense from white supremacist violence that was tolerated by southern police, fought against police brutality in race riots, and made prisons sites of revolutionary activism. More than a matter of protest tactics, these different approaches to law enforcement reflected varied intellectual critiques of the American criminal justice system among black Americans that reflected long-established traditions in black thought and the different forms that racial oppression and discriminatory law enforcement assumed across the nation.

Civil rights protests had profound implications for the operation of criminal law and the penal system. Building on and directly referencing the criminal procedure cases brought by and on behalf of African Americans in the 1920s to 1940s, a series of Supreme Court rulings in the 1960s extended almost all of the federal due process protections in the Bill of Rights to the actions of state police and courts. In *Mapp v. Ohio* (1961), the Court ruled that evidence obtained by police during an unlawful search was inadmissible under the Fourth Amendment. Further rulings in *Gideon v. Wainwright* (1963), *Escobedo v Illinois* (1964), and *Miranda v. Arizona* (1966) respectively secured defendants' rights to an attorney in noncapital trials and police interrogations, and to be informed of the right to remain silent before questioning. Much of this litigation specifically concerned cases involving black defendants, but African Americans' more significant contribution to the Supreme Court's criminal due process revolution was to reveal the depths of racial injustices and the intransigence of local law officers and political elites that not only called loudly for redress but generated broad public support for the expansion of federal power that the Court decisions encompassed.[54]

Led by the Fifth Circuit Court, the federal judiciary also used the Civil Rights Act in the mid-1960s to increase black participation on southern juries and strike down legislation against interracial cohabitation, sex, and marriage that remained in force in 16 states until 1967. Reversing decisions that had supported anti-miscegenation statutes as late as 1955, in 1964 the Court upheld the appeal of Connie Hoffman, a white woman, and Dewey McLaughlin, a black man from British Honduras, who had been convicted and fined in Florida two years earlier for interracial cohabitation. Three years later, the Court sounded the final death knell for all anti-miscegenation laws in its ruling in *Loving v. Virginia*, a case concerning the 1958 marriage of Richard Loving and Mildred Jeter in Washington DC, and the couple's subsequent arrest in Virginia for violation of the state's laws against interracial matrimony. In a deal with Virginia authorities that they struck to avoid imprisonment, the Lovings pleaded guilty and were banished from the state for 25 years, but on appeal the Supreme Court justices ruled that the state law amounted to, "invidious racial discrimination" in violation of the equal protection clause of the Fourteenth Amendment.[55]

Beyond changes to criminal law, equal employment and Affirmative Action legislation in the 1960s instigated a substantial increase in African American involvement in the administration of law enforcement. American prisons were also slowly desegregated over the following decades and the prisoners' rights movement, along with incidents such as the Attica riot, brought about reforms including expanded educational opportunities, though prison authorities also responded to prisoners' growing activism with repression, racism, and violence. There was, moreover, a cruel irony that even as the terrain of criminal justice served as a vital battlefield on which many of the greatest achievements of the black freedom struggle were won, the repressive place of law enforcement in black life was already being reconstituted for a new era. In 1964, Republican presidential candidate Barry Goldwater linked civil rights to rising crime rates in America in an appeal to southern whites disenchanted with the Democratic Party's support for black equality. The race riots and Black Nationalist movements of the late-1960s strengthened this perception, particularly as they became associated with radical student movements and antiwar protests. In the late-twentieth century, a backlash against the black freedom struggle and the expansion in defendants' rights would lead to a staggering expansion of the American penal system and the mass incarceration of black citizens.

8

The Penal State

America's criminal justice system has deteriorated to the point that it is a national disgrace. Its irregularities and inequities cut against the notion that we are a society founded on fundamental fairness.

—Senator Jim Webb (D-VA), *Parade*, March 29, 2009.

On the evening of January 20, 2009, more than 40 years after he excoriated American law enforcement as an instrument of white oppression in *Look Out Whitey! Black Power's Gon' Get Your Mama!*, SNCC veteran Julius Lester contrasted his experiences of racial injustice with the life of Barack Obama who, the following day, would be inaugurated as the first African American President of the United States. "When I look at Barack Obama," Lester wrote, "I see a man who grew up in a world in which legal racial segregation had become something read about in history classes, a man who does not remember the lynching of Emmett Till, a man who did not put his life at risk so that the words 'with liberty and justice for all' would mean what they say, and I am thrilled that he knew none of that." On the presidential campaign trail in 2007, Obama himself offered a more ambiguous analysis of the legacy of the black freedom struggle. Speaking at Brown Chapel in Selma, Alabama, where wounded marchers had found shelter on Bloody Sunday in 1965, he told an audience of civil rights veterans, "it's because they marched that the next generation hasn't been bloodied so much."[1]

Together, Lester and Obama's broad assessments of African American history since the civil rights movement serve as an insightful verdict on developments in black crime and punishment over the past four decades. Civil rights legislation, selected Supreme Court criminal procedure rulings, and wide-ranging reforms to the police and the courts, including the increasingly routine appointment and promotion of black men and women to the highest positions of American law enforcement, have combined with black political and socioeconomic advances to undermine old forms of systemic and overt discrimination and brutality. Blood still runs on American streets as a consequence of racial violence and law enforcement injustices, but it runs less freely. At the same time, there has been a punitive turn in American society and criminal justice since the 1960s that has targeted and penalized black communities disproportionately and in ways that have served to compromise the achievements and promise of the civil rights era, much as the black codes and convict leasing repressed new black freedoms in the aftermath of the abolition of slavery. Staggering increases in incarceration rates among all Americans have been accompanied by growing racial disparities in the prison population that stem in part from discriminatory policing, prosecutions, and drugs laws and have profoundly damaging economic, political, and social consequences for black communities. Courts have focused on the procedure rather than substance of law enforcement, and legislation prohibiting discrimination on grounds of race has failed to adapt to the evolving forms of racism that characterize the post-civil rights movement era. Moreover, underenforcement of law remains a persistent blight on black communities, compounding high rates of black-on-black violent crime, albeit in ways strongly conditioned by growing class differences among African Americans. This chapter explores these issues first by analyzing how race has informed recent popular understandings and political debate on African American crime and punishment. It then examines three key topics in African American experiences of the criminal justice system since the 1970s: policing, mass incarceration, and the death penalty.

The two worlds of American crime and punishment

In 1996, the independent National Criminal Justice Commission (NCJC) echoed the language of the Kerner Commission nearly 30 years earlier in concluding that "Whites and African-Americans live in completely different worlds when it comes to race and the criminal justice system."[2] The polarizing impact of race on Americans' views of criminal justice had recently been laid bare in public, media, and political responses to two high-profile trials in Los Angeles that concluded in controversial acquittals. In March 1991, officers of the Los Angeles Police Department (LAPD) were captured on film beating Rodney King, a 35-year-old African American man who had been stopped in his car following a high-speed chase. King suffered horrific injuries, including nine skull fractures, but the following year a majority-white jury acquitted four officers charged with using excessive force in securing his arrest. The verdict was met with dismay and anger in black Los Angeles and sparked a week of rioting that left 55 people dead and more than 2000 injured in one of the worst incidents of racial violence in the twentieth century. Whereas a majority of African Americans perceived the acquittal of Rodney King's assailants as evidence that the criminal justice system remained complicit in illegal police brutality, however, whites more often viewed the police violence as a justified response to a threatening suspect who was resisting arrest.

Three years after the Los Angeles riots, the African American former NFL running-back and popular movie star O. J. Simpson was found not guilty of murdering his estranged, white wife, Nicole Brown, and her friend Ronald Goldman. Once more, the case provided striking evidence that "Whites and blacks tend to perceive the criminal justice system in strikingly different terms."[3] For a majority of white Americans, circumstantial evidence and blood samples matching Simpson's DNA found at the scene of the crime left little doubt that Simpson was guilty. Black observers, by contrast, were more often sympathetic to the defense argument that Simpson was the victim of a racist frame-up by the LAPD. Led by Johnnie Cochran, Simpson's expensively assembled team of attorneys placed racial issues at the heart of the trial, drawing on long-standing black experiences of police racism and corruption. In cross-examination, the defense unpicked the racist views of Mark Fuhrman, a detective in the case and key prosecution witness, and also attacked police handling of the crime scene and procedural irregularities that left opportunities for the DNA evidence to be contaminated. They also argued that evidence might have been planted, most famously a glove, almost certainly belonging to Simpson and found at the scene of the crime covered in blood and hair fibers from both Simpson and the victims.[4]

Split-screen television news coverage of jubilant African Americans and despondent whites reacting to the O. J. Simpson verdict emphasized the racial divide in Americans' attitudes toward crime and law enforcement. In many ways, this was a simplistic conclusion that overlooked that a greater number of whites than blacks actually believed that Simpson was innocent and a substantial minority of African Americans thought him guilty.[5] These different perceptions were bound up with class and gender identities and political affiliations, but the significance of such factors was scarcely investigated in a debate fixated on black-white racial difference. On the contrary, analysis and public perceptions of the Rodney King and O. J. Simpson cases were representative of broader popular and academic understandings of the relationship between race, crime, and punishment, which John Hartigan categorizes according to "two narrative frames—white racism and black pathology." In an analysis of the Jena Six case of 2007 in which black students were charged with attempted murder of a white man after nooses were hung from a schoolyard tree in an apparent evocation of lynching, Hartigan explains that African Americans mostly viewed the case as an example of the everyday racism within the criminal justice system, whereas whites tended to attribute it to "social problems—crime, drug use, and teenage pregnancy" that they associated with African Americans.[6]

These distinct narrative frames have diverse roots. They reflect, in part, the weight of history and "the role police played in enforcing the slave codes, Black codes, Jim Crow segregation, and the ultimate form of vigilante justice, lynching."[7] As Michelle Alexander argues, in Jena (see Illustration 8.1) it was only because the nooses evoked the "old-fashioned racism" of lynching that the mainstream media picked up on the "overprosecution" of the black youths, which in itself was entirely unremarkable and unnewsworthy.[8] They are also a product of a "racial narrative of crime" in the media that recent studies suggest is positively related to public concern about crime, belief in the culpability of black offenders, and the association of African Americans with violence. The typical black offender on television news is involved in violent crime and often shown resisting arrest or restrained in police custody, whereas white offenders commonly appear in less threatening contexts. African Americans are also heavily underrepresented in the media as victims of crime and disproportionate news coverage is afforded to interracial violence. The impact of these distinctions is compounded by the disproportionate number of all news stories involving African Americans that concern crime, a failure to locate individual incidents within a broader context of crime trends and structural causes of lawlessness, and the framing of offenders in good versus evil morality narratives that invite support for punitive sanctions as the most effective means of curbing criminal behavior.[9]

Illustration 8.1 Jesse Jackson leads supporters of the Jena 6 on a march to the La Salle Parish Courthouse in Jena, Louisiana, September 20, 2007. Courtesy of Vernan Bryant/Dallas Morning News/Corbis

The potency of race in popular understandings of crime has been recognized, exploited, and reinforced by a succession of presidential candidates since the civil rights era. Building on connections between race, civil rights, and crime that were deeply engrained in American culture, in 1964 Republican presidential candidate Barry Goldwater made law and order a central campaign issue. Four years later, when Richard Nixon won the White House, punitive rhetoric and crime policies were a centerpiece of the Republican Party's successful strategy to win the votes of white southerners disillusioned with the Democratic Party's support for the black freedom struggle. During the 1988 election campaign, a television advertisement in support of George H. W. Bush played on white fears of black crime in highlighting the case of William Horton, a black, convicted murderer in Massachusetts who committed a string of offenses, including raping a young white woman, while released on a weekend furlough program that was supported by the Democratic nominee for president Michael Dukakis. The use of Horton's menacing mugshot and the diminutive name "Willie" in the advertisement was denounced as a cynical racist ploy, but it contributed to destroying the Dukakis campaign. Research indicates, moreover, that more subtle evocations of connections between race and crime remain a staple of American politics. Terms such as "welfare queens" and "inner city" are used as "racial code words" that evoke and reinforce fears of black crime without explicit reference to race.[10]

In a more nuanced and empathetic analysis, Barack Obama also addressed white notions of black criminality in a major speech on race during the 2008 presidential election campaign, describing how his white grandmother once confessed to a, "fear of black men who passed by her on the street." These comments were made in response to criticisms leveled at Obama's relationship with Reverend Jeremiah Wright, Jr., whose fiery sermons included provocative claims about American law enforcement, including allegations "that a racist U.S. government supported the infusion of drugs into black communities, frequently planted evidence against people of color, and preferred to imprison African Americans rather than provide them with the best education." Obama's speech won effusive praise from a wide-spectrum of political commentators and black scholars, but in crafting a message to appeal to white voters, Obama was also criticized for offering "a sanitized version of the United States' history of racial injustice," in which Wright's views were explained as the product of his early experiences of racism in the era before the civil rights movement, rather than a reflection of contemporary racial issues and ongoing inequality. For many black Americans, Wright's comments on crime and punishment were more consistent with their own experiences than Obama acknowledged.[11]

Policing and black communities

In 1980, a race riot erupted in Miami, Florida, following the acquittal of four white officers charged with the murder of Arthur McDuffie, an African American insurance executive beaten to death after he was stopped by police for a traffic violation. The riot occurred in the midst of high rates of black poverty and unemployment that had been exacerbated by the arrival of large numbers of Cuban refugees in the city, but it was mostly a product of black disenchantment with the criminal justice system. Prior to the McDuffie case, a string of white law enforcement officers had escaped without sanction after committing unlawful violence against African Americans, while black officials had recently been convicted on corruption charges.[12] "People like you all, killing us," one black youth explained when asked by a white man the reason for the violence. Three years later, the *Chicago Metro News* editorialized that "[i]n the Black community, police are view[ed] quite often as brutal, an army of occupation, unconcerned and cal-lous, hostile and corrupt." The black newspaper proceeded to list com-mon complaints: "Police are not available when needed"; "Police are racists"; "Police humiliate the men in the community by field inter-rogation and 'stop and frisk' procedures"; "Police do not provide ade-quate protection against crime"; "Police are not representative of the community because they refuse to appoint black officers."[13]

The Miami riot and the complaints about policing in Chicago suggested that little had changed in American law enforcement since the late-1960s. A litany of subsequent cases of police brutality and fatal shootings would reinforce this impression, but there was nonetheless also growing evidence during the 1980s that much about American policing was different from earlier eras. In many cities, policing had become more responsive to African American communities, usually as a result of black political power and African American law enforce-ment personnel serving at the highest levels of command. By 1990, there were 130 black police chiefs across the United States and their appointments contributed to improved communication with black communities traditionally hostile to law enforcement agencies and the reorientation of police priorities toward the interests of black citizens. In Houston, for example, significant reforms in the policing of black neighborhoods were overseen in the 1980s by Lee Patrick Brown, the city's first African American Chief of Police. Brown was part of the 1960s' generation of black officers who integrated American policing. He began his career in San Jose, California, obtained a PhD in crimi-nology from Berkeley, and served as a sheriff in Oregon, before he was appointed public-safety commissioner in Atlanta where he rose to national prominence leading an investigation into the murders of 28 young black men and boys.[14]

Brown arrived in Houston with a mandate for change. Although African American and Latino officers served in the city, powerful white police unions and a conservative council had long kept their numbers small and prospects for promotion bleak. Police relations with minority communities, meanwhile, were torrid, scarred by rou-tine incidents of brutality and discrimination. During an eight-year tenure in Houston, Brown cracked down on police violence, increased hiring and promotion of minority officers, and introduced a series of innovative community-policing programs. Under the Directed Area Responsibility Team (DART) program, for example, officers were assigned to specific neighborhoods where they developed local knowledge and worked with residents to jointly address local problems. DART was backed by Project Oasis, which aimed to improve living conditions so as to discourage crime, "in blighted neighborhoods characterized by vandalism, illegal drugs, burglary, theft, assault, and other crimes." The tactic brought about a marked decline in violent crime in Houston during Brown's tenure.[15]

The election of black mayors across dozens of major American cities in the 1970s and 1980s also impacted positively on policing in African American communities. A study of 170 US cities between 1980 and 1986 found that cities with black mayors—who were usually dependent on black votes—tended to have low rates of unlawful police violence. In Birmingham, Alabama, black political activists were "galvanized" in 1979 by the fatal shooting of Bonita Carter by a white police officer, George Sands, who was neither fired from the force nor indicted. The case proved instrumental in the election, later the same year, of Richard Arrington, Jr., as Birmingham's first black mayor. Cities with black mayors often also had high rates of black police officers and were early adopters of civilian review boards to investigate police violence. In Detroit, for example, complaints of police brutality fell from 2323 in 1975 to 825 in 1982 under the administration of Coleman Young, the city's first black mayor. Young abolished controversial undercover operations that were implicated in a spate of fatal police shootings of African Americans in the early-1970s, and encouraged the appointment and promotion of black officers.[16]

In the 1990s, community policing initiatives proliferated in American cities. The term captured a variety of aims and practices. It implied a proactive role for the police in preventing crime, but also a law enforcement apparatus responsive to the concerns of the public and designed to work with local residents to improve neighborhoods and combat crime.[17] These qualities were evident for a time in New Orleans, a city with the highest murder rate in America in the late-twentieth century. African American police chief Richard Pennington established the Community Orientated Police Squad in 1995 and opened Community Empowerment Centers in the city's most crime-ridden public housing projects. He also worked with the FBI to root out police corruption and brutality that flourished in deprived neighborhoods and he moved detectives out of headquarters and into district police stations to bring them closer to the people they served. As in Houston, the result was a steep decline in the New Orleans murder rate, as well as in accusations of police civil rights violations by 2000, though these trends reversed over the following years.[18]

Despite some statistical evidence of success, community policing has also proved controversial. In many cities, police implemented "broken windows" strategies that targeted "low level" crime as a means to combat more serious offences and improve public safety. Police officials in cities such as Albany and Knoxville recognized the importance of building partnerships with local communities in support of this approach, but often encountered suspicion and hostility, particularly in inner-city neighborhoods and public housing projects where predominantly black populations associated aggressive policing with discriminatory surveillance, harassment, and the criminalization of conduct that in other areas would not elicit a criminal justice response. A study of a community regeneration program in Chicago found that established residents of the predominantly-black North Kenwood-Oakland neighborhood struggled for years to make headway against serious crime problems. They lacked political influence in the city and feared that more police might bring more repressive and even violent policing. When the municipal government sought to revitalize the area, however, new middle-class residents were attracted with promises of safe streets accompanied by new investment and new approaches to law and order. At first, these developments addressed the long-standing crime complaints of old-timers in the neighborhood, but the crime crackdown quickly moved beyond serious violent and property offenses to target "quality of life" issues, which in practice often meant penalizing noncriminal behaviors of the lower classes. These involved, for example, contested ideas about appropriate use of public space, with newcomers particularly objecting to drinking on the streets, loud music, loitering, and barbecuing in parks and on sidewalks.[19]

Across the nation in the 1990s, urban black communities were targeted by new measures introduced in the name of quality of life policing, but which frequently pushed at the boundaries of legality. Ostensibly aimed at urban gang members, but in practice used far more widely, more than 150 cities in the mid-1990s introduced curfews for juveniles. Civil injunctions were also widely employed, primarily in California, to allow courts to levy six-month prison terms and $1000 fines on specified individuals for a range of noncriminal behaviors, including carrying baseball bats and crowbars, loitering on unoccupied properties, climbing over fences, and littering. In 1992, loitering ordinances were used to arrest more than 40,000 people in Chicago, few of whom were subsequently prosecuted for any crime.[20] Most of these arrests concerned mundane offenses, but they could have serious ramifications for the individuals involved. In a study of Duval County, Florida, Jerome Miller found that the "crimes" for which black citizens were most often arrested ranged from drunkenness to driving without a license and "resisting without violence," charges often stemming from police stops-and-searches that commonly targeted minorities. Unable to raise bail, and faced with waiting weeks for a court appearance, these men and women often pleaded guilty at an early hearing that saw them sentenced to time-served, but marked with a criminal record. While community policing can be a "democratizing" innovation that makes law enforcement responsive to the people, therefore, in black inner-city neighborhoods it has also served as a form of colonization that has forced disadvantaged citizens "to choose between racist policing or no policing at all."[21]

In New York City, community policing initiatives in the early-1990s were supplanted by a "zero tolerance" approach to quality of life crime and disorder following the election of Rudolph Giuliani as mayor in 1993. Rather than community engagement, the policy was based on aggressive street policing and stop-and-frisk policies that aimed to reclaim public spaces for "law abiding citizens" through targeting low-level offenses such as graffiti, begging, and minor drug dealing. In practice, the crackdown was more targeted than the rhetoric implied; certain quality of life offenses such as prostitution and gambling were largely unaffected, but misdemeanor marijuana arrests soared, from 812 in 1992 to 51,267 in 2000, as police used the charge to round up individuals suspected of more serious crimes. The crackdown was widely credited by politicians with causing a sharp downturn in felonies—between 1993 and 1997 the number of murders in New York declined by 60 percent and the number of burglaries and robberies by nearly 50 percent—but more recent analyses not only question this causal link, but also argue that aggressive street policing fundamentally compromised the benefits that accrued to poor and minority communities from New York's safer streets. These groups benefited disproportionately from falling crime due to the fact that they comprised the majority of crime victims, but they were also the primary targets of stop-and-frisk tactics and accounted for the vast majority of misdemeanor arrests.[22]

As policing in New York became tougher, so complaints of misconduct and brutality also increased sharply in heavily African American and Latino police precincts. The most serious incidents involved police killings of nonwhite men: three Latino men of African descent were shot dead in two separate incidents in 1994; Abner Louima, a Haitian immigrant, was beaten and sodomized in a police cell in Brooklyn in 1997; Amadou Diallo was shot in 1999, and Patrick Dorismond in 2000. Each case led to investigations and proposals for change from independent commissions, community groups, such as Parents against Police Brutality and Amnesty International, which in a 1996 report found, "a serious problem of police brutality and excessive force" in the New York Police Department and evidence of "marked" racial disparities "in cases involving deaths in custody or questionable shootings." Among the recommendations proposed to combat police violence were moves toward greater civilian oversight, but through the 1990s Giuliani hampered or rejected such reforms and aside from Justin Volpe, sentenced to 30 years for attacking Louima, disciplinary action against abusive officers was rare and usually limited to dismissal from the force. Assessing these cases, political scientist William Lyons argues that zero-tolerance policing in New York had the effect of "privileging the 'illegalities' of powerful public and private leaders and punishing the 'illegalities' characteristic of the least advantaged."[23]

Beyond political ambivalence, unlawful police violence can also stem from the challenging and sometimes dangerous conditions in which police officers often work. Sociologists Ronald Weitzer and Steven Tuch argue that there exists an institutional subculture of distrust toward citizens, especially minority groups and particularly among white officers whose encounters with African Americans are often restricted to hostile or problematic situations in disadvantaged neighborhoods with high crime rates. Such circumstances are conducive to unlawful police conduct due to the relative political weakness of residents to challenge the police and the perception among both police and the wider public that tough law enforcement tactics are justified in "troublesome" neighborhoods even if they impinge on the rights of law-abiding citizens.[24] Among black police officers, race and vocation can create particularly complex affiliations and conflicting loyalties. African American officers have long had strong ties to black community organizations and civil rights groups, yet black officers also identify strongly with institutional cultures that can distance them from black community criticisms of law enforcement.[25]

Color-blind justice?

Racial disparities in American crime statistics provide the most clearly measurable evidence of the different worlds of black and white criminal justice. Consistently, national statistics show that African

Americans are disproportionately victims and perpetrators of crime, stopped and searched by police, arrested, imprisoned, and sentenced to death. In 2009, African Americans accounted for less than 13 percent of the US population, but 28.3 percent of arrests. Black adults were especially overrepresented in arrests for the most serious violent crimes of murder (49.3 percent) and robbery (55.5 percent), as well as drugs offences. Racial differences in rates of imprisonment are equally striking. One in 21 black men was incarcerated in 2008, a figure more than twice the rate for Hispanic men (1 in 54) and more than six times the rate for white men (1 in 136). For young African American men aged between 20 and 34, the incarceration rate was higher still at 1 in 9. Similar patterns were repeated across the female prison population, albeit with lower rates of overall incarceration and lesser disparities between different racial and ethnic groups. Across all age ranges, 1 in 279 black women were incarcerated in 2008, compared with 1 in 658 Hispanic women and 1 in 1064 white women.[26]

These figures are a result of both high rates of black crime and the discriminatory enforcement of criminal laws, but researchers dispute the relative weight that should be attributed to each of these factors. Summarizing recent studies in 2008, Katheryn Russell-Brown argued that "[m]ainstream criminology research leads one to conclude that racial discrimination in the criminal justice system is a historical concept: some discrimination exists, but with the exception of drug offenses, it is neither intentional nor widespread."[27] Noting that most serious black crime is perpetrated against other African Americans, scholars such as Randall Kennedy and Susan Estrich argue that charges of racism in law enforcement are "overblown and counterproductive," and distract attention from the more important issue of how to improve legal protections for law-abiding black victims of crime.[28] Criminologist Alfred Blumstein concurs that efforts to address racial disproportionalities in the American prison population "will have to come from addressing the factors in our society that generate the life conditions that contribute to the different involvement between the races in serious person crimes."[29]

In a series of rulings over the past two decades, the US Supreme Court has given credibility to the notion that high rates of black arrests and imprisonment are a logical reflection of high rates of black crime by consistently refusing to uphold appeals based on evidence of racial discrimination. In subscribing to an ideology of color blindness, the Court focuses on the procedures rather than substance and outcomes of law enforcement and conceives racial discrimination in narrow

terms to include acts with an explicit racist purpose, but not unintentional discriminatory conduct, unconscious racism, or institutionalized practices that have inequitable criminal justice outcomes.[30] In
McCleskey v. Kemp (1987), for example, the Court upheld the death
sentence imposed on Warren McCleskey by a court in Georgia despite
clear evidence of pervasive racial bias in the state's administration of
capital punishment. Lawyers for the condemned presented statistical
evidence that, by a wide margin, executions in Georgia more commonly resulted from cases involving black defendants or white victims than when those racial categories were reversed. They argued
that this racial disparity made the death penalty a cruel and unusual
punishment in violation of the Eighth Amendment. For the Court,
however, statistical evidence of systemic bias was insufficient to over-
turn the death sentence, as it did not prove that racial discrimination had specifically occurred in McCleskey's case.[31] This judgment
assumed that the criminal justice system was essentially color blind
and infected by racial discrimination only in isolated cases through
the unrepresentative malfeasance of individual law officers.[32] In the
1990s and early-twenty-first century, the Court has applied similar
reasoning across a range of policy areas, including jury selection and
drugs enforcement, effectively deeming the discriminatory effects of
law in these areas to be irrelevant and consequently perpetuating judicial outcomes that engrain racial difference and black disadvantage.
The influential black legal scholar Derrick Bell described the situation starkly: "to require the defendant to produce concrete evidence
of discrimination, in effect, is to hold that defendants may almost
never prevail in race discrimination cases .... The Court's 'see no evil'
approach deprives it of any credibility as a vehicle for achieving racial
justice in our society."[33]

Critics of the color-blind interpretation of criminal justice argue
that race can infect the administration of law enforcement in diverse
ways that might be unintentional or subconscious and not apparent in
readily measurable statistical data or qualitative evidence. Case outcomes might, for example, be affected by racial language and imagery
that invokes negative stereotypes of African Americans in the courtroom. They can also reflect the racially disparate impact of facially
race-neutral laws, as well as the discretionary and largely unscruti-
nized work of key criminal justice decision makers such as public
prosecutors, juries, and parole boards. Studies of sexual assault cases
have shown that the categorizations of race, class, gender, and place
used by prosecutors and other legal agents are often evaluative as well

as descriptive and used to justify decision making. Based on "stereotypical characteristics" of the neighborhoods where crimes occur, for example, prosecutors can make assumptions about the likelihood of persuading a jury to convict, which in turn can influence how they choose to proceed with the case. A study of the overrepresentation of African Americans among Pennsylvania prison commitments from 1991 to 1995 found that for prisoners convicted of crimes that allowed for a high degree of prosecutorial discretion, such as larceny and drug law violations, less than 40 percent of the racial disproportionality in commitments was explained by different rates of offending. In Jerome Miller's assessment, such evidence reflects that "[t]he open racial bias that characterized so many courtrooms 30 years ago has been exiled to chambers and courthouse offices."[34]

Samuel Walker uses the term "contextual discrimination" to argue that while the modern criminal justice system is not affected by systematic discrimination, there is evidence of, "obvious disparities based on race and ethnicity," that reflect the diversity of law enforcement practices in different jurisdictions, at different stages of the prosecution process, and in relation to different types of crime.[35] Local political power and the racial makeup of communities, for example, can influence police priorities and the deployment of law enforcement resources. Research has found that arrest rates usually are highest in cities with large black populations and low levels of residential segregation, as these conditions heighten the perception of dominant political groups—usually whites—that social order is threatened by minorities. Practices such as the racial profiling of African American motorists are also closely related to place, with black drivers especially liable to be stopped and searched in predominantly white, suburban neighborhoods.[36] Sampson and Lauritsen further argue that African Americans suffer a cumulative disadvantage in interactions with the criminal justice system that results from "the amplification of initial disadvantages over time." They note, for example, that pronounced racial disparities in juvenile justice have significant ramifications in later life for black adults in their encounters with the police and the courts.[37]

Mass incarceration

The high rates at which African Americans are imprisoned in modern America have both fueled and been compounded by the unprecedented scale of incarceration in the twenty-first century. Rates of imprisonment in the United States were broadly stable from the early-1900s until 1975, but there then began a stark upward trend that continued for almost three decades and was unprecedented in scale in the industrialized world. By 2008, more than 1 percent of the adult American population was incarcerated in county jails or state or federal prisons, amounting to more than 2.3 million people. Including convicts on probation or parole, 7.3 million men and women were under the control of the correctional system, equivalent to more than 3 percent of the entire population. Among African Americans, the figure was three times higher at 9 percent.[38]

Increases in the prison population have only partially and inconsistently been connected to changes in rates of crime. Beginning in the 1960s, rates of violent and property crimes in the United States increased markedly, but since the early-1990s they have declined sharply and currently stand at similar levels as in 1970. The spectacular rise in incarceration rates, by contrast, persisted uninterrupted until the early-2000s and has since continued to push upward to new historic highs even though rates of almost all serious crimes fell by around 40 percent between 1990 and 2000 and by a further 15 percent for violent crime and 16 percent for property crime between 2000 and 2009.[39] It might be argued that these trends are related; there is commonsense logic to the notion that fewer crimes are committed when more criminals are in jail. However, there is little empirical evidence to support this assessment. On the contrary, in different historical periods when incarceration rates have increased, crime rates have variously fallen, risen, and remained stable. In New York City, for example, an 80 percent drop in crime between 1990 and 2009 occurred at the same time as a nearly 50 percent *decrease* in rates of imprisonment. Nationwide, one estimate suggests that, at most, 10 percent of the total fall in crime over the past two decades can be attributed to more punitive law enforcement, but this has been achieved at an extortionate cost to the taxpayer in the building and administration of new prisons, and with devastating consequences in poor and minority communities that are disproportionately represented among the incarcerated. Since the 1980s, both black crime and the percentage of African Americans among all people arrested has declined—developments that might be attributed to the impact of the civil rights movement in promoting "economic and social integration of blacks in American society"—but there has been no comparable fall in racial disparities in rates of imprisonment.[40]

The expansion of the American prison population in the 1970s was driven not by rising rates of crime, but rather by an unlikely political consensus in support of tougher punishments. On the political right, politicians associated criminality and disorder with the counterculture, liberal social upheavals, protest movements, and political turbulence of the 1960s. Denying socioeconomic explanations that crime was a product of society (particularly poverty and discrimination), that were traditionally favored by liberals and the left, politicians such as Ronald Reagan, then Governor of California, conceived crime as the result of individual choices and promoted retributive punishment rather than rehabilitation as the primary goal of the penal system. The Republican attack on the prison status quo coincided with criticisms from progressives and social scientists that rehabilitation programs had not only failed to curb reoffending, but also acted as coercive measures that extended state control over marginal groups. At the same time, the emergence of the victims' rights movement galvanized support for a crackdown on crime from unlikely quarters, including among feminists and African Americans who sought protection from violent and drug-related crime in their respective communities. This context was conducive to the passage of new, punitive legislation that led to more convicts serving longer sentences for a wider range of offenses. Tough new drugs statutes were introduced, along with determinate sentencing, mandatory minimum tariffs, and "three-strikes-and-you're-out" legislation that removed from judges and correctional officers the power to adapt punishments to the particular circumstances of individual offences and offenders. At the same time, parole was reconceived as a system to maintain monitoring of ex-offenders at the termination of their prison sentences rather than a program of regulated early-release and rehabilitation. As a result, the number of parolees returned to custody increased from 1 percent of all prison commitments in 1980 to 35 percent in 2000, with most jailed for technical violations of parole conditions, such as lack of employment or failing to attend a meeting with a parole officer.[41]

The changes in criminal law that have had the most significant impact on the African American population in recent decades concern drugs offenses. In 1973, New York governor Nelson Rockefeller condemned the state's drug treatment programs as failures and introduced the harshest drugs laws in the nation, including life sentences for dealing. The laws had little impact on drug use and by the late-1970s the state's courts and prisons were struggling to cope with the additional caseload, but the policy was widely supported by groups who felt marginalized by the civil rights reforms of the 1960s and the welfare-state model of American government that, in the opinion of one New Yorker who supported the Rockefeller laws, placed "too much emphasis on rights and the various minority groups and not enough on responsibilities and the majority." Several African American leaders supported Rockefeller's reforms, too, hoping they would address the drugs scourge in black communities, but others argued that the legislation was racially targeted and, in practice, allowed police to "round up young black kids, young black boys and put them in concentration camps."[42]

In the 1980s, the Reagan administration made drugs the number one crime concern in America. Inspired by the precedents set in New York, federal funding for drug-related law enforcement soared throughout the 1980s and investment in drug treatment programs fell. State police were given federal financial incentives to focus resources on drugs crimes, including huge investments in training and equipment and the authority to retain seized assets. As a result of the 1986 Drug-Free America Act in particular, the consequences of this realignment in policing fell disproportionately on black communities. The Act drew a significant distinction between crack and powder cocaine offences. Long mandatory minimum sentences were applied for possession of 500 grams of powder cocaine but just 5 grams of crack. This 100:1 differential was justified on account of what at the time were believed to be the more harmful effects of crack use, but because crack was disproportionately distributed in poor, inner-city black and Latino neighborhoods the policy resulted in racial disparities in enforcement as minority offenders were more often arrested, prosecuted, and sentenced to longer terms than whites. African Americans were four times as likely as whites to be arrested for drugs offenses by 1989 and by 1993 accounted for two of every five prisoners in the United States, an increase of more than 50 percent since Reagan entered the White House thirteen years earlier.[43]

Yet it was not only Republicans who embraced the war on drugs. Crime rates in America peaked in 1992, the year that Bill Clinton was elected president, but the tough-on-crime agenda persisted during Clinton's two terms in the White House. The 1994 Violent Crime Control Act was more draconian than any Republican-sponsored legislation. Among its provisions, the Act provided $10 billion of investment for federal prisons, created a range of new capital crimes, and introduced mandatory life sentences, drugs courts, and expanded powers for the FBI and the Drug Enforcement Agency that marked yet another escalation of the drugs war.[44] In the analysis of historian Robert Perkinson, this adoption by Democrats of the key aspects of the Republican law-and-order agenda reflected the "southernization" of American political culture. With the growing political influence of the Sunbelt states since the 1970s, the region's distinct "genealogy" of retributive punishment—which developed in tandem with African American slavery and Jim Crow segregation laws—was writ large across the nation, displacing the penal reform culture that was more rooted in the North and which traditional accounts identify as a defining characteristic of US prison history.[45]

Sociologist Loïc Wacquant also acknowledges the centrality of race to understanding modern American punishment, but emphasizes that its significance is conditioned by class and place. "Inmates," Wacquant argues, are "first and foremost poor people," and he maintains that "middle- and upper-class African Americans are better off under the present penal regime than they were thirty years ago." It is specifically the urban black poor who have been targeted by what Wacquant terms "hyperincarceration," which he contends has come to serve as a replacement for earlier forms of racial control stretching from slavery, through segregation, to urban ghettos. Following the advances of the black freedom struggle in the 1960s and amidst the deindustrialization of the American economy, the mass imprisonment of the inner-city black poor has, in Wacquant's analysis, come to serve as a new mechanism to regulate the black workforce, particularly the young, for casual labor in a deskilled, postindustrial, low-wage economy. Moreover, it disguises the impact of globalization and deindustrialization on minority communities by removing vast numbers of the most disadvantaged Americans from unemployment and poverty statistics. It also legitimizes the deconstruction of the American welfare state, which has proceeded in tandem with prison expansion, deploying punishment as a replacement for social support.[46]

The implications of prison expansion for offenders themselves, their families, and communities are pernicious and serve to entrench preexisting patterns of disadvantage, social instability, and violence. The financial costs of prison are manifold and often borne by inmates' partners, children, and extended family who not only have to survive on a reduced income, but also struggle to support their loved ones in prison, meeting legal fees, buying expensive prison phone cards from monopolistic private providers, and making long trips to distant and isolated correctional facilities in an effort to sustain precious personal relationships. When prisoners are released, they face limited employment opportunities and reduced earning potential that commonly results in temporary and unstable work. They are also ineligible for government-funded social support, such as welfare payments, public housing, and student loans. For the millions of convicts on probation or parole, the terms of their license can compound the struggle to find and hold down a job, and the legacy of a criminal record consequently, "acts like a hidden tax, one that is visited disproportionately on poor and minority families". Beyond these financial burdens, imprisonment systematically destabilizes family relationships, undermining the strong personal bonds and "web of obligations and responsibilities" that might otherwise discourage crime. It also leaves psychological scars on children parted from their parents that are reflected in high-school dropout rates, susceptibility to abuse, and depression. In these and many other ways, mass incarceration contributes to social and cultural conditions that are conducive to crime and violence. In some communities, prison is such a common experience—a right of passage for young black men in some urban neighborhoods—that the "violent ethics of survival" that develop inside penitentiary walls become a code of conduct for ex-offenders after their release.[47]

Mass incarceration has also undermined some of the black political gains of the civil rights era. In most American states, convicted felons can be denied the right to vote not only when incarcerated, but for years after their release from prison and in some cases for life. Jeff Manza and Christopher Uggen offer as a conservative estimate that at the time of the 2004 presidential election 5.3 million Americans were prohibited from voting on account of a felony conviction, of whom 39 percent were ex-felons no longer in custody or under postrelease supervision. A further 34 percent were on probation or parole and only 26 percent were incarcerated. In total, 1-in-40 of the voting age population was unable to vote due to felon disenfranchisement laws, but as a result of the racial disparities in the prison population the figure among African Americans was 1-in-7, a statistic that represents the continuation of legalized forms of voter exclusion that have targeted the black electorate since the antebellum era.[48] In a further link to the past, imprisonment also redistributes populations in ways that compromise black political influence. Although prisoners cannot vote, they are counted for purposes of calculating political representation, but their numbers are added to the tallies of the districts where they are incarcerated rather than their home communities. Mass imprisonment consequently artificially bolsters the political weight of majority-white rural counties where most prison building today occurs at the expense of majority-black urban areas with high rates of offenders.[49]

The racial dynamics of the American penal state are also connected to global politics. In the twenty-first century, the nation-state does not mark the limits of the prison-industrial complex that has grown up since the 1980s as private corporations have taken an ever greater role in the domestic prison system. American prisons are part of what Julia Sudbury calls, "an ever expanding network of penal repression and profit that increasingly defies national borders." The United States sits at the heart of this network, with its foreign policies, support for neoliberal global capitalism, and military and economic influence fuelling expansion in the scope of law enforcement worldwide and generating new markets for the corrections industry, which thrives—as in the United States itself—on the incarceration of people of color.[50] Racialized transnational understandings of the American penal regime have developed with particular urgency since September 11, 2001, as domestic prison policy has become increasingly entangled with global politics and the US-led "War on Terror." The brutalizing treatment of prisoners by American service personnel at Abu Ghraib and Guantanamo Bay, for example, was closely associated with practices tried, tested, and developed in domestic American prisons.[51] Sohail Daulatzai argues that the early-twenty-first century has witnessed the creation of a "transnational carceral imagination," targeted particularly at black, Muslim inmates incarcerated both in America's domestic prisons and global network of detention centers. Considering the abuse of Iraqi, Afghan, and other detainees in US custody in light of the connections between America's global and domestic prisons reveals as hollow the claim that these were anomalous events carried out by rogue individuals. On the contrary, the techniques of control and torture that were practiced at Abu Ghraib and elsewhere have been a common feature of America's domestic prisons over many decades, notably in super maximum security institutions and in the cases of black political prisoners.[52]

The death penalty

Alongside incarceration, increased recourse to the death penalty has also been a feature of the changing penal landscape of the United States since the mid-1970s. That decade marked a watershed in the history of capital punishment in the United States. In the case of *Furman v. Georgia* (1972), the Supreme Court ruled by the closest possible margin of 5 votes to 4 that the death penalty, as then practiced, violated the Eighth Amendment to the US Constitution that prohibits cruel and unusual punishment. As expressed by Justice Potter Stewart, the death penalty was cruel because it was random. There was no reasonable explanation, except for unproven racial bias, as to why most murderers and almost all rapists were not executed but a small minority were. Although the Court's ruling did not rest on evidence of racial discrimination *per se*, Justice William Douglas concurred with Stewart that the death penalty discriminated against "the Negro, and the members of unpopular groups."[53]

In the years before *Furman*, recourse to the death penalty had declined sharply and from 1967 to 1972 no executions were carried out anywhere in the United States. This effective moratorium on executions was the result of a sustained period of campaigning for abolition that was led by the American Civil Liberties Union and the Legal Defense Fund, which broadened its long-standing race-based struggle to save African Americans sentenced to death for rape in the South into a comprehensive attack on the constitutional foundations of capital punishment. While the ruling in *Furman* prolonged the suspension of executions, however, it did not abolish the death penalty altogether. Instead, during the mid-1970s states reformulated their capital punishment procedures in response to the Supreme Court's criticisms. Under the most commonly adopted new legislation, states limited the death penalty to cases of homicide and introduced a separate sentencing stage to the capital prosecution process at which a series of aggravating and mitigating factors would be considered by prosecutors, judges, and jurors to decide whether a particular offender deserved to die. Aggravating circumstances included committing multiple homicides, contract killings, and murders involving torture or committed in the commission of another felony, such as rape or robbery. Mitigating circumstances included whether a convict was a minor at the time of the offense, had mental health problems, or acted in self-defense.[54]

In 1976, in the case of *Gregg v. Georgia*, the Supreme Court upheld the new death penalty policies as a satisfactory corrective to the problems highlighted in *Furman*. This paved the way for America's death chambers to reopen and on January 17, 1977, Gary Gilmore, a white convicted murderer, became the first person executed in the United States for ten years. He was killed by a firing squad in Utah. Executions remained rare until the early-1980s, but thereafter they began to increase significantly and eventually reached a peak of 98 in 1999. Amidst rising rates of violent crime, popular support for the death penalty remained strong and few politicians with designs on national office spoke out against the growing numbers of the dead. Indeed, both *Furman* and *Gregg* had legitimized public opinion as an arbiter of the constitutionality of capital punishment and populist calls from victims and other interest groups subsequently prompted several states to increase the range of aggravating factors that could mandate execution.[55]

In total, 1277 convicts were executed in the United States between 1977 and 2011, of whom 441 (35 percent) were African Americans. As of January 1, 2012, black convicts also comprised 1335 (42 percent) of 3189 inmates on death row across the nation.[56] Notwithstanding the death penalty reforms of the 1970s, an extensive body of research indicates that these figures reflect the persistent impact of race on the prosecution of capital cases. In particular, a series of studies have shown that the race of the victim bears a particularly significant correlation to death penalty decision making. Once all other variables are controlled for, the rate at which capital convicts are sentenced to death is highest in cases involving black defendants and white victims, especially white female victims. Analysis of the more than 100 cases since 1976 in which death row inmates have been exonerated also reveals a higher incidence of wrongful convictions in cases where the accused is black rather than white. These differential outcomes reflect the impact of race on the decisions of prosecutors, the testimony of witnesses, and the composition and deliberations of juries. For example, Lynch and Haney argue that prosecutors, who overwhelmingly are white, make extensive use of peremptory challenges to select trial jurors who are, "disproportionately white, male, older, and more religiously and politically conservative." Research has found that, in comparison with all other jurors, this demographic is least likely to empathize with black defendants and that juries comprising at least five white men are far more likely to impose a death sentence than juries in which women and minorities are more heavily represented.[57]

The racial dynamics of the death penalty are also influenced by the geographical reach of capital punishment. Between 1977 and 2011, 1048 executions (82 percent) were carried out in the South compared with 229 in the rest of the nation. This discrepancy can be explained in part by higher rates of murder in the South and the low quality of defense counsel provided in many southern states for capital defendants. The data is also consistent with a distinct regional culture of violence and punishment in the southern states that has historically targeted African Americans disproportionately. Whereas in most of the Western world, including the northern United States, capital punishment has been restricted since the mid-twentieth century at least in part due to its associations with abusive state power, among southern whites crime and punishment has always been conceived as a highly localized affair and the death penalty consequently remains a cathartic form of popular justice. To an extent, state-by-state death penalty data belies this overarching picture by revealing substantial variations in the incidence of executions across the South. Almost 40 percent (477) of executions between 1977 and 2011 occurred in Texas alone, while Virginia, Oklahoma, Florida, and Missouri accounted for a further 27 percent (344). By contrast, Mississippi has conducted only ten executions in more than 30 years and Kentucky and Tennessee only three and six respectively. Even so, with the South accounting for 11 of the top 12 states ranked by number of executions since the 1970s, the region is today as distinct in terms of capital punishment as it has ever been.[58]

Since 2000, there has been a decline in the annual number of executions in the United States, several states have imposed moratoriums on the death penalty, and a smaller number have abolished the practice altogether. These developments have come about amidst growing concerns about the reliability of guilty verdicts in capital cases, scientific evidence that lethal injection is a "cruel and unusual" form of killing, and the spiraling costs and inefficiency of a system that routinely sees condemned convicts spend decades on death row while appeals slowly work their way through the courts (see Illustration 8.2). Despite these reforms, efforts to address the particular disadvantages of African American defendants within the death penalty system continue to be hampered by *McCleskey*, which has largely closed off the appellate process as a route to racial justice. There have, however, been limited moves at the state level to circumvent *McCleskey's* exclusion of statistical evidence from death penalty appeals. After six years of debate, in 1998 Kentucky passed the nation's first Racial Justice Act that allowed defendants to present evidence that race had probably been a significant factor in the prosecution's decision to seek the death penalty. Eleven years later, North Carolina enacted broader reforms in its own Racial Justice Act that allows for appeals based on statistical evidence of racial disparities in death penalty cases. Although it is too early to assess the effectiveness of this legislation, the North Carolina statute was employed for the first time in early-2012 when a Superior Court judge in Cumberland County reduced the sentence of murder convict Marcus Robinson from death to life without parole, ruling that race

Illustration 8.2 Demonstrators in Atlanta, Georgia, protest the execution of Troy Davis, September 21, 2011. Courtesy of Ed Silvera/Demotix/ Demotix/Demotix/Corbis

Note: Davis was killed by lethal injection for the 1989 murder of police officer Mark MacPhail despite grave doubts about the safety of his conviction.

had been "a materially, practically and statistically significant factor" in jury selection at Robinson's 1994 trial.[59]

In 2003, on the 30th anniversary of the passage of the Rockefeller drug laws, a coalition of drug policy reform activists and the Hip-Hop community formed Countdown to Fairness, an organization committed to raising awareness of the drug war's devastating impact on minority offenders and communities and to advocate for repeal. Six years later, Governor David Paterson signed into law reforms including the repeal of mandatory minimum sentences for low-level drug possession offenses and the expansion of drug treatment programs. Within 12 months, approximately 1000 fewer people were jailed in New York as a result of these reforms and 327 drugs offenders in custody had been resentenced and released from prison.[60] Once more following New York's lead on drugs policy, in August 2010 Congress passed the Fair Sentencing Act to eliminate mandatory minimum sentences for crack possession at the federal level and reduce from a ratio of 100-to-1 to 18-to-1 the amount of crack relative to powder cocaine that invokes possession prosecutions under federal law. A year later, on June 30, 2011, the US Sentencing Commission voted to apply the new laws retrospectively in a move that promised to reduce the sentences of 12,000 federal prisoners, more than 10,000 of whom were African Americans. Welcoming the decision, the National Association for the Advancement of Colored People called it an opportunity to "begin to mend the mistrust which has resulted between the African American community and our criminal justice system due to the disproportionate and disparate incarceration of black men and women."[61]

Like the racial justice acts in Kentucky and North Carolina, these recent reforms of America's drugs laws represent race conscious lawmaking consistent with former federal judge and historian A. Leon Higginbotham's assertion that "[r]ace consciousness by itself is not an evil but rather a reality that must be recognized even as America hopes to be and continues to strive to be a nation in which the color of one's skin is of no consequence."[62] The laws also highlight the effectiveness of protest campaigns for criminal justice reform, which have been remade in recent decades in the same way that forms of racial oppression through law enforcement have themselves adopted new guises since the civil rights movement. As those earlier protest movements—against slavery, convict leasing, lynching, and segregation— were able to exploit favorable social, economic, and political contexts to achieve change, so the current economic crisis, which places the high costs of mass incarceration under unprecedented scrutiny, today provides more encouragement for far-reaching reforms of the American penal system than at any time in a generation.

Epilogue: Remembrance, Justice, and Reconciliation

In June 2007, James Seale, a reputed member of the Ku Klux Klan, was sentenced to life in prison for the 1964 kidnap and murder of two black teenagers in Mississippi: Henry H. Dee and Charles E. Moore. Seale was the latest of more than 20 white men convicted since the mid-1990s of racially motivated killings perpetrated in the civil rights era. New investigations of these crimes were prompted by pressure from victims' families and civil rights organizations, as well as journalists and documentary makers. In 2008, the drive to secure justice for past victims of racially motivated crimes received explicit federal support with the passage of the Emmett Till Act creating new FBI offices to work with local law enforcement to investigate and prosecute unsolved cases from before 1970. The legislation was sponsored by John Lewis, the Democratic congressman for Georgia and civil rights veteran, and signed into law by Republican president George W. Bush.[1]

The prosecution of men like Seale is an important step in modern America's confrontation with its violent racial past. Convictions secured in the present can provide a measure of justice for victims' families and offer a forum for individuals, communities, and the state to recognize the occurrence of past crimes and attribute some culpability. In turn, this process can build faith in, and influence, practices of law enforcement in the present in ways conducive to justice, equality, and social cohesion. As Rita Schwerner Bender has argued, however, the belated prosecution of men accused of racially motivated crimes committed decades ago, while important, is not a panacea for the injustices of the past. Bender's husband, Michael Schwerner, was one of three civil rights workers murdered by Klansman Edgar Ray Killen in Mississippi in 1964. When Killen stood trial three years later, the jury failed to reach a verdict, but in 2004 the case was reopened and Killen was convicted on three counts of manslaughter for which he was sentenced to a total of 60 years in prison. Bender has argued that prosecuting individual perpetrators strips criminal offences of their broader context and negates the role of others who facilitated, organized, or participated in racial violence in the past. Very often this includes state officials, such as police officers who failed to protect victims, district attorneys who conducted inadequate investigations and prosecutions, and the media, which reported the crimes narrowly, focusing on the alleged perpetrators rather than the systemic roots of injustice. In reality, thousands of white people in states like Mississippi were complicit in a conspiracy of silence about the pervasive racial violence in their midst. Sensational trials of "evil" individuals obscure this silence and the routine banality of most racial injustice that it accompanied. They suggest instead that discrimination in the legal system was (and is) exceptional and a thing of the past, a notion only reinforced by the 1970-cutoff date established by the Emmett Till Act for federal funding to investigate unsolved civil rights murders.[2]

In focusing on black victims of crime alone, the reopening of civil rights era cold cases also overlooks the fate of those African American defendants who were falsely convicted of crimes against whites and abused or killed in custody. This neglect reinforces the punitive rhetoric and vilification of minority criminals that characterizes mainstream political debate on issues of crime and punishment in America today. In contrast to cases involving black victims, remembering and correcting the wrongs of the criminal justice system as perpetrated against black defendants and prisoners requires a far more problematic engagement with current issues that cannot so readily be incorporated into an uplifting history of American racial progress. It demands, for example, consideration of the wildly disproportionate rates at which African Americans are imprisoned and executed in the twenty-first century, the impact of mass incarceration on black and minority communities, and incidents of police brutality. Selective engagement with some aspects of the history of African American crime and punishment but not others therefore allows politicians, cultural commentators, and ordinary Americans to condemn racial injustices of the past while standing mute and even endorsing the current, deeply racialized regime of American law enforcement.

In recent years, the United States has engaged with past incidents of racial violence and injustice perpetrated against African Americans through many other acts of recovery, remembrance, and reconciliation that reveal a nation still divided by issues of race and law enforcement in the present as well as by confrontations with racial injustices of the past. Across the South since the 1990s, a series of "truth-telling" commissions have investigated race riots, lynchings, and murders. As South Africa recognized in establishing a Truth and Reconciliation Commission in the aftermath of apartheid, confronting past injustice through the ordinary processes of the legal system can reinforce existing social divisions by creating "a winner and a loser," who remain "divided afterward as they were before."[3] Truth-telling commissions, by contrast, are less confrontational and not constrained by the processes and narrower aims of criminal prosecutions. They therefore hold out the opportunity not just to correct specific past injustices, but to rewrite what Ronald Walters calls the "broad view" of history in a way that can serve as a basis for sustainable change. For example, Southern Truth and Reconciliation (STAR), founded at Emory University in Atlanta in 2003, promotes education and restorative justice as mechanisms for processing "incidents of racial and ethnic violence" and forming "more inclusive, whole, and functional" communities. Similarly, the Mississippi Truth Project works to "bring to light racially motivated crimes and injustices" perpetrated in the state from 1945 to 1975. In 2010, the Project began a statewide program to capture oral histories of the period that challenged a claim by the then Governor of Mississippi, Haley Barbour, that the conviction of Edgar Ray Killen had provided "closure" on the crimes of the civil rights era.[4]

The work of commissions established to investigate past acts of racial violence has sometimes been controversial. In Greensboro, North Carolina, a commission established to investigate the 1979 murder of five black communist organizers by Ku Klux Klansmen and the subsequent acquittal of the killers by an all-white jury was opposed by the city council and its work disrupted by illegal wiretapping and media leaks that "jeopardized" public hearings.[5] There were also significant political divisions in Oklahoma when a commission recommended that reparations be paid to the 118 known survivors of the 1921 Tulsa race riot. In 2001, the Oklahoma legislature passed a Reconciliation Act that acknowledged the riot's "staggering cost" to the black community, authorized medals for the riot survivors, and formed committees to design a memorial and assist in economic development and scholarships for descendants of riot victims, but it declined to fund this work or to pay compensation. This outcome contrasted with events in Florida, where the state paid $2 million in 1994 to survivors and descendants of the victims of a 1923 massacre in which almost the entire, predominantly-black town of Rosewood was burned to the ground and at least six and possibly dozens of African Americans were killed. The Tulsa riot arguably presented the stronger case for reparations, as it was instigated by local police officers and whites at the time had acknowledged the justice of African Americans' claims for redress. Nonetheless, in an indication of the continuing sensitivity of the history of white violence against African Americans, a recent analysis suggests that the Rosewood claim for financial compensation was the more successful because it was framed as a case about the violation of property rights rather than racial injustice.[6]

In early-2000, a collection of lynching photographs became the basis for "Without Sanctuary," an exhibition hosted initially at the Roth Horowitz gallery in New York City and later taken to Pittsburgh and Atlanta where it attracted tens of thousands of visitors. The photographs were also published in a glossy, coffee-table book and can now be viewed online. The collector, James Allen, hoped the material would encourage a "probing enquiry" of America's violent racial past, but he was far from certain that his goal was achieved. He often found instead that "[w]hite people feel guilty and reticent; black people look at these pictures and just get angry." In recognition of the especially raw emotions that the exhibition touched in the South, the postcards were displayed in Atlanta at the Martin Luther King Jr., National Historic Site where they were presented alongside artifacts and texts detailing interracial resistance to lynching intended to promote a constructive model for racial progress. Even so, in an otherwise positive review, historian Grace Hale noted the silences that remained in the display, questioning why visitors learned the names of the dead, but not the living, the black victims of lynching, but not the white perpetrators. Without this information, which in many cases is readily available, Hale argued that "viewers are left with an exhibit that is too close to the spectacle created by the lynchers themselves," and which presents victimhood as a defining characteristic of blackness. Moreover, by depicting whites as passive bystanders rather than perpetrators of murder, the postcards obfuscate the centrality of violence to racial domination.[7]

"Without Sanctuary" motivated Mary Landrieu, Democratic Senator for Louisiana, to introduce a resolution in the US Senate apologizing to the victims of lynching and their descendents for that body's failure to enact anti-lynching legislation in the first half of the twentieth century. Passed by voice vote on June 13, 2005, the resolution was "offered in the spirit of true repentance," and as a basis "on which improved racial relations" could be forged. Landrieu called it "a tribute to the endurance of the African American family," and Abraham Foxman, national director of the Anti-Defamation League, commended the Senate "for finally recognizing both the symbolic and contemporary importance of criminalizing this heinous practice," but others questioned the apology's significance. Julianne Malveaux, writing in *USA Today*, called it "a meaningless gesture unless it motivates a tangible and corrective course of action for our nation," while Representative Mel Watt, Chair of the Black Congressional Caucus, noted that it did "nothing substantive to compensate the victims or their families." Meanwhile, political commentator and author Earl Hutchinson highlighted that states' rights arguments similar to those that had been deployed against anti-lynching legislation in the 1930s and 1940s were used by House Republicans as recently as 2004 to impede the expansion of federal hate crimes laws. In the analysis of historian Vinay Lal, the apology, like other attempts to grapple with America's history of racial violence in the courts and legislative chambers, was "an expedient show of repentance" designed "to create some semblance of satisfaction among America's minorities" amidst the persistent injustices of the present.[8]

In January 2010, after the African American professor Henry Louis Gates, Jr. was arrested for disorderly conduct by police investigating if he had broken into his own home, Barack Obama criticized the arrest as "stupid"—a comment he would later retract—and noted that there is a "long history in this country of African Americans and Latinos being stopped by law enforcement disproportionately." Never in that long history had a white cop and a black suspect sat down to resolve their differences over a beer in the White House Rose Garden, as Gates and Officer Crowley did at Obama's invitation. Such symbolic gestures are important to the nation's ongoing struggle to understand the unique legacies of crime and punishment in African American history. As with cold cases, truth commissions, and exhibitions of lynching photographs, however, the power of such "teachable moments" is compromised without recognition that the history of racist American law enforcement does not resonate in the present only in exceptional and isolated incidents, but rather pervades and underpins the entire machinery, administration, and culture of criminal justice and the engagement of all Americans with crime and the criminal law.

Notes

Introduction

1. R. Kennedy (1997) *Race, Crime, and the Law* (New York: Pantheon Books); T. Sowell cited in K. W. Crenshaw et al. eds (1995) *Critical Race Theory: The Key Writings that Shaped the Movement* (New York: The New Press), 103; R. J. Sampson and J. L. Lauritsen (1997) "Racial and Ethnic Disparities in Crime and Criminal Justice in the United States," *Crime and Justice* 21, 355; P. Butler (2010) "One Hundred Years of Race and Crime," *Journal of Criminal Law & Criminology* 100.3, 1051–4.
2. D. Bell (2000) *Race, Racism, and American Law* (New York: Little Brown); A. L. Higginbotham, Jr. (1992) *Shades of Freedom: Racial Politics and Presumptions of the American Legal Process* (Oxford: Oxford University Press), xxiii–xxiv and 7–17; W. J. Stuntz (2010) *The Collapse of American Criminal Justice* (Cambridge, MA: Belknap), 5–7; D. M. Provine (2007) *Unequal under Law: Race in the War on Drugs* (Chicago: University of Chicago Press); G. J. Browne-Marshall (2008) *Race, Law, and American Society, 1607 to Present* (New York: Taylor & Francis), xxiii; M. Alexander (2010) *The New Jim Crow: Mass Incarceration in the Age of Colorblindness* (New York: New Press), 12–15; D. M. Oshinsky (1996) *"Worse than Slavery": Parchman Farm and the Ordeal of Jim Crow Justice* (New York: Free Press); D. Blackmon (2008) *Slavery by Another Name: the Re-Enslavement of Black People in America from the Civil War to World War II* (New York: Doubleday).
3. J. Unnever and S. Gabbidon (2011) *A Theory of African American Offending: Race, Racism, and Crime* (New York: Routledge), xvi–xvii; J. Hartigan (2010) *What Can You Say? America's National Conversation on Race* (Palo Alto, CA: Stanford University Press), 63.

1 The Slaveholders' Rule

1. H. G. Gutman (2003) *Slavery and the Numbers Game: A Critique of Time on the Cross* (Urbana: University of Illinois Press), 22–4.
2. H. T. Catterall, ed. (1968) *Judicial Cases Concerning American Slavery and the Negro, Volume II* (New York: Octagon), 57.
3. D. Brown and C. Webb (2007) *Race in the American South: From Slavery to Civil Rights* (Edinburgh: Edinburgh University Press), 126.

4. A. Kulikoff (1986) *Tobacco and Slaves: The Development of Southern Cultures in the Chesapeake, 1680–1800* (Chapel Hill: University of North Carolina Press), 132, 140–1; I. Berlin (2003) *Generations of Captivity: a History of African American Slaves* (Cambridge: Harvard University Press), 117; H. C. Frazier (2004) *Runaway and Freed Missouri Slaves and those who Helped Them, 1763–1865* (Jefferson: McFarland), 185; I. Berlin (1974) *Slaves without Masters: the Free Negro in the Antebellum South* (New York: Oxford University Press), 137 and 174–81.

5. The literature on black life in the antebellum South is voluminous. For an introduction, see D. B. Davis (2006) *Inhuman Bondage: The Rise and Fall of Slavery in the New World* (New York: Oxford University Press), 193–204.

6. A. E. Kaye (2007) "Neighborhoods and Nat Turner: The Making of a Slave Rebel and the Unmaking of a Slave Rebellion," Journal of the Early Republic 27.4, 705–20.

7. L. W. Bergad (2007) *The Comparative Histories of Slavery in Brazil, Cuba, and the United States* (Cambridge: Cambridge University Press), 234–6.

8. P. J. Schwarz (1988) *Twice Condemned: Slaves and the Criminal Law of Virginia, 1705–1865* (Baton Rouge: Louisiana State University Press), 255.

9. C. B. Dew (1975) "Black Ironworkers and the Slave Insurrection Panic of 1856," *Journal of Southern History* 41.3, 321–38.

10. N. T. Jones (1991) *Born a Child of Freedom, Yet a Slave: Mechanisms of Control and Strategies of Resistance in Antebellum South Carolina* (Middletown: Wesleyan University Press), 24; W. Dusinberre (1996) *Them Dark Days: Slavery in the American Rice Swamps* (Athens: University of Georgia Press), 123.

11. E. D. Genovese (1976) *Roll, Jordan, Roll: the World the Slaves Made* (New York: Vintage), 608, 617, 657.

12. M. Tadman (1996) *Speculators and Slaves: Masters, Traders, and Slaves in the Old South* (Madison: University of Wisconsin Press), xxx.

13. R. Follett (2007) *The Sugar Masters: Planters and Slaves in Louisiana's Cane World, 1820–1860* (Baton Rouge: University Press of Louisiana), 141–3.

14. Schwarz, *Twice Condemned*, 237.

15. F. Douglass (1892) *The Life and Times of Frederick Douglass* (Boston), 140; A. Lichtenstein (1988) "'That Disposition to Theft, with Which They Have Been Branded': Moral Economy, Slave Management, and the Law," *Journal of Social History* 21.3, 413–40.

16. S. M. H. Camp (2004) *Closer to Freedom: Enslaved Women and Everyday Resistance in the Plantation South* (Chapel Hill: University of North Carolina Press); A. Kaye (2007) *Joining Places: Slave Neighborhoods in the Old South* (Chapel Hill: University of North Carolina Press).

17. Gutman, *Slavery and the Numbers Game*, 38.

18. F. Douglass (2008) *My Bondage and My Freedom* (Stilwell, KS: Digireads), 29.

19. C. Harper (1860) "Slavery in the Light of Social Ethics: Influence of Slavery on Social Life," in E. N. Elliott ed. *Cotton is King, and Pro-Slavery Arguments: Comprising the Writings of Hammond, Harper, Christy, Stringfellow, Hodge, Bledsoe, and Cartwright, on this Important Subject* (Augusta), 572.

20. C. Tomlins (2010) *Freedom Bound: Law, Labor, and Civil Identity in Colonizing English America, 1580–1865* (Cambridge: Cambridge University Press), 417; I. Berlin (1998) *Many Thousands Gone: The First Two Centuries of Slavery in North America* (Cambridge, MA: Belknap), 17–28.

21. K. M. Brown (1996) *Good Wives, Nasty Wenches and Anxious Patriarchs: Gender, Race, and Power in Colonial Virginia* (Chapel Hill: University of North Carolina Press), 107–36.

22. T. D. Morris (1996) *Southern Slavery and the Law, 1619–1860* (Chapel Hill: University of North Carolina Press), 163–5; James Henry Hammond to Thomas Clarkson, 1845, In *Selections from the Letters and Speeches of the Hon. James Henry Hammond* (1866), 142.

23. M. J. Hindus (1976) "Black Justice under White Law: Criminal Prosecutions of Blacks in Antebellum South Carolina," *Journal of American History* 63.3, 132; Morris, *Southern Slavery and the Law*, 183; *Columbus Enquirer* (GA), March 20, 1858; *Savannah Republican* reprinted in *Daily Chronicle & Sentinel*, (Augusta, GA) February 8, 1857. See also A. Fede (1985) "Legitimized Violent Slave Abuse in the American South, 1619–1865," *American Journal of Legal History* 29.2, 122n70.

24. J. B. Wahl (1997) "Legal Constraints on Slave Masters: The Problem of Social Cost," *American Journal of Legal History* 41.1, 8.

25. *Frederick Douglass' Paper* (Rochester, NY), December 23, 1853.

26. Kaye, *Joining Places*, 51. Allston cited in Charles Joyner (1986) *Down by the Riverside: A South Carolina Slave Community* (Urbana: University of Illinois Press), 53; D. W. Blight (2007) *A Slave No More: Two Men who Escaped to Freedom* (Orlando: Harcourt), 62.

27. Moses Roper (1838) *A Narrative of the Adventures and Escape of Moses Roper, from American Slavery: Electronic Edition* (Philadelphia), 24; Charles Ball (1859) *Fifty Years in Chains, or, The Life of an American Slave* (Indianapolis), 409; Norrece T. Jones, Jr. (2003) "Rape in Black and White: Sexual Violence in the Testimony of Enslaved and Free Americans," in W. D. Jordan ed. *Slavery and the American South* (Jackson: University Press of Mississippi), 93–108.

28. B. Wyatt-Brown (2007) *Southern Honor: Ethics and Behavior in the Old South* (Oxford: Oxford University Press), 14 and 364; E. L. Ayers (1984) *Vengeance and Justice: Crime and Punishment in the 19th Century American South* (Oxford: Oxford University Press), 18.

29. P. D. Morgan (1998) *Slave Counterpoint: Black Culture in the Eighteenth Century Chesapeake and Lowcountry* (Chapel Hill: University of North Carolina Press), 259–94.

30. Chancellor Harper, "Slavery in the Light of Social Ethics," 579; Gutman, *Slavery and the Numbers Game*, 38; Joyner, *Down by the Riverside*, 54; A Small Farmer, "Management of Negroes," and H. N. McTyeire, "Plantation Life—Duties and Responsibilities," in J. O. Breeden ed. (1980) *Advice Among Masters: the Ideal in Slave Management in the Old South* (Greenwood Press), 84–7; G. McNair (2009) *Criminal Injustice: Slaves and Free Blacks in Georgia's Criminal Justice System* (Charlottesville: University of Virginia Press), 84; F. Bremer (1853) *The Homes of the New World: Impressions of America* (London), 404; W. J. Anderson (1857) *Life and Narrative of William J. Anderson* (Chicago), 22; Dusinberre, *Them Dark Days*, 156.

31. A. J. Gross (2006) *Double Character: Slavery and Mastery in the Antebellum Southern Courtroom* (Athens: University of Georgia Press), 72.

32. S. Green (2009) "State v. Mann Exhumed," *North Carolina Law Review* 87.3, 701–55; S. E. Hadden (2001) "Judging Slavery: Thomas Ruffin and *State v. Mann*" in D. Nieman and C. Waldrep eds *Local Matters: Race, Crime, and Justice in the Nineteenth-Century South* (Athens: University of Georgia Press), 1–28; *James v. Carper* (1857), *Judicial Cases concerning Slavery* vol. 2, 562–3; J. D. Martin (2004) *Divided Mastery: Slave Hiring in the American South* (Cambridge: Harvard University Press), 122.

33. W. L. Andrews (1993) "Introduction," in *William Johnson's Natchez: The Ante-Bellum Diary of a Free Negro* (Baton Rouge: Louisiana State University Press), 56–62.

34. F. L. Olmsted (1860) *The Cotton Kingdom: a Traveller's Observation on Cotton and Slavery in the American Slave States*, 351; E. R. West (2004) *Chains of Love: Slave Couples in Antebellum South Carolina* (Urbana: University of Illinois Press), 57–60; R. J. Fraser (2007) *Courtship and Love among the Enslaved in North Carolina* (Jackson: University Press of Mississippi), 52–68.

35. S. E. Hadden (2001) *Slave Patrols: Law and Violence in Virginia and the Carolinas* (Cambridge: Harvard University Press), 106–10.

36. Works Progress Administration (WPA) (1941) *Slave Narratives: A Folk History of Slavery in the United States From Interviews with Former Slaves*, vol. XIV, South Carolina, part 1 (Washington, DC), 38 and vol. IV, Georgia, part 4, 57.

37. WPA, *Slave Narratives*, vol. II, Arkansas, part 3, 35 and 294; McNair, *Criminal Injustice*, 48; Hadden, *Slave Patrols*, 104.

38. J. Forret (2006) *Race Relations at the Margins: Slaves and Poor Whites in the Antebellum Southern Countryside* (Baton Rouge: Louisiana State University Press), 115; WPA, *Slave Narratives*, vol. xiv, South Carolina, part 1, 260; McNair, *Criminal Injustice*, 48–50; Olmsted, *A Journey in the Back Country*, 476.

39. D. C. Rousey (1996) *Policing the Southern City: New Orleans, 1805–1889* (Baton Rouge: Louisiana State University Press), 13–28.

40. H. M. Henry (1914) *The Police Control of the Slave in South Carolina* (Emory, VA), 49; B. C. Wood (1987) "Prisons, Workhouses, and the Control of Slave Labour in Low Country Georgia, 1763 to 1815," *Slavery and Abolition* 8.3, 261–62.

41. J. M. Campbell (2007) *Slavery on Trial: Race, Class, and Criminal Justice in Antebellum Richmond, Virginia* (Gainesville, Florida), 30; S. K. McGoldrick (2001) "The Policing of Slavery in New Orleans," *Journal of Historical Sociology* 14.1, 411–12.

42. C. H. Latimore IV (2012) "*A Step Closer to Slavery? Free African Americans: Industrialization, Social Control and Residency in Richmond City 1850–1860*," *Slavery and Abolition*, 33.1, 119–37; E. L. Wong (2009) *Neither Fugitive nor Free: Atlantic Slavery, Freedom Suits, and the Legal Culture of Travel* (New York: New York University Press), 183–239.

43. Jeff Forret (2004) "Slaves, Poor Whites, and the Underground Economy of the Rural Carolinas," *Journal of Southern History* 70.4, 824; Forret, *Race Relations at the Margins*, 156.

44. Frederick Law Olmstead, *The Cotton Kingdom*, 253.

45. Grady v. State (1852), in Catterall, *Judicial Cases concerning Slavery*, III, 31. Camp, *Closer to Freedom*, 90–1.

46. WPA, *Slave Narratives*, vol. II, Arkansas, part 3, 253.

47. J. D. Green (1864) *Narrative of the Life of J. D. Green, A Runaway Slave, from Kentucky* (Huddersfield), 32–5.

48. S. May (1861) *The Fugitive Slave Law and its Victims* (New York: Anti-Slavery Society), 3–4; N. Brandt and Y. K. Brandt (2007) *In the Shadow of the Civil War: Passmore Williamson and the Rescue of Jane Johnson* (Columbia: University of South Carolina Press), 7–8; Wong, *Neither Fugitive nor Free*, 167–8.

49. S. J. Basinger (2003) "Regulating Slavery: Deck-Stacking and Credible Commitment in the Fugitive Slave Act," *Journal of Law, Economics, and Organization* 19.2, 338; R. J. M. Blackett (2009) "Dispossessing Massa: Fugitive Slaves and the Politics of Slavery after 1850," *American Nineteenth Century History* 10.2, 120; S. Lubet (2010) *Fugitive Justice: Runaways, Rescuers, and Slavery on Trial* (Cambridge: Harvard University Press), 5.

50. P. Finkelman (1997) *Dred Scott v. Sandford: A Brief History with Documents* (Boston: Bedford Books), 1–36.

2 Slavery and the Criminal Law

1. H. Ammon (1990) *James Monroe, the Quest for National Identity* (Charlottesville: University Press of Virginia), 189; D. R. Egerton (1993) *Gabriel's Rebellion: The Virginia Slave Conspiracies of 1800 and 1802*

(Chapel Hill: University of North Carolina Press); Thomas Jefferson to James Monroe, September 20, 1800, in P. L. Ford ed. (1905) *The Works of Thomas Jefferson*, vol. IX, 1799–803 (New York), 146.

2. Figures calculated from *Executions in the U.S. 1608–2002: The Espy File*, http://www.deathpenaltyinfo.org/executions-us-1608-2002-espy-file, date accessed August 15, 2011.

3. *The State v. Ben, a slave* (1821) cited in J. D. Wheeler (1837) *A Practical Treatise on the Law of Slavery* (New Orleans), 205.

4. R. L. Paquette (2009) "'A Horde of Brigands?' The Great Louisiana Slave Revolt of 1811 Reconsidered," *Historical Reflexions* 35.1, 77–8.

5. D. J. Flanigan (1987) *The Criminal law of Slavery and Freedom, 1800–1868* (New York: Garland), 136.

6. *State v. Benjamin Scott* (1829) in Catterall, *Judicial Cases*, vol. 2, 341.

7. J. B. O'Neall (1848) *The Negro Law of South Carolina*, 35; M. S. Hindus (1980) *Prison and Plantation: Crime, Justice, and Authority in Massachusetts and South Carolina, 1767–1878* (Chapel Hill: University of North Carolina Press), 154; Henry, *The Police Control of the Slave*, 59–60.

8. Wheeler, *A Practical Treatise on the Law of Slavery*, 213; Morris, *Southern Slavery and the Law*, 215; McNair, *Criminal Injustice*, 88, 93; H. C. Frazier, *Slavery and Crime in Missouri, 1773–1865* (Jefferson: McFarland), 87.

9. *State v. Patrick (a slave)*, in Catterall, *Judicial Cases*, vol. II, 199.

10. *Anthony (a slave) v. State* (1851), in Catterall, Judicial *Cases*, vol. III, 26.

11. P. Bardaglio (1994) "Rape and the Law in the Old South: Calculated to Excite Indignation in Every Heart," *Journal of Southern History* 60.4, 762–63.

12. G. M. Stroud (1827) *A Sketch of the Laws Relating to Slavery in the Several States of the United States of America* (Philadelphia), 100; W. Goodell (1853) *The American Slave Code in Theory and Practice* (New York), 309.

13. E. Olson (1944) "The Slave Code in Colonial New York," *Journal of Negro History* 29.2, 150.

14. A. E. K. Nash (1970) "Fairness and Formalism in the Trials of Blacks in the State Supreme Courts of the Old South," *Virginia Law Review* 56.1, 66 and A. E. K. Nash (1970) "A More Equitable Past? Southern Supreme Courts and the Protection of the Antebellum Negro," *North Carolina Law Review* 48, 237–8.

15. Nash, "Fairness and Formalism," 79.

16. R. E. Schiller (1992) "Conflicting Obligations: Slave Law and the Late Antebellum North Carolina Supreme Court," *Virginia Law Review* 78, 1222.

17. Schiller, "Conflicting Obligations," 1224–5.

18. Nash, "Fairness and Formalism," 81; W. E. Wiethoff (2002) *The Insolent Slave* (Columbia: University of South Carolina Press), 6.

19. Flanigan, *The Criminal Law of Slavery*, 138.

20. McNair, *Criminal Injustice*, 108–11.

21. A. F. Howington (1986) *What Sayeth the Law: the Treatment of Slaves and Free Blacks in the State and Local Courts of Tennessee* (New York: Garland), 210–12; McNair, *Criminal Injustice*, 107, 167; Ayers, *Vengeance and Justice*, 134; Hindus, *Prison and Plantation*, 144; calculated from Schwarz, *Twice Condemned*, 41–42.

22. R. G. McPherson (1960) "Georgia Slave Trials, 1837–1849," *American Journal of Legal History* 4.3, 269–71; *Carolina Observer* (Fayetteville, NC) 28 May, 1829; M. Wayne (2001) *Death of an Overseer: Reopening a Murder Investigation from the Plantation South* (Oxford: Oxford University Press); G. McNair (2009) "*Slave Women*, Capital Crime and Criminal Justice in Georgia," *Georgia Historical Quarterly* 93, 135–58.

23. M. P. Johnson (2001) "Denmark Vesey and His Co-Conspirators," *William and Mary Quarterly* 58.4, 938–42; *Kinloch v. Harvey* (1830), in Catterall, *Judicial Cases* vol. 2, 341; R. L. Paquette (2004) "From Rebellion to Revisionism: the Continuing Debate about the Denmark Vesey Affair," *The Journal of the Historical Society* 4.3, 298–300; J. O'Neil Spady (2011) "Power and Confession: On the Credibility of the Earliest Reports of the Denmark Vesey Slave Conspiracy," *William and Mary Quarterly* 68.2, 301–4.

24. H. I. Tragle (1971) *The Southampton Slave Revolt of 1831: A Compilation of Source Material* (Amherst: University of Massachusetts Press), 213–15.

25. D. R. Egerton (2002) *Rebels, Reformers, and Revolutionaries: Collected Essays and Second Thoughts* (New York: Routledge), 71–2; Morris, *Southern Slavery and the Law*, 237.

26. H. Jacobs, *Incidents in the Life of a Slave Girl*, 97–102.

27. W. D. Jordan (1993) *Tumult and Silence at Second Creek: an Inquiry into a Civil War Slave Conspiracy* (Baton Rouge: Louisiana State University Press), 3–4.

28. Campbell, *Slavery on Trial*; Howington, *What Sayeth the Law*; C. Waldrep (1998) *Roots of Disorder: Race and Criminal Justice in the American South, 1817–1880* (Urbana: University of Illinois Press). McNair calculated a slave conviction rate of 50 percent, compared to 27 percent for whites. *Criminal Injustice*, 114–16.

29. Hindus, *Prison and Plantation*, 142; Schwarz, *Twice Condemned*, 40–2.

30. A. Aguirre Jr. and D. V. Baker (1999) "Slave Executions in the United States: A Descriptive Analysis of Social and Historical Factors," *Social Science Journal* 36.1, 15.

31. L. Ware (1990) "*The Burning of Jerry: The Last Slave Execution by Fire in South Carolina?*" South Carolina Historical Magazine, *91.2, 101–02; Executions in the U.S., 1608–2002: The Espy File.*

32. C. B. Dew (1975). "Black Ironworkers and the Slave Insurrection Panic of 1856," *Journal of Southern History* 41.3, 338.

33. When capital cases involved several slaves from a single plantation, the absence of compensation could financially ruin the convicts' owner and in practice Missouri never executed more than two slaves for any single criminal act. W. King (2007) "'Mad' Enough to Kill: Enslaved Women, Murder, and Southern Courts," *Journal of African American History* 92.1, 40–51. Morris, *Southern Slavery and the Law*, 255.

34. Frazier, *Slavery and Crime in Missouri*, 105; Wahl, "Legal Constraints of Slave Masters," 20–1; Wheeler, *A Practical Treatise on the Law of Slavery*, 216.

35. C. Buettinger (2005) "Did Slaves Have Free Will? Luke, a Slave, v. Florida and Crime and the Command of the Master," *Florida Historical Quarterly*, 83.3, 251.

36. Chatham County Superior Court, Minutes (CCSCM), May 18, 1850, microfilm, originals in the Georgia Department of Archives and History, Atlanta, Georgia; Savannah City Council Minutes (CCM), 6 Apr., 1854, microfilm, originals in the Georgia Historical Society, Savannah, Georgia.

37. *The Revised Statutes of Kentucky, approved and adopted by the General Assembly, 1851 and 1852* (Cincinnati, 1867), 245. See also *Hamilton v. Auditor* (1853), in Catterall, *Judicial Cases*, I, 410.

38. *Miller v. Porter* (1848), in Catterall, *Judicial Cases Concerning Slavery*, I, 382; McNair, "Slave Women," 135–6; *New York Times*, July 7, 1854; W. Johnson (1997) "Inconsistency, Contradiction, and Complete Confusion: the Everyday Life of the Law of Slavery," *Law and Social Inquiry*, 22.2, 423–4; WPA, *Slave Narratives,* vol. XI, North Carolina Narratives, part 1, 134–5.

39. Campbell, *Slavery on Trial*, 104.

40. Schwarz, *Twice Condemned*, 17.

41. Campbell, *Slavery on Trial,* 107.

42. McNair, "Slave Women," 140–6.

43. M. A. McLaurin (1991) *Celia, a Slave* (Athens: University of Georgia Press), 123–36.

44. King, "'Mad' Enough to Kill," 43–5.

45. Bardaglio, "Rape and the Law," 762–3 and 768; D. M. Somerville (2004) *Rape and Race in the Nineteenth Century South* (Chapel Hill: University of North Carolina Press), 30–41.

46. J. W. Harris (2009) *The Hanging of Thomas Jeremiah: A Free Black Man's Encounter with Liberty* (New Haven: Yale University Press).

47. D. Christy, *Cotton is King*, 38 and 240–1.

48. Edgefield County Court Grand Jury Reports, October 1859 and Spring Term, 1860, Edgefield Historical Society.

49. C. Phillips (1997) *Freedom's Port: the African American Community of Baltimore, 1790–1860* (Urbana: University of Illinois Press), 204; Campbell, *Slavery on Trial*, 150–1.

50. L. B. Goodheart (2012) "Race, Rape, and Capital Punishment in Connecticut to 1830," *Patterns of Prejudice*, 46.1, 58–77.
51. L. Patrick-Stamp (1995) "Numbers that are Not New: African Americans in the Country's First Prison, 1790–1835," 119.1, 95–128.
52. *The Anti-Slavery Record*, Vol. III (New York, 1838), 164.
53. L. P. Masur (1989) *Rites of Execution: Capital Punishment and the Transformation of American Culture, 1776–1865* (Oxford: Oxford University Press), 15–19.
54. "Don't Hang Him!" *The North Star* April 20, 1849, 2.
55. D. C. Penningroth (2006) "My People, My People," in E. E. Baptist and S. M. H. Camp eds *New Studies in the History of American Slavery* (Athens: University of Georgia Press), 172.
56. J. Forrett (2008) "Violence among Slaves in Upcountry South Carolina," *Journal of Southern History* 74.3, 574; Campbell, *Slavery on Trial*, 181.

3 Reconstruction

1. The Constitution and Ordinances, Adopted by the State Convention of Alabama (Montgomery, 1865), 45.
2. *Burt v. State* (1866), in Catterall, *Judicial Cases*, vol. III, 262. The end of the Civil War spared slaves trials and punishments across the South, including in Oglethorpe County, Georgia, where two slaves convicted of capital crimes were freed without punishment in late-April 1865. See McNair, *Criminal Injustice*, 148.
3. D. G. Nieman (1989) "Black Political Power and Criminal Justice: Washington County, Texas, 1868–1884," *Journal of Southern History* 55, 413–14.
4. Ayers, *Vengeance and Justice*, 141–84; H. Rabinowitz (1996) *Race Relations in the Urban South* (Athens: University of Georgia Press), 31–59; L. F. Litwack (1980) *Been in the Storm So Long: The Aftermath of Slavery* (New York: Vintage Books), 282–91; G. Vandal (2000) *Rethinking Southern Violence: Homicides in Post-Civil War Louisiana, 1866–1884* (Columbus: Ohio State University Press), 90; Waldrep, *Roots of Disorder*, 2–3.
5. I. Berlin et al. (1985) *Freedom: A Documentary History of Emancipation, 1861–1867.* Series 1, Vol. 1 (Cambridge: Cambridge University Press), 796–806.
6. Sarah "Sallie" Conley Clayton (1999) *Requiem for a Lost City: A Memoir of Civil War Atlanta and the Old South*, ed. R. S. Davis (Macon, GA: Mercer University Press), 171.
7. S. Hahn (1997) "'Extravagant Expectations' of Freedom: Rumour, Political Struggle, and the Christmas Insurrection Scare of 1865 in the American South," *Past & Present* 157, 150.

8. E. Foner (1988) *Reconstruction: America's Unfinished Revolution* (New York: Perennial), 198–203; Jason Hawkins, "The American Black Codes, 1865–1866," http://home.gwu.edu/~jjhawkin/BlackCodes/BlackCodes.htm, date accessed 16 Mar., 2009.

9. Foner, *Reconstruction*, 198–203; Hawkins, "The American Black Codes, 1865–1866."

10. United States Congress (1866) *Report of the Joint Committee on Reconstruction, at the first session, Thirty-Ninth Congress* (Washington, DC: US Government Printing Office), 142–3; J. T. Currie (1980) "From Slavery to Freedom in Mississippi's Legal System," *Journal of Negro History* 65.2, 120; E. J. Harcourt (2002) "The Whipping of Richard Moore: Reading Emotion in Reconstruction America," *Journal of Social History* 36.2, 261–82.

11. United States Congress, *Report of the Joint Committee on Reconstruction*, 209 and 227; T. D. Morris (1982) "Equality, 'Extraordinary Law,' and Criminal Justice: The South Carolina Experience, 1865–1866," *South Carolina Historical Magazine* 83.1, 22–4.

12. Foner, *Reconstruction*, 271–91.

13. Foner, *Reconstruction*, 142–4; Ayers, *Vengeance and Justice*, 152–5.

14. P. A. Cimbala (1997) *Under the Guardianship of the Nation: The Freedman's Bureau and the Reconstruction of Georgia, 1865–1870* (Athens: University of Georgia Press), 205–7.

15. R. F. Engs (2004) *Freedom's First Generation: Black Hampton, Virginia, 1861–1890* (New York: Fordham University Press), 105.

16. S. Rapport (1989) "The Freedmen's Bureau as a Legal Agent for Black Men and Women in Georgia: 1865–1868," *Georgia Historical Quarterly* 73.1, 27–9; Ayers, *Vengeance and Justice*, 152.

17. Ayers, *Vengeance and Justice*, 152; Cimbala, *Under the Guardianship of the Nation*, 208.

18. Morris, "Equality"; M. Farmer-Kaiser (2010) *Freedwomen and the Freedmen's Bureau: Race, Gender, and Public Policy in the Age of Emancipation* (New York: Fordham University Press), 107.

19. R. A. Wilson, "Demopolis, Alabama: Monthly Report," December 31, 1868, Records of the Assistant Commissioner for the State of Alabama, 1865–1870, microfilm, reel 18.

20. J. L. West (2002) *The Reconstruction Ku Klux Klan in York County, South Carolina, 1865–1877* (Jefferson, N.C.: McFarland), 40.

21. Foner, *Reconstruction*, 426–7; West, *The Reconstruction Ku Klux Klan*, 69.

22. Harcourt, "The Whipping of Richard Moore."

23. D. A. Barnes and C. Connolly (1999) "Repression, the Judicial System, and Political Opportunities for Civil Rights Advocacy during Reconstruction," *Sociological Quarterly* 40.2, 331.

24. M. Newton (2010) *The Ku Klux Klan in Mississippi: a History* (Jefferson: McFarland), 33.

25. United States Congress (1872) *Testimony taken by the Joint Select Committee, to inquire into the condition of affairs in the late insurrectionary states*, Alabama, vol. 2 (Washington DC: US Government Printing Office), 743.
26. WPA, *Slave Narratives*, vol. II, Arkansas Narratives, part 3, 376–7.
27. Foner, *Reconstruction*, 454–9; West, *The Reconstruction Ku Klux Klan*, 116.
28. Ayers, *Vengeance and Justice*, 176.
29. Waldrep, *Roots of Disorder*, 131–3.
30. Waldrep, *Roots of Disorder*, 159–69; W. M. Dulaney (1996) *Black Police in America* (Bloomington: Indiana University Press), 116.
31. Dulaney, *Black Police in America*, 116; M. J. Mancini (1978) "Race, Economics, and the Abandonment of Convict Leasing," *Journal of Negro History*, 63.4, 343; *New York Times*, October 5, 1880.
32. D. M. Oshinsky (1996) *"Worse Than Slavery": Parchman Farm and the Ordeal of Jim Crow Justice* (New York: Free Press), 40; M. E. Curtin (2000) *Black Prisoners and their World, Alabama, 1865–1890* (Charlottesville: University Press of Virginia), 43; Rabinowitz, *Race Relations in the Urban South*, 44; S. E. Tolnay and E. M. Beck (1995) *A Festival of Violence: An Analysis of Southern Lynchings, 1882–1930* (Urbana: University of Illinois Press), 18.
33. J. Strickland (2009) "The Whole State is on Fire: Criminal Justice and the End of Reconstruction in Upcountry South Carolina," *Crime, History and Societies* 13.2, 111.
34. W. A. Blair (1995) "Justice Versus Law and Order: The Battles over the Reconstruction of Virginia's Minor Judiciary, 1865–1870," *Virginia Magazine of History and Biography* 103.2, 157.
35. D. C. Penningroth (2003) *The Claims of Kinfolk: African American Property and Community in the Nineteenth Century South* (Chapel Hill: University of North Carolina Press), 112.
36. *Savannah Colored Tribune*, April 22, 1876.
37. K. Franke (1999) "Becoming a Citizen: Reconstruction Era Regulation of African American Marriages," *Yale Journal of Law and the Humanities*, 11, 256–87.
38. Rabinowitz, *Race Relations in the Urban South*, 40 and 59.
39. C. Emberton (2006) "The Limits of Incorporation: Violence, Gun Rights, and Gun Regulation in the Reconstruction South," *Stanford Law and Policy Review* 17, 623–32; J. Saville (1996) *The Work of Reconstruction: From Slave to Wage Laborer in South Carolina, 1860–1870* (Cambridge: Cambridge University Press), 188.
40. West, *The Reconstruction Ku Klux Klan, 1865–1877* (Jefferson, N.C., 2002), 19.
41. WPA, *Slave Narratives* vol. II, Arkansas, part 1, 208 and part 3, 299 and 363; *Savannah Colored Tribune*, April 8, 1876.
42. Barnes and Connolly, "Repression, the Judicial System, and Political Opportunities," 340.

43. S. Cresswell (1991) *Mormons and Cowboys, Moonshiners and Klansmen: Federal Law Enforcement in the South and West, 1870–1893* (Tuscaloosa: University of Alabama Press), 23 and 249–58.

44. J. Novkov (2008) *Racial Union: Law, Intimacy, and the White State in Alabama, 1865–1954* (Ann Arbor: University of Michigan Press), 19.

4 The Southern Penal System

1. A. Lomax (1993) *The Land Where the Blues Began* (New York: Pantheon), 282.

2. "The New Slavery in the South—An Autobiography: A Georgia Negro Peon," *The Independent* (New York), February 25, 1904, http://docsouth. unc.edu/fpn/negpeon/negpeon.html, date accessed June 1, 2011.

3. L. P. Masur (1989) *Rites of Execution: Capital Punishment and the Transformation of American Culture, 1776–1865* (Oxford: Oxford University Press), 95.

4. M. E. Kann (2005) *Punishment, Prisons, and Patriarchy: Liberty and Power in the Early American Republic* (New York University Press), 110–17; M. Meranze (1996) *Laboratories of Virtue: Punishment, Revolution and Authority in Philadelphia, 1760–1835* (Chapel Hill: University of North Carolina Press); R. M. McLennan (2008) *The Crisis of Imprisonment: Protest, Politics, and the Making of the American Penal State, 1776–1941* (Cambridge: Cambridge University Press).

5. Ayers, *Vengeance and Justice*, 46–69; M. Colvin (1997) *Penitentiaries, Reformatories and Chain Gangs: Social Theory and the History of Punishment in Nineteenth-Century America* (Gordonsville, VA: Palgrave Macmillan), 203–4.

6. Ayers, *Vengeance and Justice*, 189; M. E. Curtin (2000) *Black Prisoners and their World, Alabama, 1865–1900* (Charlottesville: University Press of Virginia), 63.

7. *Message of His Excellency Governor J. L. Orr* (1868), 118.

8. A. D. Oliphant (1916) *The Evolution of the Penal System of South Carolina from 1866 to 1916* (Columbia: State Company), 8.

9. *Twentieth Annual Report of the Commissioner of Labor: Convict Labor* (1906), 250, 352–3 and 374–5.

10. Ayers, *Vengeance and Justice*, 196; Curtin, *Black Prisoners*, 68; A. Lichtenstein (1996) *Twice the Work of Free Labor: the Political Economy of Convict Leasing* (New York: Verso), 77–9; McLennan, *The Crisis of Imprisonment*, 97–106.

11. "The Prisoners of the United States, in 1880, by States and Territories, showing the Number Incarcerated in each Penitentiary, by Sex, Nativity, and Race," *United States Census*, 1880; T. LeFlouria (2011) "'The Hand that Rocks the Cradle Cuts Cordwood': Exploring Black Women's Lives and Labor in Georgia's Convict Camps, 1865–1917," *Labor*, 8.3, 54; Myers, "Inequality and Punishment," 314–15.

12. *New York Times*, November 12, 1886; Oshinsky, *"Worse than Slavery*, 31–49, 63–81; Curtin, *Black Prisoners and Their World*, 64–85; Mancini, *One Dies Get Another*, 98; W. Cohen (1976) "Negro Involuntary Servitude in the South, 1865–1940: a Preliminary Analysis," *The Journal of Southern History* 42.1, 56; Ayers, *Vengeance and Justice*, 217; M. T. Carleton (1971) *Politics and Punishment: the History of the Louisiana State Penal System* (Baton Rouge: Louisiana State University Press), 37.

13. Carleton, *Politics and Punishment*, 36; Curtin, *Black Prisoners and their World*, 124; LeFlouria, "Black Women's Lives," 56–8.

14. G. W. Cable (1885) *The Silent South: Together with the Freedmen's Case in Equity and the Convict Lease System* (New York), 166.

15. M. J. Mancini (1996) *One Dies, Get Another: Convict Leasing in the American South, 1866–1828* (Columbia: University of South Carolina Press), 173, 198–9; Columbus *Enquirer-Sun*, 9 Nov., 1887.

16. M. C. Fierce (1994) *Slavery Revisited: Blacks and the Southern Convict Lease System, 1865–1933* (New York: Brooklyn College), 163–5.

17. Macon *Telegraph*, March 23, 1899; V. M. L. Miller (2000) *Crime, Sexual Violence, and Clemency: Florida's Pardon Board and Penal System in the Progressive Era* (Gainesville: University Press of Florida), 26; M. N. Goodnow, "Turpentine: Impressions of the Convict Camps of Florida," in *The Survey*, May 1, 1915, 104–5.

18. Goodnow, "Turpentine," 107; Cable, *The Silent South*, 155; Miller, *Crime, Sexual Violence, and Clemency*, 11.

19. Lichtenstein, *Twice the Work of Free Labor*, 126–7.

20. Oshinsky, *"Worse Than Slavery,"* 51; Miller, *Crime, Sexual Violence, and Clemency*, 11, 34–5.

21. K. A. Shapiro (1998) *A New South Rebellion: the Battle against Convict Labor in the Tennessee Coalfields, 1871–1896* (Chapel Hill: University of North Carolina Press), 64.

22. E. L. Ayers (1992) *The Promise of the New South: Life after Reconstruction* (Oxford: Oxford University Press), 216–18, 244; J. D. M. Griffiths (1993) "A State of Servitude Worse than Slavery: The Politics of Penal Administration in Mississippi, 1865–1900," *Journal of Mississippi History* 55.1, 3; Carleton, *Punishment and Politics*, 78–9; Oshinsky, *"Worse Than Slavery,"* 52–3.

23. Macon *Telegraph*, March 23, 1899; M. J. Mancini (1978) "Race, Economics, and the Abandonment of Convict Leasing," *Journal of Negro History* 63.4, 348; *Atlanta Journal*, August 2, 1908 cited in Fierce, *Slavery Revisited*, 172; Fierce, 173–4; Gentry (AK) *Journal-Advance*, January 8, 1909, 1.

24. Lichtenstein, *Twice the Work*, 171; *Twentieth Annual Report of the Commissioner of Labor: Convict Labor* (1906); Hawkins (1984) "State versus County: Prison Policy and Conflicts of Interest in North Carolina," *Criminal Justice History* 5, 98.

25. Lichtenstein, *Twice the Work*, 179–80; *A Study of Prison Conditions in North Carolina* (1923), http://docsouth.unc.edu/nc/prison1923/prison1923.html, date accessed January 23, 2010.
26. J. Adams (2001) "'The Wildest Show in the South': Tourism and Incarceration at Angola," *TDR* 45.2, 95.
27. Oshinsky, *Worse Than Slavery*, 141.
28. J. Zimmerman (1951) "The Penal Reform Movement in the South during the Progressive Era, 1890–1917," *Journal of Southern History* 17.4, 467.
29. C. R. Henderson (1910) "Introduction," in *Penal and Reformatory Institutions, by Sixteen Leading Authorities* (New York), v.
30. *New York Times*, June 4, 1911.
31. P. Daniel (1972) *The Shadow of Slavery: Peonage in the South, 1901–1969* (Urbana: University of Illinois Press), 24–31.
32. A. J. McKelway (1910) "Three Prison Systems of the Southern States of America," in Henderson, *Penal and Reformatory Institutions*, 85–6.
33. Cohen, "Negro Involuntary Servitude," 48; D. A. Blackmon (2008) *Slavery by Another Name: the Re-Enslavement of Black Americans from the Civil War to World War II* (New York: Random House), 109; B. C. Schmidt, Jr. (1982) "Principle and Prejudice: The Supreme Court and Race in the Progressive Era. Part 2: The "Peonage Cases," *Columbia Law Review* 824, 652.
34. "How Slaves are Made," *Lawrence Daily World* June 22, 1903, 5.
35. Daniel, *Shadow of Slavery*, 50–2.
36. A. Z. Huq (2001) "Note, Peonage and Contractual Labor," *Columbia Law Review* 101.2, 354 and 387.
37. "State Must Face Issue," *Atlanta Independent* May 26, 1921, 1.
38. R. L. Goluboff (1999) "Won't You Please Help Me Get My Son Home? Peonage, Patronage, and Protest in the World War II Urban South," *Law and Social Inquiry* 24, 784.
39. McLennan, *Crisis of Imprisonment*, 196; J. J. Misrahi (1996) "Factories with Fences: An Analysis of the Prison Industry Enhancement Certification Program in Historical Perspective," 33.2, 416–19; J. Simon (1993) *Poor Discipline: Parole and the Social Control of the Underclass, 1890–1990* (Chicago: University of Chicago Press), 47–9.
40. M. E. Odem (1995) *Delinquent Daughters: Protecting and Policing Adolescent Female Sexuality in the United States, 1885–1920* (Chapel Hill: University of North Carolina Press), 119; C. S. Mangum (1940) *The Legal Status of the Negro* (Chapel Hill: University of North Carolina Press), 232.
41. "Felony Prisoners Released, By Method of Release, By States: 1938," NAACP Papers [microfilm], Part 18, Reel 7, Frame 00881.
42. S. Garton (2003) "Managing Mercy: African Americans, Parole and Paternalism in the Georgia Prison System, 1919–1945," *Journal of Social History* 3, 678.
43. G. C. Williams (1922) "The Negro Offender," *The Fifty-First Congress of the American Prison Association Jacksonville, Florida, 1921* (New York), 10.

44. J. H. Johnson (1940) "Public Welfare and Social Work: Parole in Alabama." *Social Forces* 18, 388.
45. "Statement Covering the Parole Conditions and Parole of Pete Taylor," NAACP Papers, 1940–55 (Library of Congress), Box II-B:111, Folder 21).
46. Atlanta Constitution, April 1, 1921. "The Jasper County Horror Accentuates Weaknesses and Viciousness of Georgia Laws That Commercialize Penal Labor" by James A. Hollomon. Papers of the NAACP [microfilm], Part 10, Reel 16, Frames 00665-00666.
47. R. Perkinson, *Texas Tough: the Rise of America's Prison Empire* (New York: Metropolitan Books), 216.
48. H. B. Franklin (1979) "Songs of an Imprisoned People," *MELUS* 6.1, 13; B. Jackson (1999) *Wake Up Dead Man: Hard Labor and Southern Blues* (Athens: University of Georgia Press), 29–46.
49. Willie James to Walter White, 25 Sept. 1939, NAACP Papers Part 18 B:137, F2.
50. Forest Hills to Walter White, 18 Nov., 1940, Boca Raton, F, NAACP Papers Part 18, Reel 7, Frame 00917-20.
51. Sylvester Turner to Walter White, Sylvania, Ga., 19 Jun., 1946, NAACP Papers Part 18, Reel 8, Frame 00183.
52. *Atlanta Journal*, June 28, 1949, NAACP Papers Part 18, Reel 8, Frame 00210.
53. "Ala. Escapee Wins Fight to Stay in Chicago," *Plaindealer* [Kansas], April 11, 1958, 5.
54. "Said the Governor of Georgia to the Governor of Massachusetts," *The Crisis*, October, 1937, 297–8.
55. E. Van Blue (2004) "Hard Times in the New Deal: Racial Formation and the Culture of Punishment in Texas and California in the 1930s," PhD diss., University of Texas, 238.
56. Patterson, *Scottsboro Boy*, 95–110.
57. T. Dodge (2000) "State Convict Road Gangs in Alabama," *Alabama Review* 53.4, 243–70; "Mississippi Prison," *New York Times* February 14, 1968, 28.
58. *South Carolina Law Review*, 1962.

5 Lynching and Law

1. "Mamas with Babes View KY. Hanging," *The Afro American*, August 22, 1936, 7; "Crowd Awaits Dawn and Woman Hangman," *New York Times*, August 14, 1936, 4.
2. "Kentucky 'Picnic' Hanging Draws Attack over Nation," *Kentucky New Era*, August 12, 1936, 1.
3. J. D. Hall (1993) *Revolt against Chivalry: Jessie Daniel Ames and the Women's Campaign against Lynching* (New York: Columbia University Press), 130.

4. C. Waldrep (2002) *The Many Faces of Judge Lynch: Extralegal Violence and Punishment in America* (New York: Palgrave Macmillan), 149.
5. W. Fitzhugh Brundage (1993) *Lynching in the New South: Georgia and Virginia, 1880–1930* (Urbana: University of Illinois Press), 19.
6. Lynchings by Year and Race, http://law2.umkc.edu/faculty/projects/ftrials/shipp/lynchingyear.html, date accessed February 9, 2010.
7. Brundage, *Lynching in the New South*, 105.
8. Tolnay and Beck, *A Festival of Violence*, 119.
9. Ayers, *The Promise of the New South*, 157.
10. M. Schultz (2005) *The Rural Face of White Supremacy: beyond Jim Crow* (Urbana: University of Illinois Press), 131.
11. "Another Negro Burned," *New York Times*, February 2, 1893, 1; A. Wood (2009) *Lynching and Spectacle: Witnessing Racial Violence in America, 1890–1940* (Chapel Hill: University of North Carolina Press), 1.
12. D. Garland (2005) "Penal Excess and Surplus Meaning: Public Torture Lynchings in Twentieth Century America," *Law and Society Review*, 39.4, 819.
13. J. D. Goldsby (2006) *A Spectacular Secret: Lynching in American Life and Literature* (Chicago: University of Chicago Press), 6; G. E. Hale (1998) *Making Whiteness: the Culture of Segregation in the South, 1890–1940* (New York: Random House), 205.
14. Hall, *Revolt against Chivalry*, 146.
15. J. H. Chadbourn (2009 [1933]) *Lynching and the Law* (Clark, NJ: Lawbook Exchange), 5.
16. "Lynch Law in the South," *New York Times*, November 14, 1897, 9; Project HAL: Historical American Lynching Data Collection Project, http://people.uncw.edu/hinese/HAL/HAL%20Web%20Page.htm, date accessed March 1, 2011; "Southern Race Riots. The Law Defied And Innocent Persons Lynched," *Plaindealer* [Detroit] January 3, 1890, 1; "Lynched Because Sick," *Parsons Weekly Blade* [Kansas] May 26, 1894, 1; "Fights White Man; Lynched," *Broad Axe* [Chicago] 11 May 1907, 2; "Lynched for Hog Stealing," *Gazette* [Raleigh, NC] January 15, 1898, 4; Leon Litwack, *Trouble in Mind*, 288–9.
17. Chadbourne, *Lynching and the Law*, 13.
18. B. E. Baker (2008) *This Mob Will Surely Take My Life: Lynchings in the Carolinas, 1871–1947* (London: Continuum), 104–18.
19. Brundage, *Lynching in the New South*, 169.
20. C. Waldrep (2009) *African Americans Confront Lynching: Strategies of Resistance from the Civil War to the Civil Rights Era* (Lanham, Md: Rowman & Littlefield); H. Shapiro (1988) *White Violence and Black Response: from Reconstruction to Montgomery* (Amherst: University of Massachusetts Press), 30–59; S. K. Cha-Jua (1998) "A Warlike Demonstration": Legalism, Armed Resistance, and Black Political Mobilization in Decatur, Illinois, 1894–1898," *Journal of Negro History* 83.1, 57; "*Chicago Conservator* Editorial, 1880," in H. Aptheker ed. (1990) *A Documentary History of*

the Negro People in the United States, Vol. 2 (New York: Citadel), 655; M. Vandiver (2006) *Lethal Punishment: Lynchings and Legal Executions in the South* (New Brunswick: Rutgers University Press), 149–50.

21. J. J. Royster, ed. (1997) *Southern Horrors and other Writings: The Anti-Lynching Campaign of Ida B. Wells, 1892–1900* (Boston: Bedford Books), 4–18.

22. R. Lane (1991) *William Dorsey's Philadelphia and Ours: on the Past and Future of the Black City in America* (New York: Oxford University Press); M. S. Watson (2009) "Mary Church Terrell vs. Thomas Nelson Page: Gender, Race, and Class in Anti-Lynching Rhetoric," *Rhetoric and Public Affairs* 12.1; "Gov. Bloxham, of Florida," *The Freeman* [Indiana] April 24, 1897, 4.

23. A. Fairclough (2001) *Better Day Coming: Blacks and Equality, 1890–2000* (New York: Penguin), 69–72.

24. W. F. Brundage (1997) "The Roar on the Other Side of Silence: Black Resistance and White Violence in the American South, 1880–1940," in Brundage ed. *Under Sentence of Death: Lynching in the South* (Chapel Hill: University of North Carolina Press), 277.

25. G. C. Rable (1985) "The South and the Politics of Antilynching Legislation, 1920–1940," *Journal of Southern History* 51.2, 203–4.

26. Rable, "The South and the Politics of Antilynching," 209–18.

27. R. P. Ingalls (1987) "Lynching and Establishment Violence in Tampa, 1858–1935," *Journal of Southern History* 53.4, 613–44.

28. H. M. Dorsey (1921) *A Statement from Governor Hugh M. Dorsey as to the Negro in Georgia* (n.p.); Baker, *This Mob Will Surely Take My Life*, 166–7; *The Washington Reporter*, May 21, 1925, 1; M. J. Brown (2000) *Eradicating this Evil: Women in the Anti-Lynching Movement, 1892–1940* (New York: Garland), 178–9.

29. Hale, *Making Whiteness*, 237.

30. *New York Amsterdam News*, February 21, 1934, 6.

31. G. C. Wright (1991) "Executions of Afro-Americans in Kentucky, 1870–1940," *Georgia Journal of Southern Legal History* 1.2, 334.

32. *The Afro-American*, August 27, 1927, 19; *Chicago Defender*, May 19, 1928, A2.

33. Higginbotham (1996) *Shades of Freedom*, 139–40, 148.

34. "Jury Service," Administrative Subject File, April 23, 1937, NAACP Papers [microfilm], Part 8, Series A, reel 15, frames 00506-00571.

35. G. T. Stephenson (1910) *Race Distinctions in American Law* (New York: Association Press), 255–69.

36. The race of the one other man put to death for attempted rape is unknown. *Executions in the U.S., 1608–2002: The Espy File.*

37. L. L. Dorr (2004) *White Women, Rape, and the Power of Race in Virginia, 1900–1960* (Chapel Hill: University of North Carolina Press), 18; M. J. Pfeifer (2004) *Rough Justice: Lynching and American Society,*

1874–1947 (Urbana: University of Illinois Press), 5; Vandiver, *Legal Lynching*, 1–3; T. Keil and G. F. Vito (2009) "Lynching and the Death Penalty in Kentucky: Substitution or Supplement?" *Journal of Ethnicity in Criminal Justice* 7.1, 64.

38. G. E. Gilmore (2009) *Defying Dixie: the Radical Roots of Civil Rights, 1919–1950* (New York: Norton), 335.
39. "Pink Franklin Case," Papers of the NAACP, Part 8, Series A: Legal Department and Central Office Records, 1910–1939 [microfilm].
40. S. D. Carle (2002) "Race, Class, and Legal Ethics in the Early NAACP, 1910–1920," *Law and History Review* 20.1, 117–18.
41. R. C. Cortner (1988) *A Mob Intent on Death: the NAACP and the Arkansas Riot Cases* (Middletown: Wesleyan University Press).
42. D. T. Carter (2007) *Scottsboro: A Tragedy of the American South* (Baton Rouge: Louisiana State University Press), 3–50.
43. Carter, *Scottsboro*, 52–8; H. T. Muray, Jr. (1967) "The NAACP versus the Communist Party: The Scottsboro Rape Cases, 1931–1932" *Phylon* 28.3, 279–83.
44. "Scottsboro Case," *Time* June 22, 1931; J. A. Miller, S. D. Pennybacker, and E. Rosenhaft (2001) "Mother Ada Wright and the International Campaign to Free the Scottsboro Boys, 1931–1934," *American Historical Review* 106.2, 404.
45. *The Evening Independent* (St. Petersburg, Fl.), July 20, 1931; *Pittsburgh Post-Gazette*, January 30, 1932; "Seven for Seven" *Time* November 14, 1932; Carter, *Scottsboro*, 87–103.
46. *The Daily News* (Ludington, MI), April 10, 1933; *Pittsburgh Post-Gazette*, May 9, 1933.
47. "The Negro Before the Courts During 1932," *The Crisis*, October 1933, 230. Besides Scottsboro, the cases were Downer v. Dunaway, *Lee v. State*, *State v. Lewis*, *State v. Jones*.
48. A. L. Davis and B. L. Graham, *Supreme Court, Race, and Civil Rights: from Marshall to Rehnquist* (Thousand Oaks, Ca: Sage), 158.
49. M. J. Klarman (2004) *From Jim Crow to Civil Rights: the Supreme Court and the Struggle for Racial Equality* (New York: Oxford University Press), 282.
50. J. F. Blevins (2004) "Lyons v. Oklahoma, the NAACP, and Coerced Confessions under the Hughes, Stone, and Vinson Courts, 1936–1949," *Virginia Law Review* 90.1, 434–5.
51. E. W. Rise (1992) "Race, Rape, and Radicalism: The Case of the Martinsville Seven, 1949–1951," *Journal of Southern History* 58.3, 461–90.
52. R. B. Sherman (1992) *The Case of Odell Waller and Virginia Justice, 1940–1942* (Knoxville: University of Tennessee Press), 5–12.
53. Odell Waller's Dying Statement, reprinted in Sherman, *The Case of Odell Waller*, 194.

6 Crime and Policing in the Northern City

1. Janice Monica to NAACP, April 28, 1942, NAACP Papers, 1940–55 (Library of Congress), Box II-B:111, Folder 11.
2. T. L. Smith (1966) "The Redistribution of the Negro Population of the United States," *Journal of Negro History* 51.3, 161–3.
3. G. Myrdal (1962) *American Dilemma: the Negro Problem and Modern Democracy* (New York: Harper & Row), 183–205.
4. *Chicago Defender* August 30, 1919; *The Crisis*, May 1919, 13.
5. J. Adler (2006) *First in Violence, Deepest in Dirt: Homicide in Chicago, 1875–1920* (Cambridge, Mass: Harvard University Press), 134.
6. K. Boyle (2004) *Arc of Justice: a Saga of Race, Civil Rights, and Murder in the Jazz Age* (New York: Owl Books), 105–7; C. L. Lumkins, *American Pogrom: The East St. Louis Riot and Black Politics* (Athens: Ohio University Press), 8; Chicago Commission on Race Riots (1922) *The Negro in Chicago: a Study of Race Relations and a Race Riot in 1919* (Chicago: University of Chicago Press), 341.
7. F. H. Wines (1895) *Report on Crime, Pauperism, and Benevolence in the United States* (New York: Norman Ross), 6–10.
8. W. E. B. Du Bois (1967 [1899]) *The Philadelphia Negro: A Social Study* (New York: Schocken Books), 239.
9. M. N. Work (1900) "Crime among the Negroes of Chicago. A Social Study," *American Journal of Sociology*, 6.2, 222–3.
10. K. G. Muhammad (2010) *The Condemnation of Blackness: Race Crime and the Making of Modern Urban America* (Cambridge, Mass.: Harvard University Press), 35–87.
11. K. N. Gross (2006) *Colored Amazons: Crime, Violence, and Black Women in the City of Brotherly Love, 1880–1910* (Durham: Duke University Press); C. D. Hicks (2010) *Talk With You Like a Woman: African American Women, Justice, and Reform in New York, 1890–1935* (Chapel Hill: University of North Carolina Press), 149–54.
12. Adler, *First in Violence*, 128–32.
13. Adler, *First in Violence*, 155.
14. Lane, *William Dorsey's Philadelphia*, 90.
15. Adler, *First in Violence*, 155.
16. Muhammad, *Condemnation of Blackness*, 153.
17. Chicago Commission, *The Negro in Chicago*, 343.
18. J. Fronc (2009) *New York Undercover: Private Surveillance in the Progressive Era* (Chicago: University of Chicago Press), 95–122.
19. Hicks, *Talk With You Like a Woman*, 113–4.
20. E. A. Clement (2006) *Love for Sale: Courting, Treating, and Prostitution in New York City, 1900–1945* (Chapel Hill: University of North Carolina Press), 177–8.

21. M. S. Sacks (2005) "'To Show Who was in Charge': Police Repression of New York City's Black Population at the Turn of the Twentieth Century," *Journal of Urban History* 31.6, 806.

22. K. J. Mumford (1997) *Interzones: Black/White Sex Districts in the Early Twentieth Century* (New York: Columbia University Press), 158.

23. G. C. Ward (2006) *Unforgiveable Blackness: The Rise and Fall of Jack Johnson* (London: Pimlico), 298–349, Parkin quote at 344–5.

24. K. G. Muhammad (2011) "Where did all the White Criminals Go? Reconfiguring Race and Crime on the Road to Mass Incarceration," *Souls*, 13.1, 81.

25. Hicks, *Talk With You Like a Woman*, 162–6; P. J. Giddings (2008) *Ida: A Sword Among Lions: Ida B. Wells and the Campaign against Lynching* (New York: Amistad), 548–51; S. Robertson, S. White, S. Garton, and G. White (2010) "This Harlem Life: Black Families and Everyday Life in the 1920s and 1930s," *Journal of Social History* 44.1, 97–124; J. M. Campbell (2011) "African Americans and Parole in Depression Era New York," *Historical Journal* 54.4.

26. John N. Griggs to Walter White, June 4, 1941, NAACP Papers, 1940–1955 (Library of Congress) Box II-B:111, Folder 24.

27. Hicks, *Talk with You Like a Woman*, 253–4.

28. "The Death Sentence," *New York Times*, October 29, 1875; "Indignation," *Brooklyn Eagle*, December 20, 1875.

29. Robert Butler (2005) "The Loeb and Leopold Case: A Neglected Source for Richard Wright's 'Native Son,'" *African American Review* 39.4, 555–8.

30. R. Lane (1986) *Roots of Violence in Black Philadelphia, 1860–1900* (Cambridge, Mass.: Harvard University Press), 87–92 and 157; Lane, *William Dorsey's Philadelphia*, 90–3; E. H. Monkkonen (2001) *Murder in New York City* (Berkeley: University of California Press).

31. "Administration of Justice and the Afro-American," *Chicago Defender*, November 7, 1914, p. 3.

32. C. Darrow (1932) *The Story of My Life* (New York: Scribner's), chapter 40.

33. "Negro Prisoners and the Public Defenders of the Legal Aid Society," NAACP Papers Part 12 Section B, Reel 5, Frame 0115.

34. Sacks, "'To Show Who was in Charge,'" 816.

35. D. King and S. Tuck (2007) "De-Centring the South: America's Nationwide White Supremacist Order after Reconstruction," *Past and Present* 194.1, 229.

36. *New York Times*, June 3, 1892; *Macon Telegraph*, June 3, 1892.

37. *New York Times*, March 16, 1894; Y. R. Williams (2001) "Permission to Hate: Delaware, Lynching, and the Culture of Violence in America," *Journal of Black Studies*, 32.1; P. Dray (2003) *At the Hands of Persons Unknown: The Lynching of Black America* (New York: Modern Library), 178–84, 259–60.

38. *Wilkes-Barre Times*, March 17, 1894; *Philadelphia Inquirer*, June 2, 1894.
39. *New York Times*, June 17, 1920; *Pittsburgh Courier*, May 11, 1912.
40. R. H. White (2000) "'The Spirit of Hate' and Frederick Douglass," *Civil War History* 46.1, 42–7.
41. J. M. Campbell (2010) "'You Needn't Be Afraid Here; You're in a Civilized Country': Region, Racial Violence and Law Enforcement in Early Twentieth Century New Jersey, New York, and Pennsylvania," *Social History* 35.3, 261.
42. E. Dale (1999) "The People versus Zephyr Davis: Law and Popular Justice in Late Nineteenth-Century Chicago," *Law and History Review* 17.1, 27–56.
43. *The Freeman* (Indianapolis), March 25, 1893, 1.
44. "Memorandum on Meeting of NJ State Conference of NAACP Branches, Sunday, December 13, 1936" and Walter White to Dr DeFreitas, December 8, 1936, NAACP Papers, Part 12, Series B, Reel 2.
45. J. H. Barrow (2005) "Lynching in the Mid-Atlantic, 1882–1940," *American Nineteenth Century History* 6.3, 264.
46. Gross, *Colored Amazons*, 119–20.
47. *Defender*, July 23, 1904.
48. Boyle, *Arc of Justice*, 214–19.
49. Boyle, *Arc of Justice*, 214–19 and 317; Darrow, *The Story of My Life*, chapter 34.
50. "Murder in Chicago," *The Crisis*, August 1930, 282.
51. M. S. Johnson (2003) *Street Justice: a History of Police Violence in New York City* (Boston: Beacon), 82.
52. M. McLaughlin (2007) "Ghetto Formation and Armed Resistance in East St. Louis, Illinois," *Journal of American Studies*, 41.2, 436–7 and 456.
53. V. P. Franklin, "The Philadelphia Race Riot of 1918," in J. W. Trotter Jr. and E. L. Smith eds (1997) *African Americans in Pennsylvania: Shifting Historical Perspectives.* (University Park: Pennsylvania State University Press), 319.
54. Chicago Commission, *The Negro in Chicago*, 335–6 and 345.
55. K. E. Johnson (2004) "Police-Black Community Relations in Philadelphia," *The Journal of African American History* 89.2, 120–1.
56. Boyle, *Arc of Justice*, 171.
57. *New York Amsterdam News*, May 19, 1934.
58. R. M. Fogelson and R. E. Rubenstein eds (1969) *The Harlem Riot of 1935: The Complete Report of Mayor LaGuardia's Commission* (New York: Arno), 121.
59. Mary Nowell to Charles Houston, November 27, 1937, NAACP Papers Part 8, Reel 15, frame 00707; Afro-American Echo, October 25, 1937, p. 3, NAACP Papers, Part 8, Series A, Reel 15, Frame 00709; Untitled

and undated press clipping, NAACP Papers, part 12, series B, reel 3, frame 00654.

60. M. Naison (1983) *Communists in Harlem during the Depression* (Urbana: University of Illinois Press), 116–7.

61. Fogelson and Rubenstein, *The Harlem Riot*, 11.

7 The Black Freedom Struggle

1. "Interview with Franklin McCain," in C. Carson et al. eds (1991) *The Eyes on the Prize Civil Rights Reader* (New York: Penguin), 114.

2. G. W. O'Brien (1999) *The Color of the Law: Race, Violence, and Justice in the Post-World War II South* (Chapel Hill: University of North Carolina Press), 3.

3. Fairclough, *Better Day Coming*, 207; M. L. Dudziak (2000) *Cold War Civil Rights: Race and the Image of American Democracy* (Princeton: Princeton University Press), 6.

4. "54 Southern Cities Employ 279 Negro Police," *Plain Dealer* [Kansas] November 19, 1948, 1; Dulaney, *Black Police in America*, 118; *Miami News*, February 25, 1943, 6.

5. "Nashville Negro District Terrorized by Police Brutality," *Negro Star* April 30, 1943, 4; "Negro MP's for Negro District in Nashville," *Plain Dealer* July 30, 1943, 1; "Thousands Witness Induction of Negro Police in Savannah," *Plain Dealer* [Kansas] May 16, 1947, 2; L. N. Moore (2010) *Black Rage in New Orleans: Police Brutality and African American Activism from World War II to Hurricane Katrina* (Baton Rouge: Louisiana State University Press), 28–30.

6. *Executions in the U.S., 1608–2002: The Espy File*; Dorr, *White Women*, 206–15.

7. D. McGuire (2004) "'It Was like All of Us Had Been Raped': Sexual Violence, Community Mobilization, and the African American Freedom Struggle," *Journal of American History* 91.3, 908.

8. McGuire, "'It Was like All of Us Had Been Raped,'" 929.

9. Dudziak, *Cold War Civil Rights*, 36; L. Zarnow (2008) "Braving Jim Crow to Save Willie McGee: Bella Abzug, the Legal Left, and Civil Rights Innovation, 1948–1951," *Law and Social Inquiry* 33.4, 1003–36.

10. K. Fredrickson (1997) "'The Slowest State' and 'Most Backward Community': Racial Violence in South Carolina and Federal Civil Rights Legislation, 1946–1948," *South Carolina Historical Magazine* 98.2, 178–81, 198 [quote]; T. Brown-Nagin (2011) *Courage to Dissent: Atlanta and the Long History of the Civil Rights Movement* (Oxford: Oxford University Press, 2011), 37.

11. C. Hudson-Weems (1994) *Emmett Till: the Sacrificial Lamb of the Civil Rights Movement* (Troy, MI: Bedford), 43.

12. Klarman, *From Jim Crow to Civil Rights*, 350–3.

13. K. Yasuhiro (2001) *Mississippi State Sovereignty Commission: Civil Rights and States' Rights* (Jackson: University Press of Mississippi), 39; Anders Walker (2009) "The Violent Bear it Away: Emmett Till and the Modernization of Law Enforcement in Mississippi," *San Diego Law Review*, 46.2, 461 and 479–89; J. A. Kirk (2002) *Redefining the Color Line: Black Activism in Little Rock, Arkansas, 1940–1970* (Gainesville: University Press of Florida), 1.

14. "We'll Walk On and On," *The Afro-American* [Baltimore], March 3, 1956, 6.

15. C. Coleman et al. (2005) "Social Movements and Social Change Litigation: Synergy in the Montgomery Bus Protest," *Law and Social Inquiry* 30.4, 679–80.

16. Coleman, "Social Movements and Social Change Litigation," 665–6.

17. Brown and Webb, *Race in the American South*, 296; D. C. Catsam (2009) *Freedom's Main Line: The Journey of Reconciliation and the Freedom Rides* (Lexington: University Press of Kentucky), 109; Fairclough, *Better Day Coming*, 243.

18. Raymond Arsenault (2006) *Freedom Riders: 1961 and the Struggle for Racial Justice* (Oxford: Oxford University Press), 352–7.

19. C. G. Fleming (1994) "Black Women Activists and the Student Nonviolent Coordinating Committee: The Case of Ruby Doris Smith Robinson," *Irish Journal of American Studies* 3, 41; H. A. Baker (2010) *Betrayal: How Black Intellectuals Have Abandoned the Ideals of the Civil Rights Era* (New York: Columbia University Press), 17; Catsam, *Freedom's Main Line*, 109; Fairclough, *Better Day Coming*, 243; "Diane Nash," in D. W. Houck and D. E. Dixon (2009) *Women and the Civil Rights Movement, 1954–1965* (Jackson: University Press of Mississippi), 156; Arsenault, *Freedom Riders*, 352.

20. R. Hohle (2009) "The Rise of the New South Governability," *Journal of Historical Sociology* 22.4, 502.

21. *Philadelphia Tribune*, March 28, 1964, 1 and 4; Brown-Nagin, *Courage to Dissent*, 235–43.

22. M. Stanton (2003) *Freedom Walk: Mississippi or Bust* (Jackson: University Press of Mississippi), 145–8.

23. *Afro-American*, March 23, 1963, p. 3.

24. Baker, *Betrayal*, 26.

25. J. M. Thornton (2002) *Dividing Lines: Municipal Politics and the Struggle for Civil Rights in Montgomery, Birmingham and Selma* (Tuscaloosa: University of Alabama Press), 566.

26. J. E. Luders (2005) "Civil Rights Success and the Politics of Racial Violence," *Polity* 37.1, 115–16.

27. John Dittmer (1995) *Local People: The Struggle for Civil Rights in Mississippi,* 109, 215; R. Hofstadter and M. Wallace (1970) *American Violence: a Documentary History* (New York: Knopf), 434; C. Van

Woodward (1972) *The Strange Career of Jim Crow*, 3rd revised edn (New York: Oxford University Press), 184.

28. L. Washington, *Black Judges on Justice: Perspectives from the Bench* (New York: New Press), 80.

29. D. O. Linder (2002) "Bending Toward Justice: John Doar and the Mississippi Burning Trial," *Mississippi Law Journal* 72.2, 731–79.

30. L. Hill (2004) *The Deacons for Defense: Armed Resistance and the Civil Rights Movement* (Chapel Hill: University of North Carolina Press), 39–40; C. Strain (2005) *Pure Fire: Self-Defense as Activism in the Civil Rights Era* (Athens: University of Georgia Press), 3.

31. R. F. Williams, "Is Violence Necessary to Combat Injustice? For the Positive: Williams Says 'We Must Fight Back,'" in Carson, *The Eyes on the Prize Civil Rights Reader*, 110–12; T. Tyson (2001) *Radio Free Dixie: Robert F. Williams and the Roots of Black Power* (Chapel Hill: University of North Carolina Press), 220–7.

32. Hill, *The Deacons for Defense*, 69, 149, 153–9.

33. H. K. Jeffries (2009) *Bloody Lowndes: Civil Rights and Black Power in Alabama's Black Belt* (New York: New York University Press), 104–5 and 144; Hill, *The Deacons for Defense*, 2; S. Vaught (2006) "Narrow Cells and Lost Keys: The Impact of Jails and Prisons on Black Protest, 1940–1972," PhD Dissertation, Bowling Green State College, 194–5.

34. F. Shapiro (1964) *Race Riots: New York, 1964* (New York: Crowell), 43–62.

35. J. Sides (2004) *L.A. City Limits: African American Los Angeles from the Great Depression to the Present* (Ewing, N.J.: University of California Press), 174–6.

36. U. S. Riot Commission (1968) *Report of the National Advisory Commission on Civil Disorders* (Washington: US Government Printing Office), 202.

37. D. Livingstone (1997) "Police Discretion and the Quality of Life in Public Places: Courts, Communities, and the New Policing," *Columbia Law Review*, 97.3, 571.

38. T. J. English (2011) *The Savage City: Race, Murder, and a Generation on the Edge* (New York: William Morrow), xvi.

39. J. Lester (1968) *Look Out Whitey! Black Power's Gon' Get your Mama!* (New York: Dial), 23.

40. D. Wainstock (2009) *Malcolm X, African American Revolutionary* (Jefferson, N.C.: McFarland), 43–5.

41. W. Churchill and J. V. Wall (1988) *Agents of Repression: The FBI's Secret Wars against the Black Panther Party and the American Indian Movement* (Boston: South End), 63; Y. R. Williams (2008) "Introduction," in Williams and J. Lazerow eds *Liberated Territory: Untold Local Perspectives on the Black Panther Party* (Durham: Duke University Press), 7.

42. Moore, *Black Rage in New Orleans*, 72–82.

43. P. Alkebulan (2007) *Survival Pending Revolution: The History of the Black Panther Party* (Tuscaloosa: University of Alabama Press), 5–6; R. Wilkins, "Whither 'Black Power'?" *The Crisis*, August–September 1966, 353.

44. D. Lindorff (2005) "Justice Denied: Race and the 1982 Murder Trial of Munia Abu-Jamal," in R. Asher, L. B. Goodheart, A. Rogers eds "Murder on Trial: 1620–2002" (New York: SUNY Press), 92; Director, FBI, to SAC, Albany, August 25, 1967, "Re: Counterintelligence Program Black Nationalist—Hate Groups Internal Security," and SAC, Philadelphia to Director, FBI, August 30, 1867, COINTELPRO: The Counterintelligence Program of the FBI. Black Nationalist Hate Groups [microfilm], Reel 1.

45. C. Sellers and R. L. Terrell (1973) *The River of No Return: the Autobiography of a Black Militant and the Life and Death of SNCC* (New York: Morow), 257.

46. Sides, *L.A. City Limits*, 173; A. Alonso, "Out of the Void: Street Gangs in Black Los Angeles," in D. Hunt and A-C. Ramon eds (2010) *Black Los Angeles: American Dreams and Racial Realities* (New York: NYU Press), 148.

47. P. S. Foner, ed. (1970) *The Black Panthers Speak* (Philadelphia: Lippincott), 84; Moore, *Black Rage in New Orleans*, 79–80.

48. C. R. Garry, "The Persecution of the Black Panther Party," in Foner ed. *The Black Panthers Speak*, 259.

49. Churchill and Wall, *Agents of Repression*, 61.

50. Hill, *Men, Mobs, and Law*, 276.

51. C. E. Smith (1993) "Black Muslims and the Development of Prisoners' Rights," *Journal of Black Studies* 24.2, 131–46.

52. G. Jackson (1970) *Soledad Brother* (New York: Bantam Books), 31.

53. Hill, *Men, Mobs, and Law*, 309; G. Benjamin and S. P. Rappaport (1974) "Attica and Prison Reform," *Proceedings of the Academy of Political Science* 31.3, 200; L. Bernstein (2007) "The Age of Jackson: George Jackson and the Culture of American Prisons in the 1970s," *Journal of American Culture*, 30.3, 310–23.

54. D. J. Garrow (2008) "Bad Behavior Makes Big Law: Southern Malfeasance and the Expansion of Federal Judicial Power, 1954–1968," *St. Johns Law Review* 82.1, 25–6.

55. C. F. Robinson II (2003) *Dangerous Liaisons: Sex and Love in the Segregated South* (Fayetteville: University of Arkansas Press), 137–41.

8 The Penal State

1. J. Lester, "Thoughts on the Day before the Inauguration," January 19, 2009, http://acommonplacejbl.blogspot.com/2009/01/thoughts-on-day-before-inauguration.html, date accessed June 1, 2010; D. Remnick (2010) *The Bridge: the Life and Rise of Barack Obama* (New York: Picador), 20.

2. S. R. Donzier (ed) (1996) *The Real War on Crime: The Report of the National Criminal Justice Commission* (New York: Harper), 99.
3. R. J. Weitzer and S. A. Tuch (2006) *Race and Policing in America: Conflict and Reform* (New York: Cambridge University Press), 5.
4. G. Fisher (1997) "Review: The O. J. Simpson Corpus," *Stanford Law Review*, 49.4, 1000–2; W. L. Hixson (2002) "Black and White: The O. J. Simpson Case (1995)," in A. Gordon-Reed ed. *Race on Trial: Law and Justice in American History* (New York: Oxford University Press), 226.
5. K. Russell-Brown (2008) *The Color of Crime: Racial Hoaxes, White Fear, Black Protectionism, Police Harassment, and Other Macroaggressions* (New York: New York University Press), 54–5.
6. Hartigan, *What Can You Say?*, 62.
7. Russell-Brown, *The Color of Crime*, 35.
8. Alexander, *The New Jim Crow*, 210.
9. V. J. Callanan (2004) *Feeding the Fear of Crime: Crime-Related Media and Support for Three Strikes* (New York: LFB Scholarly), 70; T. L. Dixon (2008) "News Exposure and Racialized Beliefs: Understanding the Relationship between Local News Viewing and Perceptions of African Americans and Crime," *Journal of Communication* 58.1, 116–17.
10. J. Hurwitz and M. Peffley (2005) "Playing the Race Card in the Post-Willie Horton Era: The Impact of Racialized Code Words on Support for Punitive Crime Policy," *Public Opinion Quarterly* 69.1, 109–10.
11. E. Utley and A. L. Heyse (2009) "Barack Obama's (Im)perfect Union: An Analysis of the Strategic Successes and Failures in his Speech on Race," *Western Journal of Black Studies*, 33.3, 159.
12. "Miami Still Tense in Wake of Riots," *The Dispatch* [Lexington, N.C.], May 20, 1980, 2.
13. "Policing the Police," *Chicago Metro News*, October 1, 1983, 9.
14. L. P. Brown (1987) "Innovative Policing in Houston," *Annals of the American Academy of Political and Social Science* 494, 132.
15. W. Marvin Dulaney, "Black Police in America," 93–4; P. Blauner, "The Rap Sheet on Lee Brown," *New York Magazine* January 22, 1990, 32–8; D. D. Watson (2005) *Race and the Houston Police Department, 1930–1990: A Change did Come* (College Station: TAMU Press), 143–8.
16. D. Jacobs and R. O'Brien (1998) "The Determinants of Deadly Force: a Structural Analysis of Police Violence," *American Journal of Sociology* 103.4, 858; M. D. Holmes and B. W. Smith (2008) *Race and Police Brutality: Roots of an Urban Dilemma* (Albany: SUNY Press), 18; M. Wilson and J. Lynxwiler (1998) "The Federal Government and the Harassment of Black Leaders: A Case Study of Mayor Richard Arrington Jr. of Birmingham," *Journal of Black Studies*, 28.5, 548; G. H. Saltztein (1989) "Black Mayors and Police Priorities," *Journal of Politics*, 51.3, 541; "Detroit Officials Defend the Police," *New York Times* September 26, 1983, B10.

17. D. Livingstone (1997) "Police Discretion and the Quality of Life in Public Places: Courts, Communities, and the New Policing," *Columbia Law Review* 97.3, 573–6.

18. Moore, *Black Rage in New Orleans*, 238–43.

19. M. Pattillo (2010) *Black on the Block: The Politics of Race and Class in the City* (Chicago: University of Chicago Press), 265.

20. Livingstone, "Police Discretion and the Quality of Life in Public Places," 554–6.

21. J. G. Miller (1997) *Search and Destroy: African American Males in the Criminal Justice System* (Cambridge: Cambridge University Press), 22–4, 108; L. K. Brown (2004–5) "Officer or Overseer? Why Police Desegregation Fails as an Adequate Solution to Racist, Oppressive, and Violent Policing in Black Communities," *New York University Review of Law and Social Change*, 29.4, 766.

22. F. E. Zimring (2011) *The City that Became Safe: New York's Lessons for Urban Crime and its Control* (New York: Oxford University Press), 205; J. A. Greene (1999) "Zero Tolerance: A Case Study of Police Policies and Practices in New York City," *Crime and Delinquency* 45.2, 171–2.

23. W. T. Lyons (2002) *Law, Meaning and Violence: Politics of Community Policing: Rearranging the Power to Punish* (Ann Arbor: University of Michigan Press), 3; Amnesty International (1996) "Police Brutality and Excessive Force in the New York City Police Department," http://www.unhcr.org/refworld/publisher,AMNESTY,,USA,3ae6a9e18,0.html, date accessed July 1, 2011; Lyons, *Law, Meaning and Violence*, 3–4.

24. Weitzer and Tuch, *Race and Policing in America*, 25.

25. P. Knepper (2008) "Rethinking the Racialization of Crime: the Significance of Black Firsts," *Ethnic and Racial Studies* 31.3, 517.

26. *Pew Center on the States* (2008) One in 100: Behind Bars in America 2008 (Washington, DC: The Pew Charitable Trusts), 34.

27. Russell-Brown, *The Color of Crime*, 26.

28. R. Kennedy (1994) "The State, Criminal Law, and Racial Discrimination: A Comment," *Harvard Law Review* 107.6, 1256.

29. A. Blumstein (2005) "On the Racial Disproportionality of United States' Prison Populations," in S. L. Gabbidon and H. T. Green eds *Race Crime and Justice: A Reader* (New York: Routledge), 52.

30. Provine, *Unequal Under Law*, 127.

31. S. B. Bright (1995) "Discrimination, Death, and Denial: The Tolerance of Racial Discrimination in the Infliction of the Death Penalty," *Santa Clara Law Review* 433, 62–3.

32. Hartigan, *What Can You Say?*, 61–4.

33. Provine, *Unequal Under Law*, 131, 147; Bell, *Race, Racism, and American Law*, 513–14 and 545–6.

34. K. Russell-Brown (2004) *Underground Codes: Race, Crime, and Related Fires* (New York: New York University Press), 9–14; R. L. Allen and

M. D. Austin (2000) "Racial Disparities in Arrest Rates as an Explanation of Racial Disparity in Commitment to Pennsylvania Prisons," *Journal of Research in Crime and Delinquency*, 37.2, 216; Miller, *Search and Destroy*, 61.

35. S. Walker, C. Spohn, and M. DeLone (2004) *The Color of Justice: Race, Ethnicity, and Crime in America* (Belmont, CA: Wadsworth/Cengage Learning), 357.

36. Holmes and Smith, *Race and Police Brutality*, 17; A. J. Meehan and M. C. Ponder (2005) "Race and Place: The Ecology of Racial Profiling African American Motorists," in Gabbidon and Green eds *Race, Crime, and Justice*, 207.

37. R. J. Sampson and J. L. Lauritsen (1997) "Racial and Ethnic Disparities in Crime and Criminal Justice in the United States," *Crime and Justice*, 21, 311.

38. Pew Center, "One in 100: Behind Bars in America 2008," 5; Pew Center on the States (2009) *One in 31: The Long Reach of American Corrections* (Washington, DC: The Pew Charitable Trusts), 1.

39. Uniform Crime Survey 209 Table 1a. http://www2.fbi.gov/ucr/cius2009/data/table_01a.html, date accessed August 1, 2011.

40. Zimring, *The City that Became Safe*, 88 and 223–5; Tonry and Melewski cited in Steffensmeier et al. (2011) "Reassessing Trends In Black Violent Crime, 1980–2008: Sorting Out the 'Hispanic Effect,' in Uniform Crime Reports Arrests, National Crime Victimization Survey Offender Estimates, and U.S. Prisoner Counts," *Criminology*, 49.1, 199.

41. M. Gottschalk (2006) *The Prison and the Gallows: the Politics of Mass Incarceration in America* (Cambridge: Cambridge University Press), 11; Alexander, *The New Jim Crow*, 93.

42. J. Kohler-Hausmann (2010) "'The Attila the Hun Law': New York's Rockefeller Drug Laws and the Making of a Punitive State," *Journal of Social History* 44.1, 76, 82.

43. Provine, *Unequal under Law*, 127; G. C. Loury (2008) *Race, Incarceration, and American Values* (Cambridge, MA: MIT Press), 16.

44. Alexander, *The New Jim Crow*, 55.

45. Perkinson, *Texas Tough*, 8. See also M. Lynch (2009) *Sunbelt Justice: Arizona and the Transformation of American Punishment* (Stanford: Stanford University Press).

46. L. Wacquant (2002) "From Slavery to Mass Incarceration: Rethinking the 'Race Question' in the US," *New Left Review* 13, 41–60; L. Wacquant (2010) "Class, Race and Hyperincarceration in Revanchist America," *Daedalus*, 139.3, 74–90.

47. B. Western (2006) *Punishment and Inequality in America* (New York: Russell Sage), 7 and 131; G. De Jong (2010) *Invisible Enemy: the African American Freedom Struggle after 1965* (Chichester: Wiley-Blackwell), 69; D. Braman (2004) *Doing Time on the Outside: the Hidden Effects of*

Incarceration on Families and Communities (Ann Arbor: University of Michigan Press), 156; Miller, *Search and Destroy*, 97.

48. J. Manza and C. Uggen (2006) *Locked Out: Felon Disenfranchisement and American Democracy* (Oxford: Oxford University Press), 9–10 and 79–80.

49. P. S. Karlan cited in Loury, *Race, Incarceration, and American Values*, 52.

50. J. Sudbury (2002) "Celling Black Bodies: Black Women in the Global Prison Industrial Complex," *Feminist Review*, 70, 65–9.

51. S. Daulatzai (2007) "Protect Ya Neck: Muslims and the Carceral Imagination in the Age of Guantánamo,' *Souls*, 9.2, 132–47.

52. M. Brown (2005) "'Setting the Conditions': for Abu Ghraib: The Prison Nation Abroad," *American Quarterly* 57.3, 986.

53. D. R. Dow (2002) "How the Death Penalty Really Works," in D. R. Dow and M. Dow eds *The Machinery of Death: the Reality of America's Death Penalty Regime* (New York: Routledge), 12; D. Garland (2010) *Peculiar Institution: America's Death Penalty in an Age of Abolition* (New York: Oxford University Press), 225–6.

54. S. Banner (2002) *The Death Penalty: an American History* (Cambridge, MA: Harvard University Press), 247–50 and 269–75.

55. Dow, "How the Death Penalty Really Works," 13; Gottschalk, *The Prison and the Gallows*, 217–24; J. Simon and C. Spaulding (2001) "Tokens of Our Esteem: Aggravating Factors in the Era of Deregulate Death Penalties," in A. Sarat ed. *The Killing State: Capital Punishment in Law, Politics, and Culture* (Oxford: Oxford University Press), 100.

56. "National Statistics on the Death Penalty and Race," http://www.deathpenaltyinfo.org/race-death-row-inmates-executed-1976, date accessed May 2, 2012; "Death Row U.S.A. Winter 2012" (NAACP Legal Defense Fund), 2.

57. M. Lynch and C. Haney (2011) "Mapping the Racial Bias of the White Male Capital Juror: Jury Composition and the 'Empathic Divide,'" *Law and Society Review* 45.1, 73–80.

58. "Number of Executions by State and Region since 1976," http://deathpenaltyinfo.org/number-executions-state-and-region-1976#region, date accessed May 28, 2012; S. F. Messner, R. D. Baller, and M. P. Zevenbergen (2005) "The Legacy of Lynching and Southern Homicide," *American Sociological Review*, 70.4, 633–55; Banner, *The Death Penalty*, 278–9.

59. R. Paternoster and R. Brame (2008) "Reassessing Race Disparities in Maryland Capital Cases," *Criminology*, 46.4, 971–1008; S. Kotch and R. P. Mosteller (2010) "The Racial Justice Act and the Long Struggle with Race and the Death Penalty in North Carolina," *North Carolina Law Review*, 88.6, 2087–8; G. Stassen (2008) "The Death Penalty is Losing," *Tikkun*, 23.4; "Judge Blocks Death Sentence Under Law on Race Disparity," *New York Times*, April 20, 2012.

60. "The End of the Rockefeller Drug Laws: A Hip-Hop Victory," *Health & Medicine Week*, April 13, 2009, 3464; "Preliminary Impact of 2009 Drug Law Reform October 2009–September 2010," http://criminaljustice. state.ny.us/drug-law-reform/documents/interim-drug-law-reform-update-10-07-2010.pdf, date accessed May 28, 2012.
61. "U.S. Sentencing Commission Votes to Apply New Crack Cocaine Sentencing Guidelines Retroactively," http://www.naacp.org/news/entry/u.s.-sentencing-commission-votes-to-apply-new-crack-cocaine-sentencing-guid, date accessed May 28, 2012.
62. A. L. Higginbotham, A. B. Francois, and L. Y. Yueh (1997) "The O. J. Simpson Trial: Who Was Improperly 'Playing the Race Card'?," in T. Morrison ed. *Birth of a Nation'Hood: Gaze, Script, and Spectacle in the O. J. Simpson Case* (New York: Pantheon Books), 49.

Epilogue

1. "NAACP-Supported 'Emmett Till Unsolved Civil Rights Crime Act' Signed into Law by President Bush," http://leadership500.naacp.org/get-involved/activism/alerts/110thaa-2008-10-08/index.htm, date accessed October 26, 2009.
2. R. L. Bender (2008) "Searching for Restorative Justice: The Trial of Edgar Ray Killen," *Souls* 10.2, 155–64; J. L. Dickerson and A. A. Alston (2009) *Devil's Sanctuary: An Eyewitness History of Mississippi Hate Crimes* (Chicago: Lawrence Hill Books), 319–20.
3. B. Lang (2009) "Reconciliation: Not Retribution, Not Justice, Perhaps Not Even Forgiveness," *The Monist*, 92.4, 613–14.
4. "Southern Truth and Reconciliation: the Road to Justice for Human Rights Abuses," http://www.fcd360.com/SouthernTruth/, date accessed March 1, 2012; "Mississippi Truth Project," http://www.mississippitruth. org/, date accessed February 9, 2012; Ronald Walters (2009) Price of Racial Reconciliation (Ann Arbor: University of Michigan Press), 3.
5. "Executive Summary," Greensboro Truth and Reconciliation Commission, http://greensborotrc.org/exec_summary.pdf, date accessed February 9, 2012.
6. A. Brophy (2002) Reconstructing the Dreamland: the Tulsa Riot of 1921 (New York: Oxford University Press), 114; C. Henry (2007) Long Overdue: the Politics of Racial Reparations (New York: New York University Press), 89–91.
7. D. Apel (2003) "On Looking: Lynching Photographs and Legacies of Lynching after 9/11," American Quarterly 55.3, 462–3; G. Hale (2002) "Review," Journal of American History 89.3, 993–4; J. Allen et al. (2000) Without Sanctuary: Lynching Photography in America (Santa Fe: Twin Palms); "Without Sanctuary: Photographs and Postcards of Lynching in America," http://withoutsanctuary.org/, date accessed August 1, 2011.

8. Lynching Victims Senate Apology resolution, 109th Congress, June 13, 2005; "ADL Welcomes Senate's Apology," ADL Press Release, June 15, 2005; "Lynching Apology Fine, but inadequate," USA Today, June 16, 2005; "Senate Weights Apology," National Public Radio, June 13, 2005, http://www.npr.org/templates/story/story.php?storyId=4700498, date accessed May 10, 2010; Vinay Lal, "Enduring Mythography of American Justice," *Economic and Political Weekly*, August 6, 2005.

Index

African American history has been scarred by violent and discriminatory law enforcement—from the mass executions of rebel slaves through to the present day in which more black citizens are incarcerated than ever before. This book provides an in-depth overview of crime, punishment, and justice in African American history. It presents cutting-edge scholarship on major issues of criminal justice history in the United States, and explores everyday African American experiences alongside famous trials and court decisions. It also highlights the ways in which resistance to oppressive policing, punishment, and vigilante justice has advanced the broader struggle for black freedom, and driven an ongoing process of criminal justice reforms.

JAMES CAMPBELL is Lecturer in American History at the University of Leicester, UK. He is the author of *Slavery on Trial: Race, Class, and Criminal Justice in Antebellum Richmond, Virginia* and co-editor (with Rebecca Fraser) of *Reconstruction: People and Perspectives.*

American History in Depth

Series Editors: A. J. Badger and Stephen Tuck